THE VOTE COLLECTORS

THE

VOTE

COLLECTORS

THE TRUE STORY OF THE SCAMSTERS, POLITICIANS, AND PREACHERS BEHIND THE NATION'S GREATEST ELECTORAL FRAUD

★ ★ ★

MICHAEL GRAFF AND NICK OCHSNER

SECOND EDITION

With a new preface by the authors

A Ferris and Ferris Book

THE UNIVERSITY OF NORTH CAROLINA PRESS

Chapel Hill

This book was published under the
MARCIE COHEN FERRIS AND WILLIAM R. FERRIS IMPRINT
of the University of North Carolina Press.

Designed by Richard Hendel
Set in Utopia, Klavika, and Patriotica types
by codeMantra
Manufactured in the United States of America

Cover image © iStockphoto/BackyardProduction.
Interior image of button © iStockphoto/koya79.

ISBN 978-1-4696-7964-8 (paper; alk. paper)
ISBN 978-1-4696-7965-5 (epub)
ISBN 978-1-4696-7966-2 (pdf)

The Library of Congress has cataloged the original edition of this book as follows:
Names: Graff, Michael (Journalist), author. | Ochsner, Nick, author.
Title: The vote collectors : the true story of the scamsters, politicians, and preachers
behind the nation's greatest electoral fraud / Michael Graff, Nick Ochsner.
Other titles: Ferris and Ferris book.
Description: Chapel Hill : The University of North Carolina Press, [2021] | Series:
A Ferris and Ferris book | Includes bibliographical references and index.
Identifiers: LCCN 2021021866 | ISBN 9781469665566 (cloth) |
ISBN 9781469665573 (ebook)
Subjects: LCSH: Harris, Mark, 1966 April 24- | United States. Congress. House—
Elections, 2018. | Republican Party (N.C.) | Elections—Corrupt practices—North
Carolina—Bladen County. | Elections—North Carolina—History. | African
Americans—Civil rights—North Carolina—History—19th century. | North
Carolina—Race relations—History—19th century. | BISAC: HISTORY / United
States / State & Local / South (AL, AR, FL, GA, KY, LA, MS, NC, SC, TN, VA,
WV) | POLITICAL SCIENCE / Political Process / Campaigns & Elections
Classification: LCC JK1994 .G73 2021 | DDC 324.6/60975632—dc23
LC record available at https://lccn.loc.gov/2021021866

CONTENTS

★ ★ ★

PREFACE

Spring 2024

Dear reader,

We've discussed this book with library lovers and bookstore junkies and partisan hacks throughout the country over the past couple of years. Perhaps the sharpest and most succinct comment came after our talk with students and faculty in a 300-level political science course at Davidson College called Campaign Strategy.

After a lively discussion about election fraud, an audience member approached us and said, "So . . . the ones who smelt it dealt it?"

Well. Yeah. You might put it that way.

Election fraud is, we suppose, like a bad fart in a crowded room. It affects everybody, turns friends into skeptics, and casts doubt on future gatherings. And often the most offended person winds up revealing himself as the offender.

Such was the case in Bladen County, the sprawling rural county in eastern North Carolina where this book is set, a county known for centuries as "the Mother County." It was here on this sandy soil where, in late 2016, a Republican political operative named McCrae Dowless accused his Democratic rivals from the Bladen Improvement Association PAC of running an illegal ballot-harvesting operation. But a state board of elections hearing over Dowless's complaints that December brought a surprising twist: during questioning, Dowless nearly incriminated himself and admitted to his own ballot-harvesting operation. The turnabout set off a bizarre series of events over the next several years that became the threads of *The Vote Collectors*, which ends in 2020.

Four years later, the stench of broader national election scandals is unmistakable as America turns its attention to the 2024 presidential election. This paperback is scheduled to publish during primary season, and the only prediction we are comfortable making is this: come November, millions of Americans will not believe the results.

This is not new, of course. Many still don't believe the 2020 results, including former president Trump, who's been indicted on multiple charges for his efforts to overturn them. Others still question the validity of the 2016 election.

The distrust goes beyond that, though, as we detail in this book. In eastern North Carolina, white folks in Bladen County argued that the 2010 sheriff's race was rigged. Long before that, Black voters in Wilmington knew for certain that the 1898 election was stolen; many of them were prevented from voting at gunpoint. Same for 1870, when Democrats seized legislative power in the state by force, then trumped up charges to impeach Republican governor William Holden.

This year's threats are more modern and less brute, but they're driven by the same twisted thirst.

In the 2024 election, misinformation concocted by humans and repackaged by artificial intelligence will sway voters as much as any stump speech. But while the tools used to sow doubt have changed, one constant of the American condition remains. This is both a flaw and a strength of our country: people simply can't fathom that their side can lose, or should lose.

We watched the fallout from the 2020 election in disbelief. What if, we wondered, people had paid more attention to Bladen County in 2018 and 2019? It certainly was a preface.

Mark Harris, a Republican pastor, claimed victory on election night in 2018 in the Ninth Congressional District. His lead over Democrat Dan McCready was slim, a few hundred votes out of tens of thousands cast. A month later, the state elections board declined to certify the results, citing voting irregularities in Bladen County. Three months later, the race became the first overturned federal election in at least a generation.

After the race was thrown out, Dowless—a small-town, chain-smoking political operative—was indicted on charges related to election fraud, along with several people who worked for him. They were accused of harvesting absentee ballots in service of Harris. The scandal drew breathless national headlines. But soon attention shifted to the 2020 campaigns, and the people of Bladen County were left to assess their tarnished reputation.

The lessons from Bladen County aren't tactical. The methods people use to game a system are less important than why they feel compelled to game it in the first place. Thus, this book.

From Donald Trump to McCrae Dowless to the members of the Bladen Improvement Association to Mark Harris, people accused of election tampering almost always maintain their innocence. This often isn't defiance, either. Over the course of our reporting, we met people on all sides of the

Bladen County scandal of 2018, and we came to understand that what bonded them was a sincere-to-a-fault belief that they did nothing wrong.

The guiding question of this book, then, the one that steered us through our reporting, is this: How far are these characters—hell, how far are we all—from being who they believe themselves to be?

A great deal has changed in the years since the hardcover edition of *The Vote Collectors* was published in 2021.

The fallout from the 2018 election and its ensuing circus lingered over Bladen County like fog over a cotton field. Lifelong friendships were spoiled. Elections officials quit or were fired.

A New York Times/Serial Productions podcast from Zoe Chace called *The Improvement Association* sparked infighting that ultimately splintered that group. The Bladen County Improvement Association, which for years had helped elect Black politicians in a rural county, disbanded.

Dowless was also sidelined, first by his criminal charges and then by cancer. He died in April 2022 in a hospital bed in his daughter's house.

Nick visited him a few days before he passed. Dowless looked at Nick and said, "I'm glad I never lied to you, and that I didn't have to," a thing most people don't feel like they have to say to someone they've never lied to.

We went to the memorial service for Dowless and wrote about it for the North Carolina publication *The Assembly*. Several of his closest friends used their eulogy time to bash our book and us. One, hamburger heir Pat Melvin, tried to go nose to nose with Michael in the parking lot while the pallbearers loaded the casket in a hearse. On the other side, the state board of elections investigator who led the inquiry into Dowless's operation left a review that said the book was one-sided . . . toward Dowless. We figure the contradictory criticisms are a sign we did the story justice.

In all of our conversations, before and after the book published, Dowless never conceded that he could be guilty of the charges he faced, even after being indicted twice in two years. He would tell us about all the people he couldn't trust in Bladen County while appearing to remain unaware of the reasons people wouldn't trust him.

He saw himself as a simple "country boy," but he was a numbers genius and a master schemer who was at the center of a scandal that tore apart the county he loved.

He had countless contacts saved in his phone. In the end, though, he had few true friends. Of all the politicians he'd worked for in his career, only a couple showed up to his funeral.

Mark Harris, the tainted candidate, did send in a video message for the service.

A little more than a year later, Harris announced that in 2024 he would make another run for Congress. In his launch video, Harris, who in 2019 called for a new election himself as evidence mounted to show he knew more about Dowless's operation than he let on, said, "In 2020, Democrats stole the election from President Trump. The year before, they did it to me."

The national environment has changed, too. For one, Trump and many of his associates have been indicted in an election-related racketeering case in Georgia, leading to an unprecedented mugshot of a former president that somehow turned into a fundraising tool. Several of Trump's codefendants have pleaded guilty in Georgia as of this writing.

More than that, the conversation around fraudulent elections has shifted, in a positive way, we believe.

For years, lawmakers and attorneys focused on election fraud's less destructive cousin, voter fraud. There is a difference between the two, one that became clear in North Carolina long before the rest of the country caught on.

Voter fraud is most often an individual act—a lawyer in Ohio voting in two states, a Wisconsin man who thought he could vote while on parole. These are isolated cases—the Associated Press found fewer than 500 in six key battleground states in 2020—and if you added them together they wouldn't change the outcome of even one district, let alone an entire presidential contest.

Election fraud, however, is a grander and more sinister scheme. It's organized crime—racketeering charges, for instance, are commonly associated with the mafia—and a plot to change the course of hundreds of thousands of votes. Election fraud requires powerful people and money.

On May 4, 2023, Trump's 2024 presidential campaign fired off a fundraising email with a striking message: he was setting up a *ballot harvesting* operation and needed money to help get it going.

Yes, the same Trump who cited ballot harvesting and, more generally, any use of absentee ballots as a basis for his false claims that the 2020 election was stolen was now trumpeting absentee ballots and a scheme to have people go around and pick up those ballots. Where it was legal, of course, the campaign noted.

Ballot harvesting, the act of collecting voters' absentee ballots and returning them to the board of elections, is legal in some states and not explicitly illegal in others.

In North Carolina, harvesting has been illegal for years, but the state legislature nearly unanimously strengthened the law in the weeks following the Ninth District scandal. Left-leaning activists protested, but Democrats here voted for it anyway, given all the trouble harvesting had caused. Now, only the voter—or a near relative or legal guardian—is permitted to handle and return a person's ballot.

Since 2020, lawmakers in more than two dozen states have introduced legislation to limit who can return a ballot. In Alabama, only the voter can handle a ballot, and lawmakers want to make it a crime for *any other person* to do so.

But Alabama already is a deep-red state, as are most of the states with the strictest laws.

The Trump-led Republican shift to a pro–early voting, pro-harvesting playbook is a staggering change in rhetoric. But it's designed, say Republicans, to make gains in swing states, and even blue states, where the practice is legal.

"Do I think it's the most secure way of voting? No," said Republican National Committee chairwoman Ronna McDaniel in late spring 2023. "But if it's the law, we're going to have to do it just like the Democrats are."

Trump was more blunt in his fundraising email: "Either we ballot harvest where we can, or you can say goodbye to America!"

When we read that, we nearly yelped. In tone and in logic, it sounds exactly like the things we heard in Bladen County—except there, people said them more than a decade ago.

In 2010, Bladen County elected a Black sheriff for the first time in its history. White Republicans couldn't believe the results. They still don't. They cried foul and blamed the Black-led Bladen Improvement Association, saying the organization's get-out-the-vote efforts were illegal.

But by the time the next sheriff's race rolled around, in 2014, those white Republicans had hired McCrae Dowless to lead their campaign to take back the office. Their candidate won. Time and again, when we asked Bladen County's Republican leaders why they felt the need to shift their strategy toward harvesting, they said the same thing: "Well, if the Democrats are doing it, we have to, too."

Now we're hearing the same words again, but at a national level. The narrative that follows, then, seems to be more than a story about what happened in a forgotten county in a forgotten period of time. It may well be an indicator of what's ahead for the United States.

It's certainly appropriate that Bladen County's nickname is "the Mother County."

—MICHAEL GRAFF AND NICK OCHSNER

THE VOTE COLLECTORS

PROLOGUE

Morning in Mother County December 2018

★ ★ ★

A blazing pink sky decorates the tops of flat fields along the two-lane road that leads to the town of Tar Heel. It's just before seven on a Friday morning in December 2018. The thatch remnants of whatever had been growing in late summer still lean toward the Cape Fear River, two months after Hurricane Florence's floodwaters receded.

Men in jeans and flannel shirts ache and groan as they climb the steps of Tar Heel Baptist Church for the weekly Friday men's prayer breakfast. Around the low-ceilinged fellowship hall are thirty-five men of different races and political persuasions, bonding over sunrise, prayers, and bags of Hardee's. "Ham biscuits on the right," a man says, "sausage on the left."

They talk quietly. They give firm handshakes and a few hugs. They are Black and white and Latino. They've been through hell with the hurricanes lately. Some lost their entire fall crop. Some might soon lose a farm. On top of that misery, they've been made fun of all over the world.

Tar Heel, population 150, holds two distinctions: its name matches the nickname and logo of the University of North Carolina in Chapel Hill, 115 miles to the northwest; and it's the home of the Smithfield packing plant, the world's largest hog-processing operation.

But over these few weeks in December 2018, reporters from New York and Washington have rented cars and come here to ask questions about the door-to-door ballot-collection program that upended the midterm election. It's big news elsewhere, for whatever reason small-town shit becomes big news. A congressional race got held up. Dan McCready, the boyish-looking Democrat, got close to turning a very red district blue for the first time in almost four decades. He'd lost to Mark Harris, the preacher with the good hair, by less than a thousand votes. But a month after Election Day—the week after Thanksgiving—the state board of elections said it couldn't certify the race because something was crooked with the ballots of Bladen. They said it had been going on for years and that now, after such a close election, it had to stop.

That was about a week before the prayer breakfast in the fellowship hall. In the days between, people in suits used the scandal to point fingers at other people in suits, to justify whatever political beliefs they have. The president hadn't done them any favors, tweeting out lies about Democrats and voter fraud and immigrants who cast ballots illegally. Now some people on his own side were caught, which would be bad enough even if it didn't mean that all the left-leaning news organizations in the Western Hemisphere were hitching their assumptions to the story and using it as a reason to say, "See, Republicans are the cheaters!"

Stephen Colbert even devoted four minutes of his monologue to the scandal around the door-to-door ballot collections here.

"They're like Jehovah's-I-hope-there-aren't-witnesses," Colbert said.

The men in the church are tired of it. *Y'all didn't give a damn*, they keep saying to outsiders, *when the chemical company an hour north contaminated the drinking water.*

Didn't give a damn when water rose to the roofs of homes and businesses in the county seat during Hurricane Florence.

Didn't give a damn when hog farmers needed help defending themselves against slick Texas lawyers who filed those multimillion-dollar nuisance lawsuits on charges that hog farms stink. No shit.

But now here they were, these people from all over, giving a damn about Bladen County, North Carolina, chasing down a few scribbles on ballots and saying it's the home of the biggest political story outside the Beltway.

Where, they wonder, *have y'all been?*

To understand how election fraud happens, and how a small place like Bladen County became a siren of a fracturing democracy years ahead of the 2020 election and violent attempts to overturn it, you can't make simple assumptions. You have to understand how big-city prejudices about race and class can be flipped upside down in places like this. You have to understand that it's a story about nothing and everything. You have to understand the land.

Bladen used to be the ocean floor. Millions of years ago, saltwater waves crashed against the Uwharrie Mountains, about 150 miles inland from the current Atlantic coastline. Over time the sea slipped east and left behind a grainy, sandy soil, ripe for peanuts and soybeans and longleaf pines. It left behind the coastal plain, the region of flatlands where Bladen County sits.

The ocean tells the story of the past, but also the future. A series of devastating floods have amounted to the ocean's way of saying it wants to reclaim some of what it left behind.

Already some places have conceded. Way out on North Carolina's eastern elbow, the last three residents of the once-thriving maritime port Portsmouth Island left in the 1970s, mostly in response to a series of hurricanes. The only occupants left in the village now are the mosquitoes and biting flies. The federal government turned Portsmouth into a national park, with some of the softest sand you'll ever encounter, and the park staff keeps up maintenance on a few cottages, an old church, and the post office. They stand there neatly still today, as if their occupants will be right back.

The closer you look at the flood maps and predictions, the more you wonder if places like Bladen County are next. What was a county with 35,000 inhabitants in 2010 now has only slightly more than 30,000 in 2020. Eastern North Carolina has a bit of a history with vanishing settlements. The first European child born in North America, Virginia Dare, was delivered on Roanoke Island here in 1587. She was part of what's still known as the Lost Colony, a group of settlers who disappeared but still live on through a glittery outdoor theater production designed by the Broadway legend William Ivey Long.

The first European settlers who survived in North America called Bladen the Mother County, and its original boundaries stretched from these flatlands near the Atlantic Ocean all the way west to the sandstone tips of the Great Smoky Mountains. Over time they chopped off sections. It's now shaped like a low-top boot, and at 874 square miles, it's the fourth-largest of North Carolina's 100 counties. Its southeastern toe is only thirty miles from the Atlantic Ocean, and its northwestern heel about seventy.

It is a forgotten stretch of sand and peat. Poor laborers line up each morning inside the Smithfield packing plant to slaughter 35,000 hogs a day. In the past three years, two of the wettest hurricanes in history have flooded entire towns and put family farms out of business. The poverty rate is 20 percent, and the median household income of about $32,000 is half the national median. The population decline can be traced to any number of underlying causes, as some depart to find employment, others to leave flooded-out houses, others on the solemn wings of an opioid overdose.

These are the table settings for the small-scale fraud that fudged the result of a congressional race. They are the foundation for the distrust that led not just to the Ninth Congressional District mess, but to the years-long preoccupation with election fraud that led to the insurrection at the U.S. Capitol in 2021. Perhaps the most worrisome thing about what happened here in

2018 is how unworried most locals were about it. Fraud, to many people in Bladen County, was just a fact of democratic life. Hoax or be hoaxed.

Bladen is not alone, though. It is a most accurate representation of eastern North Carolina and of the rural South. It's a place most people come to know only because they pass through it on the way to the beach, or when someone's in trouble. It is a series of rivers pushing into the vast and low stretch of land like fingers deep in a glove.

Water defines life here. Most of the rivers spill into a network of estuaries, which are bodies of mixed water—the freshwater from the rivers rushing along the surface while the saltwater from the sea scrapes the bottom, density working as the dividing line. The estuaries breed the most diverse marsh classroom: egrets and heron, shrimp and oysters, striped bass and red snapper, sea turtles and snakes, dragonflies and fire ants, red wolves and black bears. The eastern North Carolina watershed reminds us of the order of a world without politics.

But it can also be an exact reminder of the order of politics. A predator in one situation can, in another, become prey.

We love this place. Nick grew up about thirty minutes from Bladen in Hope Mills, a town in the Sandhills known mostly as a bedroom community for Fort Bragg, the largest military installation in the country. Nick's father was a Special Forces soldier, a Green Beret who was killed in 2005 by a roadside bomb in Afghanistan. Nick was just a teenager when three men in Class A uniforms came to his home to deliver the news. He spent the next several years of his life trying to understand the why and how. He's devoted his career as a television reporter to trying to make things right. The thrust of his job at North Carolina's oldest television station, WBTV, is to investigate corruption and fraud.

That's how Nick found himself back in Bladen County in December 2018, knocking on doors about the election fraud scandal there. His connections gave him access to some of the main players. In this book you'll read stories from McCrae Dowless, who hasn't done interviews with anyone else, stories that started flowing only after Nick told him he grew up not far from here.

Michael, meanwhile, spent four years working at the *Fayetteville Observer* during the heart of the Iraq and Afghanistan wars. He was, as it happens, a reporter at the paper when Nick's father died. Michael's covered eastern North Carolina extensively since then, from stories about wildlife to long-form pieces about the rural healthcare crisis. Michael's father was a charter fisherman and crabber, and the way of life in eastern North Carolina reminds him of where he grew up.

Over the course of our work in Bladen County, we've found ourselves reporting not just as observers but also sometimes as participants. For those reasons, you'll see that from time to time we become characters in this book. Nick, mostly. In some of the strangest moments, Nick would receive a press release or call saying McCrae Dowless was being charged with a crime. Nick would call McCrae's number and find out the cops hadn't shown up yet—McCrae didn't even know they were coming. In some ways, those encounters were metaphors for the overall story of Bladen County, a place that's often a little bit behind.

Because if Bladen County is the Mother County, it is more of a guiding light than an annoying flicker. We shouldn't dismiss the election fraud that happened here as an outlier but recognize it as an early-stage disease. And given that the person at the center of that disease, a low-budget operative named McCrae Dowless, has worked for both political parties in his career, we shouldn't treat it as a Democrat disease or a Republican disease: it's an American disease. And Bladen County is an indicator.

Bladen gave birth to the state's most prominent Black family, the Spauldings, who went on to start Black Wall Street in Durham. And from that family came one of the most important Black politicians of all time, George Henry White. Born in a rickety house in a swamp along the Bladen-Columbus county line, White served in Congress from 1897 to 1901. He was the last Black congressman before Jim Crow laws truly took effect, the last Black congressman in the United States for a generation, and the last Black congressman in North Carolina for ninety years.

In this book we will draw clear connections between White's years in Congress and the 2018 election. The 1898 campaign that drove him from office and the campaign of 2018 are merely distant cousins, separated by only two generations and 120 years of racism in rural politics.

Like most of the country's issues with race, this story is one of fits and starts, progress and retaliation. So we split the book into three parts: the first builds toward the 2018 election through the main characters on the Republican side, particularly McCrae Dowless and Mark Harris, and shows how they became the defendants in the case of *Democracy v. Bladen County*. This part explains how the election was part of a white backlash to the election of a Black sheriff eight years earlier.

Events in Bladen County today have clear predecessors. Part 2 tells the history of race in eastern North Carolina through its defining Black characters. George Henry White, for sure. But also an aging schoolteacher named Delilah Blanks, civil rights attorney Irving Joyner, and other modern civil rights activists who in the late 1990s built the Black political powerhouse that resulted in the white backlash of the 2010s. One thing that's consistent throughout time is that the poorest and most vulnerable people come out worse off. Those in power in eastern North Carolina in George Henry White's day and those in power today were experts at sorting people into groups, at making it impossible for a poor white man to see himself standing alongside a poor Black man, even if that relationship would be mutually beneficial. What was true then remains true today: a few figures from each race emerge with the fortune and power, while their neighbors suffer.

And part 3 brings the stories together in the winter of 2018, when all of Bladen County, Black and white, rich and poor, became lumped together as one, under searing and unforgiving national attention that simply made them out to be jokes of the backwoods.

What those stories all missed, of course, is that what happened in Bladen County could happen in any community where desperation rules. In any place where white people confuse race with power, and where Black people want power for their race. In any place where the rivers are rising higher and higher each fall with every named storm, where entire neighborhoods sit empty and rotting, where the small family farmers sold out to the middle-man farmers who sold out to the industrial farmers who sold out to foreign investors.

Most of the men in the church reception hall worked the tobacco fields every summer as a kid, and spent the money they made on new coveralls to wear to school each fall. When consumers finally came to believe warnings about the links between tobacco and cancer in the 1980s and 1990s, Bladen County's cash crop became worthless. The people here had to come up with another way to make a living. They turned to pork.

Today there are twenty-nine hogs for every person in Bladen County.

Agriculture has always been the way to survive here. During the American Revolution, the Patriots used chicken eggs to defeat the Tories in Elizabethtown. For several weeks, a woman named Sally Salter took the eggs to the loyalist camp and reported back to the Patriots to tell them what she'd seen. Eventually a young rebel colonel named Thomas Robeson used the information to surprise the Tory camp, forcing them down a hill and into a ravine.

The Tories retreated, Robeson got a county named after him next door, the British abandoned Wilmington, the ravine became known as Tory Hole Park, and Bladen County went on farming food for the rest of the country.

"This nation has forgotten where their food comes from," Colon Roberts, a farmer at the prayer breakfast, tells Michael. Roberts raises chickens and cows. His parents grow peanuts and cotton and corn. They're in their seventies, and they've lost all of their savings in the past three years, thanks to crop losses from floods related to Hurricanes Matthew and Florence.

These people who believe they have little to no say in Washington politics instead spend all their energy on local political races—sheriff, county commission, even the Soil and Water Conservation Board. Meanwhile, congressional candidates keep doing whatever it is congressional candidates do.

They've bickered in their quest to top their neighbors in local politics, sure, but they never thought it was more than punching a hole in the wall of their own house. Yes, they knew that after the church breakfasts break up, the Black men in the room would rally around Black candidates, and the white men in the room would rally around white candidates. That's how it is. Yes, they knew that the sheriff's office wielded more power than any sheriff should. Yes, they knew McCrae Dowless was crooked long before he was on the front page of every major paper.

But they don't believe those things define them.

At the end of the breakfast the men at Tar Heel Baptist Church pass around an offering plate. They collect $158, mostly in singles, fives, and change. They plan to donate all of it to a local drug abuse and rehabilitation center.

"One bad man don't make a county," Roberts, the chicken and beef farmer, tells Michael. "It's all the good people. You saw what these men did this morning. They took money out of their pockets and gave it to people hooked on drugs."

The visiting pastor gives a fifteen-minute sermon at the meeting, a message of positivity and hard work and resilience.

He tells the men that their mission for the month is to "go throughout Bladen County and tell people that God loves them."

Much of the coverage of the scandal turned Bladen County into the land of hicks and hillbillies, druggies and dolts. Attention spans being short, national audiences distilled the ordeal into good guys and bad guys, with no villain more evil than McCrae Dowless. His portrait became the face of election tampering. Democrats, especially, turned him into a meme of rural life, a skinny and conniving white, rural Republican in the Trump era. In this book, we'll show that McCrae Dowless couldn't care less about Donald Trump. We'll show that he's merely the only one prosecuted in a much larger system of corruption, a fall guy for a country that struggled to acknowledge its racist past and the role of big-money politics in exacerbating inequities.

He's not innocent. He's also not guilty. He was mostly the next man up in a system that rewards people for hauling votes, at whatever cost, for the people who hold the cash.

Thank God for Bladen

★ ★ ★

The Missing Piece April 6, 2017

★ ★ ★

Can you think of a more comfortable place to have a meeting?
RAY BRITT

The preacher swung open the door to Ray's Furniture Liquidators. A gas range and leather recliner, marked down to sell, lined the sidewalk. A few buildings away on the main street, the early lunch crowd, all suspenders and jeans and sun-worn farm faces, lined up for the famous $2.25 flat-top hamburgers wrapped in paper at Melvin's, established 1938.

Most folks in Elizabethtown, Bladen County's biggest city, population 3,469, had spent the previous night watching weather forecasters break into regularly scheduled programs with tornado watches. A few inches of rain fell and the wind roared like hell, but there were no funnel clouds. This time, at least. In this little eastern North Carolina city, where there's not much to do but worry about the weather and everybody else's business, that's a blessing.

The preacher had come a long way for the meeting. He'd driven three hours from his home in the sparkling city of Charlotte. He looked a little out of place, his head of silver hair parted too neatly, his nose too straight, and his smile too warm. He looked like someone who'd come to tell you what you want to hear, with the unspoken expectation that you'll return the favor.

The furniture store's faded brown shingles hung low like a brow over the storefront windows. A square sign, red and yellow, read "Ray's Inc." The store's owner, a fellow by the name of Ray, walked from behind a counter to greet his guest. The preacher introduced himself as Mark Harris. He's a family man, a husband, and father. A solid-as-stone conservative. A Baptist minister. In this part of the Bible Belt, God's still a pretty good sales pitch.

The showroom furniture was arranged in neat rows across the floor: sofas, loveseats, and chairs of every color imaginable basked in fluorescent yellow lighting.

11

Ray Britt wore his hair combed back, too, but his was a little slicker than Harris's. Ray's a county commissioner, and he was honored to host some of the most important Republicans in Bladen County to meet with Harris here. On their way were bona fide local celebrities like Pat Melvin, maybe the richest person in the county—the man whose family name is on the hamburger joint—and Walter McDuffie, the county's Republican Party chairman. The sheriff was supposed to come too, but had to swing by a funeral first.

The final and most important guest was a sixty-one-year-old man with a sandy beard and wrinkles on the sides of his eyes. His name was McCrae Dowless.

A former felon with a steady smoking problem, McCrae is an unassuming character whose mind stays on politics and numbers. On a drive through his county, McCrae can point to each home and tell you the owners' political parties and whether they voted in the most recent election. He had a knack for winning elections that would soon elevate him from unknown, slump-shouldered, short-sleeved local boy to a man known around the world as the "political operative" at the center of the biggest election fraud scandal in the country's history. Not that he thinks he deserves the attention.

They settled into the living room furniture on the right-hand side of the store.

"Can you think of a more comfortable place to have a meeting in Bladen County?" Ray Britt said.

Harris, the preacher, opened the session. He was a little nervous: "I came down here because, you know, I'm considering running for the Ninth District, and I would like for you all . . . to sort of explain to me . . . what the landscape of politics in Bladen County looks like."

Harris finished within a whisker of the Republican nomination in 2016, losing by only 144 votes out of about 26,000 cast. So on this April 2017 morning, he'd backed out of the long concrete driveway of his 3,500-square-foot brick home in Charlotte's wealthy apron and pointed east toward Bladen County because he believed that the people in this room—these cursing and smoking and yessir-sayin' country boys—had the power to deliver him to Washington.

The two corners of the Ninth District couldn't be more different. Charlotte is the fastest-growing city in the Southeast, the second-biggest banking center outside of New York, the city that gave birth to Bank of America. Bladen County, some 150 miles east of the skyscrapers and tower cranes, has lost 4 percent of its population in the past decade. Many of those who remain spend their days plowing fields or working on the line at the world's largest hog-slaughtering operation.

Harris found a receptive audience in Bladen County that day. The Republicans in the showroom were shopping for a new political partner. They'd grown sick of the one they had in office, Robert Pittenger. The second-term congressman and real estate investor was far richer than even Harris, with a mansion along the seventh fairway at Quail Hollow Country Club in Charlotte's haughtiest neighborhood. Pittenger won the office in 2014 by just 5 percentage points over his opponent in the general election, the narrowest victory by a Republican in the district since 1986.

To the Pat Melvins and McCrae Dowlesses of Bladen County, Pittenger was just another representation of Washington: a distant man who didn't visit enough. All around eastern North Carolina, rural hospitals were closing, opioids were slicing families apart, hurricanes seemed to pour harder every year, and the only thing people of all politics and races could agree on is that crooks in Washington don't give a damn about them.

Harris seemed to care. From his haircut to his jawline to his family portrait, he looked like the ideal politician, almost a Southern Baptist version of Mitt Romney. He was from a rural area of North Carolina himself, he told them. Grew up idolizing Billy Graham. He'd been the president of the state Baptist Convention, and his audience in the discount loveseats liked that. They knew and he knew that the majority of the votes in the Ninth District were in Charlotte and the counties closest to it. But still he was here, talking to them, way out in Bladen County, and that mattered to them.

Harris was here because he believed they could be the difference. He believed they could turn his close loss in 2016 into a victory in 2018. He believed he needed to connect in places his neighbors in Charlotte can't find on a map. He believed he needed to connect with people like those in Ray's furniture store. One of them more than the others.

It's a short drive from one America to another.

Let's ride, for a minute, with Mark Harris across the Ninth Congressional District that morning. First you slip out of his neighborhood, surrounded by two- and three-story brick homes, through rows of mature trees and luxury SUVs. Then you turn left onto a busier street called Providence and pass a Shell gas station. Of all the Shell gas stations in the world, this is the one where white supremacist Dylann Roof stopped and used a debit card to buy snacks in June 2015, the morning after he killed nine Black people at a Bible study at Mother Emanuel church in Charleston.

From that gas station, you merge onto Charlotte's beltway, a sixty-mile loop named Interstate 485. A few miles later you might spot one of those cell phone towers with fake greenery on top, as if it's fooling anyone. Then comes the exit for Highway 74, the east–west transportation lifeline of the region.

Nicknamed Andrew Jackson Highway, U.S. 74 is a four-lane divided strip of asphalt that runs across the Ninth District like a belt. At first it's a maddening stop-and-go stretch through suburban Union County, before opening up just east of Marshville, the birthplace of country music legend Randy Travis.

Then you head through the service stations and fast-food stops in Anson County. Past farm stands and a peach ice cream shop. Then you'll struggle to keep your eyes open as the road cuts through the miles and miles of pines. There's Richmond and Scotland Counties, which have the fiercest high school football rivalry in the state but not much else these days. A few miles off the highway, the old Rockingham Speedway, "The Rock," sits empty, a concrete tomb to a time when NASCAR was the state's most important sport.

Beyond that, you may be jarred awake by a sign that says the highway is now nicknamed the "American Indian Highway." It's a striking shift considering that everywhere else the same road is named for the president responsible for Indian Removal. But these sorts of contradictions abound as you enter Robeson County, home of the Lumbee Indian tribe. As you pass through Lumberton you might consider that just six months before Harris's trip, Hurricane Matthew dumped so much rain here that the river lapped against the overpasses you're crossing.

Life has sharper edges in this wing of the state. Flooded-out strips of public housing rot in plain sight. A penitentiary with barbed wire pops up on your left. The red clay of the Piedmont gives way to the sandy soil of the coastal plain, and floodline marks can still be seen, high on the longleaf and cypress trees. Basketball legend Michael Jordan's father, James Jordan, was murdered in this spot in 1994 after he pulled over to take a nap in his Lexus.

Lumberton's claim to fame, other than being home to the largest Native American tribe east of the Mississippi, is that it gave birth to a Black Panther named Afeni Shakur Davis, who gave birth to a hip-hop icon named Tupac Shakur. Otherwise, it makes its way into the news most often for violence. If it's not Jordan's killing, it's the time a few rebels took the small-town newspaper hostage in 1988, pointing their guns at the heads of sports writers and copy chiefs because the men wanted to bring attention to the corruption in the area. As it happens, they were absolutely right about the corruption. In the years since, as funnel clouds and hurricanes came and went, leaving countless families staring at rubble that was once a home, politicians both local and statewide withheld disaster money again and again.

This hard, compromised land is where the white preacher with the good hair needed to win enough votes to flip the next election.

Curve down the long cloverleaf exit ramp in Lumberton. From here you'll pass a mash-up of abandoned old hotels, industrial buildings, and aging strip malls. Just when it feels like the end of the earth, you know you have half an hour left to Elizabethtown.

Not far beyond the Bladen County line, you'll notice the smell.

Pigs outnumber people here. The Smithfield Foods hog-processing plant stretches for nearly a mile along the highway. The hard, physical labor of turning pigs into food provides a livelihood for thousands in the area who otherwise wouldn't have anywhere to work.

Not far from there, four lanes drop to two as you enter Elizabethtown. Just inside the town limits, you'll pass a Mexican restaurant in an old, faded yellow barn. Across the street is the Tractor Supply store and a Walmart. Then a string of churches, Elizabethtown Town Hall, and a few lawyers' offices, until you hit the main drag and see the building with the faded brown shingles.

Now you're in front of Ray's Inc., in the seat of the Mother County, the humble setting for a meeting that would change the landscape of North Carolina politics.

In the beginning, it was just five Republicans on discount furniture. The meeting had been arranged by no less than a judge. Marion Warren spent a few years running North Carolina's court system and wielding his conservative political clout in Raleigh.

It was Warren who, shortly after the 2016 primary, called Harris to tell him how he'd lost to Pittenger. Warren said that a third candidate, Todd Johnson, had won 221 out of 226 mail-in absentee ballots. Harris won 4. Pittenger—a sitting U.S. congressman—won 1.

How's that possible? Harris wondered. Warren, his longtime friend, had the answer.

"Man, I would have given anything if I could have introduced you to McCrae Dowless before Todd Johnson got to know him," Warren said.

"Well, who's McCrae Dowless?" Harris asked.

"A good ol' boy. Todd Johnson didn't beat you. McCrae Dowless and his get-out-the-vote program did."

Warren continued: "If you ever think about running for office again that would include Bladen County, I would encourage you to let me know, and I'll be personally willing to take you down there and introduce you . . ."

McCrae grew up in Bladen County, the youngest child in a blended family to which his father and mother each brought a handful of children from previous marriages. To hear him tell it, his father was a strict man, the quiet type who believed in showing his children tough love. Except for McCrae. His dad bailed him out of every jam and out of every jail whenever he needed it.

McCrae spent most of his working life in construction. It was a good job that took him to far-flung places like California and Puerto Rico. Paid him enough money to get in trouble with women and booze, and to fund his pack-a-day cigarette habit. Eventually the smokes left him with a faulty heart, which sidelined him from full-time employment and forced him to stay at home, where he had time to shine up his new hobby.

Some people in Bladen County collect cars. Others, coins. Many more sell drugs. And still others just sit and watch the trucks go by.

McCrae Dowless counts votes.

He got so good at counting votes, in fact, he could tell you how many his candidate would collect before the returns were in, just like any eastern North Carolina farmer could tell you how many pounds of peanuts his crop would yield that year.

Now Harris was here with McCrae, the prince of rural politics himself. From his armchair, McCrae gave Harris a quick lesson on the county's changing political landscape. For decades, Bladen had been a majority-Democrat county. But in recent years the county commission had gone from one Republican to four. Momentum. The mention of a Republican presidential candidate carrying the county a generation earlier would cause some of their ancestors to turn in their graves. But in 2016, Donald Trump won Bladen by nine points and they cheered.

What they failed to mention to Harris was that the reason for the shift had less to do with politics than with race: the people fleeing the Democratic Party were almost all white. And in this area, even though a few white residents still hoard most of the county's wealth, the mere perception of losing power to Black residents is all the motivation white people need to start crafting exotic plans to win elections.

The tension between Black people and white people, ever-present in Bladen County and the rest of eastern North Carolina, was surging again that day when Harris stepped into the furniture store, and so were Republicans.

"And a lot of that is owed to this man, McCrae Dowless, and the work that he's been doing," one of the others said to Harris.

"Well," Harris said, turning to McCrae, "what makes you so special? And what do you do?"

★ ★ ★

The Ballad of the Flim-Flam Man October 1995

The only thing I got left is my integrity.
MCCRAE DOWLESS

The prison bus hummed along the faded asphalt. McCrae Dowless was thirty-nine years old, broke, divorced a couple of times already. Tall pines flickered past the window as his chariot made its way down Prison Camp Road, the two-lane country strip that leads to the Columbus County Correctional Institution.

It was October 1995, warm and muggy. On one side of the road McCrae could see the jail, a series of one-story redbrick buildings surrounding a prison yard. On the other side, in a sweeping field dotted with tin-roofed showrooms, Columbus County's fair was in swing. It's the only fair across the two counties, has been for half a century. Bladen County put a ban on fairs and carnivals in the 1950s after a traveling Black carnival worker was arrested for raping and murdering a white woman. That made Columbus County the entertainment leader of the region. If you craved a pig race and cotton candy and 4-H club exhibits and country music, Columbus County's fair was the biggest show around.

Most of the people McCrae Dowless knew in this life were on one side of the road or the other.

He'd already been gone for a few months, locked away in a prison a couple of counties over. Columbus County Correctional would be an improvement over that one, at least. Here he knew half the guards and inmates by name and address.

As the prison bus turned left into the jail instead of right into the fair, McCrae had a few months left on a two-year sentence. He'd taken out an insurance policy on a dead man, you see, then cashed it in. He called it a paycheck; the court called it insurance fraud. Still, after stints in prisons around the state, he was being transferred home, and he couldn't wait to get back.

Prison guards and other authority figures could look after him, give him cushy jobs like sweeping the floors. It pays to know people inside barbed-wire fences. On McCrae's first day at the new jail, an employee stopped by with an offer.

"I don't give a shit what you do," the employee said, and then he pointed to the yard. "Go out there and take a rake, rake a little bit. That's two days off of your time."

"Hell," McCrae told him, "I'll do that every day. Give me two or three days off every time."

What was supposed to be a few more months of a sentence soon turned into just a few weeks. One day before Thanksgiving, McCrae Dowless walked out a free man. He had nothing to his name other than the clothes he wore. But he still had his people.

McCrae's dad and brother greeted him on the other side that day. They took him home and gave him two shirts and two pairs of pants and got ready for the annual turkey supper.

It was time to start his new life.

Nowadays, the first thing you notice when you step into the home of the man who became the nation's most notorious country-boy political operative is the smoke.

McCrae's house is situated on the outskirts of Bladenboro, near an airport that consists of an aluminum garage and a grass runway. The humble brick ranch has a short driveway that slips into a carport. Visitors use the front door, but anybody who knows any better comes through the carport door that opens into the kitchen. There's a No Trespassing sign on a post now, a recent addition meant to deter people holding cameras and notepads.

Across the street is an aging mobile home, neighboring a plot of land that's filled with rusted cars, metal parts, and junk accumulated over time.

From 2018 to 2020, we spent about fifty hours in McCrae's kitchen. Nick made the initial contact, back in 2018 after the scandal broke and McCrae became a national news story. Working on the story for his TV job, Nick had gone through an acquaintance of an acquaintance of an acquaintance to get McCrae's number.

At the time, the only picture circulating of McCrae was a grainy black-and-white photo where he was in the background. It made him sort of the Loch Ness Monster for big-city political observers who were looking out into the rural sea for the first time. From Charlotte and Washington and New York and London they found their way here, hoping to be the first to get him on record. But Nick could say something none of them could: "I grew up in Hope Mills." This is probably the first and only time Hope Mills, a bedroom community for Fort Bragg about thirty miles from McCrae's house, has been used as a way to gain an advantage of any sort. McCrae stayed on the line. "I just want to hear the other side," Nick told him.

McCrae invited him over.

He was standing in his driveway wearing khaki pants and a blue button-down. And he had, like he always has, a lit Newport between his fingers. He still has a full head of hair in his early sixties, always combed back, and he stands about five foot eight or five foot nine, depending on how high that hair's grown. He's lean with dark eyes and a narrow stare.

"You're going to have a real good story once you see this," McCrae told Nick, tapping on his shirt pocket and drawing attention to a rectangular outline of a folded slip of paper.

That began a two-year relationship. When Nick told McCrae that Michael would be joining him for interviews, McCrae was skittish. He'd promised to share his story with one reporter, not two. And certainly not a writer from liberal Charlotte.

The day Michael met McCrae for the first time, we stopped by the office of McCrae's attorney, Cynthia Adams Singletary, who goes by Cindy. Her law office is in an old building in Elizabethtown, just across the street from the courthouse. The office lobby was dark, after hours, when Cindy invited us back through a door near the receptionist's desk. She led us to a conference room with a long table surrounded by wood-paneled walls. A globe sat in the corner, propped open at the equator, and when Michael asked what was inside Cindy said, "Liquor. You want a drink?"

Michael said no, and she laughed.

Unprompted, she said that her favorite writer was renowned southern author Pat Conroy, then informed Michael he was "no Pat Conroy." She said her favorite movie was the adaptation of the John Berendt novel *Midnight in the Garden of Good and Evil*. In the movie, John Cusack plays a writer who travels into the Deep South to work on a lighthearted travel story, only to be witness to a murder and find himself stuck there for months, trying to solve the case while townspeople manipulate him and lie to him.

Cindy's eyes scanned Michael up and down, then she chuckled at him and said, "You're like John Cusack."

These sorts of interactions happened over and over again in Bladen County. It's a place that is, by most economic or health measures, shriveling up and dying. The people who remain here haven't had so much as a county fair in seventy years. The biggest festival is called the Beast Fest, which is an entire weekend of concerts and collard sandwiches (collard greens stuffed between flat pieces of cornbread) in honor of a mythical beast that supposedly tormented farmers and pet owners in the 1950s by stealing and killing animals in the middle of the night. When a place like this is home, your imagination goes wild. And when you're a writer spending your nights and weekends in a place like this, you start to wonder how much of what you're hearing is true, how much is a lie a person is telling to protect their own interests, and how much is made up just to mess with you.

McCrae's life flipped upside down in the two years we visited him in that kitchen, through summer and winter in 2019, as he got indicted and arrested and set free. He'd regularly have Carolina Pick Three lottery tickets folded up on the counter, waiting on his luck to turn. One constant was a potholder hanging from an eye-level cabinet that read, "Today is a beautiful day."

For a good portion of 2019 one of his ex-wives lived with him, on the couch in the living room, while she dealt with a blood circulation problem that doctors said could have threatened her legs. Other times we were there when the latest news story would break about him.

"That's bullshit," he'd say at any charge.

The checkered tablecloths and wood-paneled walls (every wall in Bladen County has wood paneling, it seems) in his kitchen have seen and heard quite a bit. The kitchen is where McCrae conducts most of his business: ballot counting, phone calls, visits with county officials. He has a bowl full of papers, mostly printouts of election laws and vote totals from elections gone by.

He usually sits in an office chair at the head of the table. Metal-framed chairs surround the rest of the space. There's no question who is king in this kitchen.

Smoke fills your eyes and throat as you sit with him, and it soaks into your hair and clothes. Spend more than fifteen minutes inside and you'll emerge smelling like a honky-tonk. One evening in August 2019, Michael settled into a chair at McCrae's table, turned on the recorder, and marked the number of cigarettes. At 6:33 P.M., McCrae had seven butts in the ashtray. By 7:22, eleven were in there and he lit up a twelfth.

The next day, we all met outside a restaurant instead.

"Oh, hell," McCrae told Nick, "he got tired of me smoking yesterday, Mike did. Burnin' 'em down!"

"I did not say a word to you about that," Michael replied.

"I didn't say you did to me. You did to Nick," McCrae shot back, ever capable of reading people.

Another thing you'll notice is that his phone rings about as often as he lights up a new cigarette. Sometimes he'll carry two phones on him, sometimes just one. Never an iPhone or Android. Instead, McCrae keeps a flip phone in his pocket. He knows how to read a text message but isn't sure about typing responses.

But he can talk. It's not unusual in any given conversation to be interrupted one, two, three, maybe four times by the preset jingle of a phone made nearly twenty years ago.

He'll answer it, "What's *goin' oooooooon*."

For a Loch Ness Monster, McCrae lives to talk with other people. He couldn't wait for our visits, and seemed to grow dependent on Nick's calls. We saw the seasons change through his decorations. In early December 2018, the table was covered with a festive tablecloth with snowmen on it. Months later, after the holiday had passed, the glass top sat exposed. By the time the next year rolled around, on November 12, 2019, he already had his Christmas tree decorated.

"Fellas, that's the difference between the rural areas and the city," he told us. "Out here we just wish Santa Claus would go ahead and come on."

Not once in our time with him did we get to a point where we trusted McCrae Dowless completely, even though McCrae would often point out to Nick that he'd never lie to him. It's just the kind of thing a con man would tell his mark. He was charming, funny, and always welcoming. And he was loyal, even when it was self-imposed. He told us our interviews would always remain exclusives, though we never asked him to do that. Once, when *This American Life* reporter Zoe Chace called while we were recording, he said, "Zoe, I am busy, real busy today, and really I, Zoe, I really don't have any comments on, on."

It was a polite conversation. After it was over, McCrae said, "See, she's got a, she does the recording stuff. Not satellite. And if you say anything, hell, they can take that part out. They, they take stuff out of context."

Then he said he didn't plan to participate in the *This American Life* interviews.

"I don't talk but to one man and he's sitting in front of us," McCrae said, nodding to Nick. "And I made a promise to him from day one."

"You're always free to talk to whoever you want," Nick said.

"I made a promise and I'm keeping that promise," McCrae said.

"I appreciate that," Nick replied.

And then McCrae said, "The only thing I got left is my integrity."

There was never a visit to that kitchen when we didn't walk out and wonder how much of what he told us was real. But it's worth saying that doesn't make him different from most people we talked to. Nor is that any different from the feelings anybody in that county has toward anybody else. Trust in Bladen County is traded like a white-elephant gift—you may have it for a moment, but you'll probably either give it up later in the game, and if not then, certainly next year.

And in no interaction is the trust more shallow than in one between a Black person and a white person. The racial divisions in this county that is 57 percent white and 38 percent Black are astounding. To the point where it's more an accepted fact than anything worth fixing.

"Racial tension is worse here than anywhere I've ever been," a white man named Jim McVicker told Michael one October at the Beast Fest.

"Why?" Michael asked.

"Well, they don't wanna work with us," McVicker said of Black residents.

McVicker, we should point out, is the sheriff.

Duly elected, of course, with a good bit of help from the man in the swivel chair in the wood-paneled kitchen.

Leslie McCrae Dowless Jr. was born on January 3, 1956. On front pages around the country that morning was a story of a woman in Pennsylvania who gave birth to quadruplets, much to the surprise of her store-clerk husband, who made sixty-five dollars a week. Also that morning, an Associated Press story made its way to the *Robesonian* newspaper in Lumberton, just twenty-five miles from where McCrae was born. The story was about a newspaper editor out of Charleston, South Carolina, who was making the case against desegregation in the South.

McCrae was the only child Leslie Sr. and Monnie Margie Pait had together, but he was the youngest of eleven children they'd had, all told. Leslie Sr. had fathered seven in previous relationships; Monnie gave birth to three before McCrae came along.

Harry, Herman, Peggy, Mertie San, Sheldon, Filena, Ronnie, Barbara Jean, Nancy, Libby: McCrae never considered any of them half-brothers or half-sisters, just brothers and sisters. He trusted some and didn't trust others. Mostly he looked up to his dad.

McCrae spent his first ten years on a 200-acre peanut farm off of Red Hill Road in Columbus County. Their home was so far back in the woods "you had to pump sunshine in," he says. No indoor plumbing or heat. In the winter, his mother gave the family hot water by boiling it on the stove. In the summer, McCrae and his brothers took baths in a fifty-five-gallon drum.

McCrae wouldn't enjoy the luxuries of an indoor toilet until he was old enough to go to school.

"Back then, you shit outside and smoked inside," McCrae says. "Now you shit inside and smoke outside."

When he was ten, his mother and father moved him and the family across the county line to Bladenboro, the biggest place he ever lived, with a population of 783. He'd run around turning faucets on and off, marveling at how water could be cold and hot inside the same home. He flushed the toilet with delight. How on earth, he thought, did he get so lucky to live in a mansion like this?

His dad and uncle built a store and sold fertilizer off of Highway 41 in 1966. McCrae, who was ten then, worked at the store throughout his teenage years, pumping gas and loading trucks with farm goods.

Bladen County was growing at the time, its fortune riding the tobacco wave. For every ad man in New York City who needed a smoke to make a deal, there was a boy like McCrae Dowless working the hot tobacco fields of North Carolina. The state led the country in tobacco production for more than a century.

McCrae understood how farms worked, and understood numbers, even if he was never worth much in school. He knew what a dollar of fertilizer was worth to the seller and to the buyer, knew what an acre of tobacco was worth, and around here, there wasn't a whole lot else you needed to know.

As he grew older, he picked up a job or two at the cotton mill in Bladenboro. It wasn't a huge operation like those around Charlotte, but it was enough to make a buck. To a teenage boy in the late 1960s and early 1970s, the people who worked in the mill always seemed a little tougher and rougher. McCrae looked up to a few longtime lintheads he still remembers as Mousey, Punky, and Skipper.

"They didn't give a shit, man," he remembers. "Good people. Just wasn't gonna take no bullshit. These people were raised up hard on the cotton mill here."

Being the youngest in his family meant McCrae didn't have as many rules as his ten siblings. His father was lenient with him. He paid no mind when McCrae would head out at night, running to Elizabethtown to play pool at Melvin's Pool Hall, which was just behind Melvin's Hamburgers. Both were run by a man he knew as Mr. Melvin, who happened to have a boy about McCrae's age named Pat.

McCrae was hardly a hustler, but was pretty good at winning a pool game and finding a way to sneak a sip of alcohol. One day Mr. Melvin tried to cut him off before the drinking got out of hand. "McCrae," the old man said, "I better not hear of your ass drinking like these other boys do because I will whip your ass."

McCrae looked at the man, his breath half lit but his eyes somehow convincing, and said, "Mr. Melvin, I don't do that shit." Then Mr. Melvin would turn his head and McCrae would find another sip. At least that's how he remembers it: a simple story of a teenage boy getting away with something.

But Mr. Melvin was watching McCrae closely, because he had a tendency of sneaking out the back door of the hall without paying his tab.

Until late 2018, the most famous person in Bladen County was probably Guy Owen.

The late novelist grew up on a tobacco farm near Clarkton in the 1920s. His best-known work was the lighthearted 1965 book *The Ballad of the Flim-Flam Man*. It's the story of a con artist named Mordecai Jones, who travels eastern North Carolina weaseling money out of unsuspecting people.

The book became a George C. Scott movie, which includes a scene where the con man tells his accomplice about a plan to hustle people in a local card game. "That's your line, is it?" the accomplice asks.

"Greed's my line, lad," Mordecai says. "Greed."

Many people in Bladen County see McCrae Dowless as the modern-day flim-flam man.

Some folks have stories of getting scammed by him forty years ago. "I don't shake his hand. He stuck me," longtime Republican Charles DeVane says. "I used to be in the jewelry business, and he stuck me twice back in the sixties. He bought something and didn't pay for it. He [did it] one time under McCrae Dowless and then one time under Leslie Dowless."

The second time, DeVane said to Leslie McCrae Dowless, "Do you know McCrae Dowless?" and Dowless responded, "Yeah, that's my brother."

In the book version of the flim-flam man, Owen plays up the Mordecai Jones character's southern folksiness and uses it as a cover for his genius. "You can't cheat an honest man," Mordecai tells a young man. "You might say I'm one who puts his trust in the taint of corruption in the human heart."

Even though the book is a work of fiction and the movie was absurd, that faith in human fallibility has characterized real con men throughout time. In his 2013 book *Blood Will Out*, the author Walter Kirn writes about Christian Gerhartsreiter, a con man and murderer who eluded the law for years by coming up with aliases, including "Clark Rockefeller." Kirn and Gerhartsreiter engaged in their own battle of wits while working on the book, and Kirn eventually found out that in any con artist situation, the audience is as much to blame as the artist. "The last bastion of the human ego is the belief that you cannot be deceived," Kirn said in an interview in 2019. "It's not that we're dishonest; it's that we all want a little more than we deserve."

And how did "Rockefeller" dupe people for so many years? "Three words: Vanity. Vanity. Vanity," Kirn recalled Gerhartstreiter telling him once. "I find out who you wish you were but fear you're not, and I treat you like the person you wish you were."

McCrae Dowless calls both of us "buddy." He asks how we're doing, makes jokes about Nick's taste for high-dollar whiskey, and compliments Michael's Ford truck, even though he's never liked Ford much, he says. He's a salesman, at the very least. He has a way of making other people feel better about themselves, and worse for him.

When Owen's book was published, critics said the Mordecai Jones character wasn't believable. They said Owen played up too much of the character's folksiness. No way, the critics thought, would it be possible that a man like Jones would actually give himself the distinguished degrees "M.B.S., C.S., D.D.—Master of Back-Stabbing, Cork-Screwing, and Dirty-Dealing."

It does seem like a stretch.

Then again, in the fall of 2019, while he waited for an update on the fraud charges against him, McCrae Dowless started selling T-shirts to make ends meet.

Scripted on the front of the shirt was the line "McCrae Dowless: Political Operative."

Of all the vices a person can have, McCrae's was pretty clear from a young age: he had a particular weakness for women. Or at least new women.

McCrae has been married eleven times to nine different women.

"I tried to have one for every day of the week," he says.

Of them all, Sandra is the one that's made him fall the hardest and caused him the most pain. She's the reason he no longer keeps a bank account: he says she cleaned out all the money about thirty years ago.

It was Sandra's idea, McCrae says, to run a scheme that landed him in prison.

McCrae was managing a used car lot in the late 1980s with Sandra. They weren't married yet—Sandra didn't think he had enough money to support her—but they were living together. The car lot was where they met Charlie Simmons. Charlie was in his early twenties and had just moved back to North Carolina after leaving for Florida. His father, Charlie Sr., was in and out of jail for most of his childhood. In May 1990, the elder Charlie died and his son came home and found work at the used car dealership with Dowless. One day Charlie asked for a day off to go to nearby Whiteville. He was riding in a small Datsun with a friend when the car flipped and threw Charlie out. He died instantly.

A few weeks later, an insurance salesman came to the house McCrae shared with Sandra. She had an idea. The salesman sold Sandra a life insurance policy on Charlie. McCrae wrote the check to buy the policy and backdated it to before the young man died. It brought them instant money. McCrae and Sandra cashed in that life insurance policy on their dead former employee for $163,000.

That's when Sandra decided McCrae had enough money to marry, and the two went off to Vegas. She moved into his home with her ten-year-old daughter, Lisa Britt.

Not long after the wedding, they were being investigated for insurance fraud. McCrae would be charged with multiple felonies and prosecuted by a crooked, chubby-faced district attorney named Rex Gore.

Both McCrae and Sandra pleaded guilty. Sandra's sentence was just community service. McCrae would eventually go to prison. To this day, McCrae believes he shouldered the bulk of the punishment for the crime Sandra hatched.

"There was another person way more involved than I was," McCrae says, referring to her. "You can't take an old poor-ass country boy and put him in the life of the fast lane. He can't live like that. I wasn't brought up like that. You know. Not in the fast lane."

So why did Gore, the district attorney, push for McCrae to go to jail, then?

"I guess he didn't like me."

After the conviction, the feeling was mutual. McCrae spent a good portion of his prison sentence obsessing over Gore and plotting out various paths of revenge. The most satisfying, in his eyes, would be to one day watch Gore lose an election.

After he left the jail that Thanksgiving week in 1995, McCrae went home with his father and decided he wanted to start over. He moved to California to take a construction job. He says he put the lessons of hard work he learned farming peanuts and pumping gas at his daddy's store to good use, diving into fifteen-hour days on a construction site seven days a week.

After six months, McCrae returned home with $40,000 worth of checks in his pocket.

McCrae used that money to buy some land and a house. He continued working as a construction foreman, but he never could get Gore, the district attorney, out of his mind. So he picked up a new hobby: politics.

In 1998, McCrae took a job handing out campaign literature for Gore's opponent. Gore still won, but McCrae was enthralled by the process—in particular, the idea that campaigns knew, to the voter, how many votes to expect from each precinct.

A flim-flam man pays attention. Far better than you might expect. Mc-Crae doesn't miss much. He even has a habit of finishing sentences for you, mumbling the last words as if he knew them before you did. Your own words. He'll point to you as he says them, not only to make it clear he knew what you were about to say, but to validate it for you in the process. It's a remarkable trick, and one that comes natural to him.

In the 1998 campaign against Gore, McCrae sponged up everything he could about elections. He loved the maps on the walls that showed where people lived and who they were likely to vote for. In a world that hardly made sense to him sometimes, elections had boundaries and numbers.

The campaign gave him one more thing that he never received in any other job: respect. Out here, telling people who to vote for and seeing how it could result in a person of power being stripped of it overnight, he saw a future for himself.

And it should be noted—and highlighted and circled—that McCrae Dowless believed his future in politics would be with an organization that was growing in size and influence, one built to ensure that Black people had positions in office. McCrae Dowless's team back then was the Bladen County Improvement Association PAC.

To understand how the election fraud of 2018 happened, we have to go back not just to McCrae's days with Bladen Improvement, but to the organization's earliest days and its rise as a powerful, necessary political force.

★ ★ ★

A Girl, Born into the Jim Crow South April 1936

★ ★ ★

If we're going to fight for democracy, we would like to experience it.
DURHAM COMMITTEE ON NEGRO AFFAIRS

In the spring of 1936, out on a tobacco farm in an unincorporated area of far eastern Bladen County that's closer to Wilmington than it is to Tar Heel, Delilah Bowen was born.

She was the daughter of Archie and Lena Bowen. She had a white grandfather and a Native American grandmother. Family portraits in her house decades later show many shades of skin. Delilah's had freckles.

Her dad was a farmer, first a tenant farmer and then an owner. He grew tobacco, corn, and soybeans. She liked that he was a farmer. She thought it made her rich. She learned how to work the land, too, like kids in her day did. She was hanging tobacco to dry before she was a teenager. But she loved school more. She went to East Arcadia School in a small wooden building that housed children from elementary school through high school. Career opportunities were hardly in abundance for Black children at the time, but in that wooden schoolhouse during World War II, Delilah could see a profession that seemed available, and attainable, and respectable. Right there and then, she set out to become an educator.

There was a train stop not far from her parents' home, and she had a habit of running down to see who was getting on and who was getting off. She befriended one of the train employees who helped with baggage. He learned how much she loved to read, and he would pick up a newspaper from Wilmington for her whenever he knew he was coming through East Arcadia. He gathered loose books left behind by passengers. As the train slowed down on its way into town, he'd toss the newspaper and books in her family's backyard.

She knew as a kid what many of her friends would realize later in life: nothing was as important to the civil rights movement that would soon erupt in the South as education.

Eight months before Delilah was born, a young Black man who'd grown up about twenty miles west of her house, CC Spaulding, joined six men at the Durham Tennis Club to form the Durham Committee on Negro Affairs.

Spaulding was from one of the most prominent Black families in North Carolina, one that traced back to Benjamin and Edith Spaulding, a freed slave and a Native American who'd accumulated hundreds of acres of land along the Bladen-Columbus county line. The Spauldings formed schools and churches in Bladen County, and their family reunions had grown into some of the biggest parties of the year. They became politicians, too. One of CC's ancestors, John, was Bladen County's first Black county commissioner. CC's illustrious cousin, George Henry White, served in the U.S. House and was the country's last Black congressman before the Jim Crow era.

When eastern North Carolina became the center of the hostile and deadly white supremacy campaigns of the late nineteenth century, several Spaulding descendants moved to Durham, a small city with a reputation for welcoming Black entrepreneurs. One, Aaron McDuffie Moore, cofounded the North Carolina Mutual Life Insurance Company. Moore was CC Spaulding's uncle, and CC took over the company after Moore's death in 1923.

CC Spaulding would turn North Carolina Mutual Life into the country's largest Black-owned business. He and his fellow businessmen would make Durham the capital of the Black middle class. They formed a Black Wall Street there, taking the name after white supremacists burned down Tulsa's Black Wall Street in 1921. But they knew that to maintain it, and to avoid the same fate as Tulsa, they needed Black political influence.

The hot August night they formed the committee, their mission was to bring Black people together to discuss community issues and determine which political fights were most worth taking on. They intended to tackle them as a group, all Black people of Durham, in order to try to gain representation. Unity was the goal. If Black people would all agree to support one issue or one candidate, they knew they would have more sway.

CC Spaulding was known as a more conservative member of the Black community, someone who was able to appease whites while still making progress. His friendships with the city's white leadership often frustrated his friends and neighbors, but he didn't believe he had a choice. He had learned how to maneuver the fields of white supremacy the hard way. He'd come to Durham in the 1890s from the family land in Bladen and Columbus Counties, finished high school here and worked a mess of "Negro jobs," from dishwasher to bellhop. He worked his way up in business.

His success made him a natural selection as the first chairman of the Durham Committee on Negro Affairs (DCNA). While the group had several more progressive characters, Spaulding possessed the temperament and skills to drive change. "He wasn't a man to carry any ill feeling," Conrad Odell Pearson, another DCNA founder, said later. "He was just a man who had succeeded with a country background."

Change came soon after the committee formed. Durham went from 50 registered Black voters in 1928 to more than 3,000 by 1939. In 1938, they ran a Black candidate for elected office. Over the next decade, Black people would become firemen in Durham, and police officers.

They engaged in a battle for a new bus station in Durham. They'd long since accepted that the station would have white entrances and Black entrances, but to put the Black entrance on the sign with the garbage dumpsters was unjust, they argued. "If we're going to fight for democracy," another committee member said at the time, "we would like to experience it."

The state utilities commission denied the request, but the case and the publicity around it set the stage for Black organizing in the state. The Durham Committee on Negro Affairs would engage in countless battles over separate and unequal schools and other civil rights matters. It was the first Black political action committee (PAC) in North Carolina, and its work in those early years fathered dozens of followers around the state for the next half century. Its model was replicated everywhere from Charlotte to Greensboro to a small political committee for Black people in eastern North Carolina known as the Bladen Improvement Association PAC.

The era of Jim Crow, which took its name from a nineteenth-century minstrel show character in blackface, lasted six decades in eastern North Carolina. It officially began when Homer Plessy boarded a "whites only" train car in Louisiana in 1892, leading to the Supreme Court's *Plessy v. Ferguson* "separate but equal" decision four years later.

But in North Carolina, the era is probably best defined as the time between CC's cousin George Henry White's departure from Congress in 1901 and 4 P.M. on February 1, 1960, when four Black students from North Carolina A&T sat down at a Woolworth's lunch counter in Greensboro and launched the sit-in movement throughout the South. One of those students was a young man named Joseph McNeil, who grew up in Wilmington, where his most distinct memory as a child was the time his dog, Trigger, got sick. McNeil rushed the dog to the vet, who looked at the boy and said, "We don't take colored dogs."

McNeil and his friends went to college as angry young men, McNeil once told Michael. The Greensboro sit-in sparked a political moment for righteous, justified fury just like theirs. Young Black people sat down at lunch counters in Durham and Greensboro and Winston-Salem and Charlotte, and then so did people in Charleston and Nashville. Many of them were defying their Black parents and grandparents and the established Black newspapers warning the young people that their "radical" steps would set back Black progress. A high school boy who started the sit-in movement in Charleston, South Carolina, didn't even tell his parents what he was doing. He organized it with friends through quiet channels, then made the move without alerting anyone in his family. That teenage boy, Harvey Gantt, went on to become the first Black student at Clemson University, and then the first Black mayor of Charlotte.

Of course, the 1950s were full of incidents that set the foundation for the 1960s. The *Brown v. Board of Education* high court decision to desegregate schools led to a widespread rush to integrate everything else. In 1955, six Black men in Greensboro, led by a dentist named George Simkins, went to the public golf course and asked to play. They put down the greens fees, but the course manager told them to leave. They dropped the money and played anyway, only to be arrested that night. The case went to the Supreme Court, which ruled against the course, helping to open public recreation spaces for Black people in the South.

Meanwhile, on the morning of September 4, 1957, a fifteen-year-old Charlotte girl named Dorothy Counts buttoned up the neck on a checkered dress made by her rural seamstress grandmother and hopped in the backseat of her father's car to go to school. When Dorothy opened the door to get out, a crowd led by the White Citizens Council greeted her. She walked right through that crowd, through spit and rocks and insults, to desegregate the city's schools. A picture of Dorothy landed on the front page of the *New York Times* the next day, right next to a picture of Elizabeth Eckford of the Little Rock Nine in Arkansas.

But none of those things could've happened without the earlier work of organizations like the Durham Committee on Negro Affairs and other Black political action committees throughout the South.

In those committees' earliest years, the 1930s and 1940s, they knew that if they wanted representation that could lead to desegregation, they needed eligible Black voters. And if they wanted eligible Black voters, they had to educate people to pass the absurd literacy tests, which sound easier than they actually were. The tests were minefields that measured far more than one's ability to read.

Probably the best-known example is young Rosanell Eaton, just thirteen years older than Delilah. Eaton was born in the northeastern North Carolina town of Louisburg. Not long after her twenty-first birthday in 1942, Eaton took her family's mule-drawn wagon to the courthouse to vote.

The writer Vann R. Newkirk II, who grew up in the eastern North Carolina town of Rocky Mount, wrote of Eaton's experience in a 2016 article in the *Atlantic*:

> In order to even prove herself eligible to vote, Eaton recalled, she had to put her hands by her side, stare straight ahead, and recite the Preamble to the Constitution, verbatim. Whether those three administrators were aware of the staggering irony of their demand or not, she stood straight, stared at a spot behind them on the wall, and aced the recitation, word for word. Apparently, so few black people had even been bold—or foolhardy—enough to even take the test that the registrars had no thought of intimidation beyond that point. "You did a mighty good job," one man told Eaton. "Well, I reckon I have to have you to sign these papers."

These are the things fledgling political committees in North Carolina worked toward in the mid-twentieth century. They not only needed their voters to be educated—they needed their voters to be *better educated* than white voters. The growing state NAACP joined in support. Lost to time, or perhaps better described as overshadowed by the 1960s, are stories about how many wins they actually had in the years leading up to the sit-ins.

"The amazing thing is that in North Carolina, in the forties and fifties, African American teachers were paid at the same level or higher than white teachers," the professor and civil rights attorney Irv Joyner told us. "The key to overcoming Jim Crow was seen to be education: *We educate our folk. We educate them and get them ready to go out there and challenge in the marketplace. And that will result in Jim Crow crumbling."*

That work in the 1940s paved the way for *Brown v. Board of Education* in 1954. Four other cases were rolled into *Brown*, including *Briggs v. Elliott*, a case filed in rural South Carolina, where some Black kids were walking twelve miles to and from school.

Widespread movements are often reduced to a few moments or flashpoints. But the organizing that occurred throughout North Carolina in the 1930s and 1940s was vital to setting up what was to come.

Delilah Bowen, the little girl who waited for the newspapers and books to come flying out the train window in eastern Bladen County, went on to a double major at Shaw, a historically Black college in Raleigh, then went straight into teaching high school in eastern North Carolina. She married Eddie Windell Blanks, giving her the name that she'd carry into her political work and activism for the next six decades, Delilah Blanks.

It's the name that rolls from the mouths of people in Bladen County whenever we ask who the most influential Black political figure of the past fifty years has been.

"*Deliiiiilah Blanks,*" Charles Ray Peterson, a white county commissioner, said with a smile. There's something about the way the three *l*'s buddy up next to the vowels in her name that make it like a thirteen-letter southern lyric.

"He hates me and loves me at the same time," Blanks told us of Peterson.

Blanks moved back to Bladen County in the early 1960s and took jobs with the county's social services department as a child welfare employee. Then she moved on to college instruction as an assistant professor of social work at UNC Wilmington.

Her story is important not only to Bladen County but to all of eastern North Carolina. And not just because of what she would go on to do after that, but because of what she represented. During a generation in which hundreds of thousands of Black families hustled out of the South on midnight trains, Delilah had something in common with George Simkins, who led the Greensboro golf course protest, and Dorothy Counts, who desegregated Charlotte's schools: they came back home and fought.

Delilah was hellbent on making sure future generations of Black children had equal access to everything from parks to politics, same as any of the other great leaders of her generation. But she was doing it in Bladen County, which was dozens if not more years behind other areas of the state.

Just one or two generations before her, the white terror campaigns of the late 1800s had been especially brutal in eastern North Carolina. Families had been torn apart, Black businesses burned to the ground. So any viable political movements took a little longer to form than they did in places like Durham.

Blanks and the organization she led, the Bladen Improvement Association, didn't gain momentum until the 1980s. They won a court case to expand the board from five members to nine, securing at least three districts that were predominantly Black. They rallied around candidates in district and at-large races and, over time, integrated the local elected offices.

As the 1980s became the 1990s and then the 2000s, Blanks and the Improvement Association became the dominant political forces in the county. They were the manifestation of the idea Bladen native CC Spaulding had seventy-some years earlier when he founded the Durham Committee on Negro Affairs.

Still, by the spring of 2010, the biggest and most important office in the county had eluded them: sheriff.

That year Delilah Blanks looked to her son-in-law, a fifty-year-old captain in the Bladen County Sheriff's Office named Prentis Benston, to fix that.

The Black Sheriff 2010

The only man who can remove me is a Superior Court judge or death.
INTERIM SHERIFF EARL STORMS

The first time McCrae Dowless allowed Nick into his home, in December 2018, McCrae assembled a couple of local Republican dignitaries, including Ray Britt, the chairman of the county commission and owner of the discount furniture store.

Nick sat at the table in the smoky kitchen and expected to take notes on the 2018 election. But facing worldwide attention for his county's role in a congressional election that would later be declared a fraud, Britt launched into an entirely different set of grievances.

"It all goes back to 2010," he said, before lowering his voice to emphasize the words that have since become the motif of GOP-led election fraud claims, "and *the nursing home.*"

★   ★   ★

The 2010 election was crucial in North Carolina. It was the first midterm of the Obama administration, and a census year. That meant the party that claimed the state legislature would have license to draw the congressional district maps for the next decade. Democrats had controlled the legislature for more than a century, but a budding Republican state house member and minority whip named Thom Tillis, who just a few years earlier was best known as a youth sports coach, launched a county-by-county, door-to-door campaign to rally Republican support.

Tillis, a fit dad with close-cropped hair who'd built a nice suburban life as an IT consultant, connected with people. Speaking with a heavy Tennessee twang, he told voters that they needed to go conservative, not only to counter the Obama administration and the controversial Affordable Care Act that was passed that spring, but to take back both houses of the legislature for the first time since 1896.

If they did that, they could draw congressional districts that would effectively erase North Carolina Democrats' considerable registration advantage over Republicans.

Bladen County in 2010 had 15,591 Democrats on the rolls, compared to 2,819 Republicans. The disparity may be surprising, especially when you consider that the county has almost twice as many white voters as Black voters. But many Democrats in Bladen were white descendants of the Dixiecrats, who opposed extending civil rights to Black people in the mid-1900s, and they were beginning to vote Republican.

Into this volatile political concoction—the national resistance to Obama, the statewide GOP organization, and the local divide between white Democrats and Black Democrats—stepped Prentis Benston. On February 9, 2010, the second day for filing in Bladen County, Benston launched his campaign for sheriff, and Bladen County hasn't been the same since.

He was by then fifty years old and bald on top, with hair wrapping from ear to ear around the back of his head. He always wore glasses and looked more like a teacher or professor than a police officer. But he'd served for more than two decades in law enforcement, the last several as a captain in the Bladen County Sheriff's Office. He helped lead torch runs for the Special Olympics and several other feel-good campaigns. But more than anything, to a significant portion of Bladen County's population, Prentis Benston was defined by one characteristic: he was Black, and now he was running for sheriff.

White people could deal with Black politicians, Black business owners. But a sheriff? Designed to shape and enforce the law? Few things could stir up deep-rooted racism like the thought of that.

Whites quickly circulated fearful rumors reminiscent of post-Reconstruction eastern North Carolina. That spring the local paper ran several stories and op-eds that painted Benston as a nice man, but one who was aloof and distant and would probably lead the county down a lawless path.

Black people in the county brought their own fire, though. For more than a century since the Civil War, they'd had their lives and minds and bodies policed by men who didn't look like them. From nights in the 1860s when men on horses would threaten to hang a Black man who voted, to the decades during Jim Crow and highway stops on lonesome country roads when the only witnesses were pine trees, Black people here dreaded interactions with law enforcement. For some, Benston was the uniformed embodiment of emancipation.

To McCrae Dowless, the only color that matters is green—and even though that's an old cliché, with him it's true, especially considering he still doesn't have a bank account.

In a county where racism permeates everything, McCrae Dowless simply could not care about anything else but scratching together dollar bills. If you were to hold an online competition for, let's just say favorite southern dessert, and he was in charge of piling up votes for pecan pie, and you were droning on about your love for banana pudding, McCrae Dowless would make an enemy out of you.

Throughout the early stages of his political career, McCrae worked as an apprentice in the Bladen Improvement Association PAC, the organization that gets out the Black vote.

After getting that initial taste of politics, McCrae became an obsessive. He printed six-foot-square maps of the county, put them on his walls, and drew district borders. Many followed the straight lines of country roads. Some families that lived across the road from each other were in different districts and needed different yard signs. He requested voter rolls and estimated vote totals for each candidate.

In those early years, a Black man named Harold Ford was the treasurer of the Improvement PAC. Ford was one of the most respected figures in the county, Black or white. He fought in Korea and came home to teach and coach football and basketball at the segregated Booker T. Washington High. He did enough good work there that the superintendent made him the basketball coach at the integrated Clarkton High in 1970.

Michael met Harold Ford in January 2020, after Ford had ridden as the grand marshal in the local Martin Luther King Jr. parade. At eighty-nine, Ford smiled and laughed through each question he didn't hear. His daughter-in-law answered many of them for him. He beamed when he talked about his service and days coaching high school. He said he'd won "seven or eight" state championships at Clarkton, but who can keep count? He's one of those older men in a rural county whose every birthday makes the newspaper, a man for whom guys from the American Legion will line up to shake a hand and say goodbye. McCrae Dowless called him "Mr. Harold Ford." He was the only person Dowless called "Mr." in all of our conversations.

McCrae learned all of the tools of get-out-the-vote from the Improvement PAC. For instance, he learned that when you're working the polls or mailing pamphlets, a list of Bladen Improvement–endorsed candidates is only as good as the voter holding it. Dowless called upon a lifetime of knowledge in the county to sort out who would be receptive. And often in those early years, it wasn't as simple as spotting a Black person and handing her a sheet. Dowless knew which Black people were likely to vote against the powerful PAC's choices, and he knew which white people would vote for them. Within a few years, he didn't even need to hand out anything—people just called him to ask for his recommendation.

If you were a candidate, you wanted Dowless not because you liked him or because you wanted to be his friend, but because you knew that he was worth far more than just his one vote. If you had him, you knew that he would bring hundreds more. Not only would those hundreds of votes now be added to your column, they would be subtracted from the opponent's count as well. Double the influence.

"I could sit right here at the house, and if they bring me a sheet with the names on it of who's voted, I can still give you how the election's gonna go," he tells us. It's bluster; it's also a fact.

But McCrae's relationship with the Improvement PAC soured after a man named Horace Munn took over. McCrae maintains that he has a good relationship with Munn to this day. But sometime during the late 2000s, McCrae realized that he, as a white man, would hit a ceiling in the organization. So he went out on his own and took many of his people with him. The Bladen Improvement Association still reigned as the most powerful political organization in the county. It wouldn't be easy to compete with them, he knew.

At first he was a fairly bipartisan freelancer—in May 2009 he even hosted a bipartisan Politician's Appreciation Dinner at a local vineyard. "It's really a good thing for the people to get out and meet who represents them," he told the local paper, sounding like the county's convener in chief. "If you're new to the area and don't know who your representatives are, you can come out to meet them."

Problem is, there weren't many people who are "new to the area" in Bladen County. So for his operation to really take off, he needed a big, public, flag-in-the-ground election. Then, in the spring of 2010, Lieutenant Eric Bryan, a white man, announced he would run against Prentis Benston in the Democratic sheriff's primary.

McCrae saw it as an opportunity to rebrand himself. He went to work for Bryan.

And one of the nastiest primary elections in county history—Benston/Blanks/Improvement PAC versus Bryan/Dowless/white conservatives—was on.

In early April 2010, Lieutenant Eric Bryan asked his superiors if he could take a leave of absence to campaign. The question rose to the level of the county commission. Delilah Blanks, the mother-in-law of Bryan's opponent, rallied seven votes to deny his request.

Then, on April 15, on the eastern edge of the county where she'd grown up, Delilah cast her ballot at her home polling station in East Arcadia. The next week, one of McCrae's workers called him with big news: they'd seen Blanks pull into a different polling station at the public library. She went in to ask to vote, but poll workers had stopped her. She told the *Bladen Journal* that she was just "testing the system" and that she'd notified the elections board director. The director said that no such conversation took place.

Meanwhile, the outgoing white sheriff threw his support behind Bryan—and undercut the county commission by granting Bryan his leave of absence in defiance of their vote.

Blanks, whose political ties extended all the way to Raleigh and Washington, responded by filing charges with the federal Office of the Special Counsel, alleging that Bryan was in violation of the Hatch Act, which prohibits public servants from engaging in partisan activities.

Each accusation elevated the tension. All the while, stranger and stranger things were happening in Bladen County. That same spring, a popular at-large county commissioner died of pneumonia. The board quickly appointed a longtime board of education administrator to fill the seat. Then that man steered his 2000 Honda passenger car into oncoming traffic on a rural two-lane road. An eighteen-wheeler struck the car, killing the new commissioner and his mother.

The board then appointed a Black farmer to the cursed seat. The farmer was well-liked by white people, but the Bladen Improvement PAC threw their support behind another Black man, who would challenge the farmer.

It was a lot of drama for one small-town primary election in 2010—and it wasn't over yet.

With Dowless's help, Bryan claimed the most votes in the May primary—209 more than Benston. But in the five-person race, Bryan's percentage of votes was only 38.6 compared to Benston's 36. A candidate needs 40 percent to avoid a runoff, and the rematch was set for late June. That's when the election turned truly strange.

As early voting began for the runoff in early June, Bryan told McCrae he didn't want his help, that he wanted to keep it simple. "Eric, if you don't do early voting, you're going to lose," McCrae warned him.

Bryan relented and allowed Dowless in. Within just a few days, Benston's team planted a story in the *Journal*. It said that Bryan, as a candidate for county sheriff, had hired a convicted felon—McCrae Dowless.

McCrae ignored the bad press and got to work. He printed a list of all the voters in the county and scoured it, name by name, marking the ones he knew would vote for Bryan and the ones who would vote for Benston. This was still the primary, so every name still had a D beside it. But McCrae knows his county, and all he needed were names and addresses to run the rough tally. "I'm not saying I'm the best there is doing elections," McCrae says, "but I know the people in Bladen County."

Mostly it came down to race. Dowless picked out the white voters—and the few Black voters he knew would vote against Benston—and made sure they had wheels to the polls. He arranged rides for those who didn't. The strategy isn't illegal, as long as the hauler isn't offering bribes to woo people in the vehicle. Day after day, Dowless and his operation shuttled people to the local board of elections in Elizabethtown, the only place to vote early in Bladen County.

Benston's campaign manager was a mustached white man named Jens Lutz. Just a few days before the primary, Lutz sent a letter to the state board alleging that McCrae was doing more than driving people to the polls. He said that some people in "public housing boasted of being paid" for working for McCrae.

After the story of McCrae being a convicted felon came out, *someone* alerted the *Journal* that Benston had accepted a $4,000 donation from a registered sex offender. Benston returned the check, but each new day brought new punches, and McCrae kept rolling up to the polls with a van full of people. Jens Lutz boiled every time he saw a new load of voters. McCrae even set up a pop-up canopy across the street, in a lot with loading docks and dumpsters and trash cans.

One day McCrae was standing where the parking lot meets the road when he heard a motorcycle. He looked over and saw it was headed toward him. He jumped back. The bike missed him. When he looked up, he saw Jens Lutz driving it. He'd tried to run over McCrae.

One of McCrae's friends ran toward the idling motorcycle and its unhinged driver. "Buddy," the friend said, "there ain't gonna be none of this here today."

On the morning of the primary election runoff, June 22, the *Bladen Journal* ran a headline: "One for the Record Books: Board of Elections has been swamped with residents voting early for sheriff."

Nearly 3,000 had taken advantage of early voting, and 715 absentee ballots had been received. By night's end, 39 percent of the county's registered voters participated. In North Carolina at the time, municipalities rarely saw more than 10 percent turnout in a local primary. Bladen was having a runoff in the dead of summer, with temperatures nipping 100 degrees, and damn near 40 percent of the people voted.

A skeptical person might say the number was too high to be true, but for McCrae Dowless and Jens Lutz, the votes were the fruits of hard work.

Local officials set up a big-screen television in the courthouse in Elizabethtown on election night. They told visitors they had a new technology system in which the poll workers would bring a flash drive to the election office, and then the elections board would upload those results to the state board and they'd show up on the screen.

About a hundred people came to the courthouse watch party. First they saw the early-voting and absentee numbers, the ones that mattered most to the ballot harvesters. Benston had a 583–302 edge in early votes, and a 447–299 edge in absentee. That's 429 total votes he was up.

Then came the precincts. They would show Benston winning 3,878–3,583, or by 295 votes. In other words, the race was won in early and absentee voting.

You could call McCrae Dowless every name in the book, and you could tell him his mama couldn't cook and his daddy couldn't farm, and you tell him he was a failure as a car salesman, and you could tell him he was a crook and a flim-flam man, but there's not a thing in this world that could hurt his ego more than telling him he was responsible for the difference in a losing election.

"Prentis Benston has won the election," the elections chairman, who happened to be Ray Britt of Ray's Inc. at the time, said in the courthouse that night. "There will not be another runoff."

People gasped. Black people hugged each other around the neck. Benston hopped from his seat and shook Bryan's hand. His chin quivered while he addressed the crowd: "I have to thank God for this."

To McCrae Dowless and other white conservative Democrats, one explanation for Benston's primary victory made more sense than divine intervention: he must've cheated.

That was just the primary!

Overnight, conservatives rallied around Billy Ward, a white man who had been a Democrat but now signed his name as unaffiliated. He hurriedly gathered signatures to become eligible to compete in the fall general election.

On July 1, the sitting sheriff retired. The commissioners swore in retired sheriff Earl Storms to run the department on an interim basis, just until the general election. Storms had been sheriff from 1976 to 1994, and he agreed to take the interim post only because the commissioners asked him to.

Storms was a Benston supporter. The day of his swearing in, his first official business was to rehire detectives and deputies. He decided not to rehire Eric Bryan. Just like that, with no explanation, Bryan went from a few votes short of becoming sheriff to out of a job altogether.

Storms then quickly installed progressive reforms aimed at reducing Black incarceration. He told his deputies not to conduct vehicle stops. He ordered radar guns removed from sheriff's vehicles. It all but confirmed the white conservatives' worst fears—that Prentis Benston was already directing the department down the road toward lawlessness, with Storms just serving as a temporary swinging door. They called a meeting of the commission to discuss Storms's conduct.

Storms didn't attend the meeting.

"The only man who can remove me is a Superior Court judge or death," Storms said.

Whether Storms's motives were pure and he truly believed he was fighting for justice didn't really matter in the end. His brief tenure seemed to give the county residents a glimpse of what they might expect from Benston. A feverish group of white supporters emerged to back the unaffiliated candidate in the general, Billy Ward. In the meantime, the racial divisions within the sheriff's office were being laid bare, with employees siding with one candidate or another.

"Right now," a deputy told the *Journal* that month, speaking anonymously, "Bladen County is a criminal's paradise."

"DO NOT VOTE A STRAIGHT TICKET!! VOTE BILLY WARD FOR SHERIFF—UNAFFILIATED!!!" Billy Ward wrote on his Facebook page, hoping the all-caps message resonated with his audience, many of whom filled out an all-Democrat ballot for decades. He posted the message over and over during early voting.

To many others—especially white Democrats—the sixty-year-old opened their eyes to an avenue out of the party. It was the summer of 2010, the same season when WikiLeaks dumped about 90,000 pages of classified documents about the U.S. efforts in Afghanistan, the same summer when the Deepwater Horizon spill pumped millions of barrels of oil into the Gulf of Mexico.

As the calendar turned to October and early-voting season began, Bladen's opposing political forces poured everything they had into the get-out-the-vote efforts. The polling stations looked like shuttle bus stops—one minute a car with Bladen Improvement PAC people pulled up, the next came a group of folks from McCrae's side.

More than 7,000 voters cast early ballots in Bladen County in the fall of 2010—nearly half the overall vote total. And more than 6,100 of those early voters made a selection in the sheriff's race. Benston won the absentee by mail vote, 481–279.

As Election Day drew closer and it became clearer that the Bladen Improvement Association PAC was more organized than McCrae was, conservatives in the Ward camp started building their last-gasp defense to try to prevent a Black man from becoming their sheriff. They began circulating a story of something they claimed took place two blocks from the board of elections office.

Elizabethtown Healthcare and Rehabilitation Center is a one-story building with a light brown roof that has about ninety-four beds for residents, just outside the main downtown strip in Elizabethtown. As the general election approached that fall, conservative Democrats like Pat Melvin and McCrae Dowless came to believe that the Bladen Improvement PAC was going into nursing homes to peel votes from people who were in various stages of cognitive decline.

"They would go to nursing homes. They would get people unconscious to get an absentee ballot. They'd go to the graveyard," Charles DeVane, a contractor and longtime GOP donor, told us in 2018. "The Bladen Improvement Association does not represent the majority of the Black people in Bladen County. The majority of the Black people in Bladen County would have nothing to do with something if it was illegal. But they take the poor and the ignorant and lead 'em."

Several Ward supporters launched their own investigation into the matter. They found, they insist, a batch of questionable ballots. Among them were eight that were locked away at the board of elections office for safekeeping. But those eight nursing home votes didn't make a difference in the end.

Benston won the November election, 6,398 to 5,844—a margin that was more votes than the total absentee difference. When talking to supporters on election night at the courthouse, Benston started his victory remarks by simply saying, "It has been a long nine months."

That same night, Republicans were celebrating across the state of North Carolina. The Thom Tillis–led conservative movement swept nearly everywhere through the state. Republicans went from down ten seats to up ten in the state Senate, and from down seventeen in the House to fifteen up.

But in Bladen County, somehow, Democrats swept nearly every race, including the only one that mattered, the only one that ever matters: sheriff.

The losses left Bladen County conservatives incensed. Over the next two years, and especially over the next four years under Sheriff Benston's administration, white Democrats fled the party in waves.

But that wasn't all they were going to do. "You have to fight fire with fire," DeVane told his friends.

Those eight nursing home ballots were what Ray Britt and McCrae Dowless wanted to talk to Nick about that day in 2018 when they first met in Dowless's kitchen. Their conversation, as it turns out, foreshadowed the election fraud claims that would spread throughout the nation over the next few years. From Georgia to Michigan, election losers have accused winners of stealing nursing home votes, echoing the stories that Bladen County's operatives have been telling since 2010.

Ray and McCrae say they took the complaint to the state and county elections leaders. They say those leaders called a meeting two years later and told everybody to knock it off. But nobody bothered to do anything formal. In fact, Britt said, the state elections director denied ever receiving a complaint.

To check the story out, Nick visited the county board of elections to see if the ballots were still there. The elections office looks like it could be one of those old photocopying businesses. Just inside the door is a tall front desk, almost shoulder height for a medium-built person.

A woman at the desk seemed not to know what Nick was talking about. She summoned Jens Lutz—the man from the motorcycle years earlier—who was now vice chairman of the county board of elections. Lutz said no such ballots from 2010 were at the elections board office.

By coincidence, at that very moment state elections director Kim Strach walked in with the board's lead investigator. "Let's go in here and talk," Strach said to Lutz. Nick watched the three disappear into a conference room.

Now with the room to herself, the same front-desk worker who just a few minutes earlier had professed ignorance now whispered to Nick that she would go retrieve the ballots for him. Sure enough, she came back with all eight. All with related material and still locked in a small safe inside the county board of elections. She removed the contents carefully and set them on the counter.

The papers showed that the eight ballots were cast by people who lived in the same nursing home. Some of them, the notes showed, had never voted before—or even registered to vote, for that matter. The materials included fax cover sheets showing transmissions to an investigator for the state board of elections and a card for a special agent with the SBI.

There were the ballots, and there was the proof they'd been sent to the authorities. What wasn't there was any evidence showing that anything had been done to investigate them after that.

★ ★ ★

The Backlash 2014

★ ★ ★

Am I a white nationalist or a white supremacist?
PAT MELVIN

Nobody fumed over Benston's victory in the sheriff's race like Pat Melvin.

The hamburger heir is the most influential conservative in Bladen County. A short man with glasses and a spit-shined bald head, Melvin speaks a speedy brand of southern that suits his career as a real estate agent. He's a classic small-town character, the man who came from money and tilled it up to make more money on top of that.

The flat-top hamburger place his father started in 1938 achieved road-trip royalty status. The *Washington Post* stopped in once to write about it. *Our State* magazine, the lifestyle Bible for rural North Carolina, named it one of the hundred foods you have to eat in the state. Pat bought the business from his dad in 1971 but eventually got tired of all the grease and sold it in the early 2000s, sending it out of the family after almost seventy years.

Underneath that smile and slaw recipe, Pat can be bristly. His family line goes straight back to the establishment of Elizabethtown as the Bladen County seat in 1773. That history is one reason Pat's vowed to never run for political office: "You can go down to the courthouse and see how many slaves we owned," he says.

But there's another, more likely reason Pat Melvin's never run for office: he doesn't need to. A job on the county commission would be a step down on the power hierarchy. He's never backed away from a fight with any town or county board, on any subject from elections to the size of an awning outside the Bladen Hardware building he owns.

The *Bladen Journal*'s called him "hard-headed and stubborn" and has implored elected officials to stand up to him. In an editorial a few years ago, the paper saw fit to remind city leadership: "This is Elizabethtown, not Melvinville."

Melvin's forefathers settled in Bladen County around the same time three brothers with the last name Helms migrated here. Their descendants spread throughout eastern North Carolina and into the Piedmont. One of them, born in 1921, was a boy by the name of Jesse.

Jesse Helms would go on to serve more terms in the U.S. Senate than any other person in North Carolina history. A polite description of Helms might be to call him the architect of modern conservatism; a more pointed one might describe him as a race-baiting segregationist who depressed civil rights for Black people and gay people throughout his thirty-year run in the Senate.

One of Helms's most famous campaigns was the 1990 effort against Harvey Gantt, who'd served as Charlotte's first Black mayor. Gantt ran a campaign that explicitly avoided the topic of race, and he was ahead in the polls going into the last month of the race. That's when Helms launched the notorious "Hands" advertising campaign, which included a simple close-up of a white person crumpling up a piece of paper while a narrator says, "You needed that job and you were the best qualified, but they had to give it to a minority because of a racial quota. Is that really fair? Harvey Gantt says it is." Helms won the election the next week. He won another one six years later.

Pat Melvin's entry into politics was working on local campaigns for Jesse Helms. To this day, Pat still identifies with the term conservative Democrats in eastern North Carolina used to describe their support of Helms: "Jessecrats."

Melvin has a Martin Luther King Jr. picture in the back corner of his office. He's talked about race with Michael several times in that office. In one case he even opened the conversation with it: "So tell me, Mike, you're the media. Am I a white nationalist or a white supremacist?"

This was sarcasm. He went on to say that journalists of today seem to label every white conservative by one epithet or the other. But as always, this kind of sarcasm brings with it some strands of truth. Melvin has lots to say on the subject of race. In one conversation, with that MLK picture still sitting over his right shoulder, he said, "What, what if I called people a Black nationalist or Black supremacist? They'd go ballistic. But that's all right for us? We can also have the United Negro College Fund. What if we had the United White College Fund?

"In other words, they don't get any backlash, but let us do it."

And after Prentis Benston's election, they did it.

State Republicans did everything they promised to do following the 2010 takeover. They redrew the congressional districts, held quiet public hearings about them at the state museum of history, then cast them in southern lore. A state that has more Democrats than Republicans was now almost certain to have ten Republicans in Washington and three Democrats. The legislators carved out three surefire Democratic districts by creating river-shaped boundaries that conveniently pulled in most of the state's Black people.

The conservative swing wasn't just about race, though. Another matter would capture the attention of the country moving into 2012: North Carolina's effort to ban same-sex marriage. Especially in rural places like Bladen, it was an issue that crossed the color line. And one of the architects of the campaign was a preacher from Charlotte with good hair named Mark Harris.

Harris was born about seventy miles northwest of the Ninth District, in Winston-Salem, at what was then known as Baptist Hospital. In 1980, when he was fourteen years old, he spent three days a week volunteering at the "Americans for Reagan" campaign offices in his hometown. From there he went to Appalachian State and majored in political science. He'd been planning to go to law school in the fall of 1987 when he asked Beth to marry him. That summer, he worked as a full-time youth minister and felt called to another profession.

"It happened two weeks before my wedding, and I told Beth that she was not marrying an attorney, she was marrying a preacher," Harris once told the *Charlotte Observer*.

Two years later, he had his first job at a church in a Winston-Salem suburb. The church's Sunday School membership was 50; over the next decade he was there, it grew to nearly 800.

He brought that momentum to First Baptist Church in Charlotte in 2005. He started as co-pastor, filling in while his predecessor, who was dying of cancer, served his final months. The burden of a Baptist church leader in Charlotte goes beyond the walls of one building or one congregation. This is the city, after all, that gave birth to Billy Graham.

Harris willingly stepped into his first major controversy in 2010. That's when a coalition of atheists and agnostics purchased space on billboards in six North Carolina cities in an attempt to show that nonreligious people too can be patriotic. One ad popped up alongside Billy Graham Parkway in Charlotte. It read, "One Nation Indivisible," and intentionally left out the words "Under God."

Harris said the placement of that billboard was "at best in poor taste and, at worst, a disgrace."

The next year, in November 2011, Harris's profile jumped significantly when he was elected president of the Baptist State Convention of North

Carolina. It was his first venture into an elected office of any sort. At the same meeting where he was chosen to lead the 1.3 million North Carolinians in the convention, the group voted to endorse a state constitutional amendment to ban same-sex marriage.

That amendment officially went on the ballot the following May, during the presidential primary. It was called Amendment One, and it was written on yard signs from the coast to the mountains.

When time came to vote, the campaign led by Harris and the reinvigorated conservatives of North Carolina won in a landslide. Sixty-one percent of the state's voters said yes to the marriage ban. It was the lowest moment for the North Carolina Democratic Party in a generation.

In Bladen County, 83 percent of voters were for the ban. For comparison, President Barack Obama received just 57 percent of the vote in Bladen's primary—and he was running unopposed.

The county lost 600 registered Democrats from 2010 to 2012. It kicked off a decade-long voter spill for Democrats, who dropped to nearly 10,000 registered voters by 2020, down from nearly 16,000 at the beginning of the decade.

By the time Prentis Benston was up for reelection in 2014, his mere presence as sheriff had reshaped the entire Bladen County Democratic Party.

This point should be made very clear: Bladen County was, by nearly every statistical measure, safer under Prentis Benston. The violent crime rate dropped by 33 percent, from 346 instances per hundred thousand people the year before he took over to 233 in the final year of his first term. Robberies, larceny, assault, and property crimes—all down.

He even made ceremonial efforts to appeal to conservatives. In the months following the 2012 mass shooting at an elementary school in Newtown, Connecticut, Benston joined hundreds of sheriffs around the country in pledging to uphold the Second Amendment.

But the campaign to oust him was on from the minute he was elected, and it happened to mesh perfectly with the hearty rightward shift in North Carolina politics.

Melvin and the new Republicans had handpicked their favorite choice in their most important sheriff's race. It was Jim McVicker, a retired highway patrolman. Melvin would pour his life into McVicker's election. "That's the only thing I really, really care about," Melvin told us of the sheriff's races. "It's the only thing you really get your bang for your buck. Protection."

McVicker is a bald white man in his seventies whose left upper lip curls up when he smiles. He's about six feet tall, and his head is constantly tilted down. He looks like he sprouted from the sandy, hot, poor lands of southeastern North Carolina like a sunflower, and now, in old age, he's wilting over it. He graduated from a high school in the tiny town of Rowland, near the South Carolina line, less than three miles from the famous South of the Border amusement park, which has highway signs up and down Interstate 95. When he was twenty, he joined the police department in Lumberton, where corruption and racism ran rampant, and still do.

He joined the highway patrol in 1977 and spent most of the rest of his career there. Both of his boys went on to join the highway patrol, too. McVicker retired in 2002 and dipped into a comfortable life teaching law enforcement at the local community college. Then came the call to run for sheriff from Bladen's burgeoning Republican Party.

On the Democratic side, Benston didn't have nearly as much trouble in 2014's primary as he did in 2010, picking up 62 percent of the vote. But his concerns that spring were far deeper than votes.

His wife died on April 15. She was just fifty-four years old.

At the next county commission meeting, Reverend Larry Hayes of Good News Baptist Church, Bladenboro, provided the invocation: "Remembering the loss of Dr. Delilah Blanks' daughter and Sheriff Benston's wife, Sherri Benston."

It wasn't Benston's last bout with tragedy that year.

In August 2014, Bladen County woke up to the horrifying story of a seventeen-year-old high school junior who was found hanging from a swing set in a park. Lennon Lacy was a Black boy, a member of the West Bladen football team. Bladenboro's police department, convinced from the get-go that Lacy's death was suicide, put together a half-hearted investigation. And at every step, Lacy's family says, Bladen County's systems failed them.

District Attorney Jon David said there was no evidence of foul play. The state medical examiner's office ruled that Lacy died of asphyxia from hanging. But this is the same district attorney who'd been under investigation for a scheme that involved starting a program to send low-level traffic offenders to a driving class, then awarding the contract for the class to a company run by one of his top campaign donors. And this is the same state medical examiner's office that just one year earlier had so badly botched an investigation into mysterious carbon monoxide deaths at a motel that several more people died from the same gas leak in the same motel.

Outside support poured into the family. The Reverend William Barber, then the president of the North Carolina NAACP and perhaps the most noteworthy civil rights activist of the modern era, rallied organizers for marches and demonstrations in Bladen County. To them, Lacy's death was a clear example of a modern-day lynching. Still, no charges.

Prentis Benston remained distant from the discussion. His name appears alongside Lacy's in only a handful of stories. The death would grow into the most significant and frustrating civil rights case in a generation in eastern North Carolina, the subject of a PBS documentary and stories from here to London, and the prime example of a study that showed countless Black bodies turning up as suicides with little explanation.

At home, though, white Republicans led by Pat Melvin wrote the death off as a suicide and kept on with their lives. They had a sheriff's office to take back, after all.

They started to pinch people who hedged. Take, for instance, what they did to gaming parlor owner Jeff Smith.

In September, McVicker's campaign manager paid Smith a visit. The campaign manager told Smith, who is white, that Benston planned to raid Smith's parlors. Shaken, Smith wondered what he could do. As Smith later recalled, the campaign manager gave him the obvious answer: support Benston's opponent, McVicker.

Smith tried to hand them a check right there. No, they told him, that wouldn't do them any good because they'd have to report it on campaign finance reports. Instead, they told him to take it out in cash, and hand it to McCrae Dowless directly. The next day, McCrae had a stack totaling $4,000. And Smith gave him an additional pair of $900 donations over the next few weeks, while Dowless ramped up his absentee program.

McCrae Dowless is very good at his job in any circumstance. But as a general rule, with him, you get what you pay for. And now he was being paid well.

Jim McVicker won the very close sheriff's race that November, beating Benston by a mere 349 votes out of 11,579 cast. A state board of elections subpoena issued years later would claim that Dowless was connected to more than 800 absentee ballots.

In his concession speech, Benston asked the people of Bladen County to work with the new sheriff.

The next month, District Attorney Jon David held a press conference to announce that he was handing the Lacy investigation over to the FBI. McVicker was one of twenty or so people who attended the meeting, watching on as the newly elected sheriff.

Six months later, on May 29, 2015, McVicker and David joined up to send one of their first joint messages as a power duo: they would not tolerate illegal gambling in Bladen County. They organized a raid of Aladdin I and Aladdin II sweepstakes parlors in the tiny town of Dublin.

The parlors were owned by Jeff Smith, which makes for a telling tidbit about how power works here. The year before, Smith had given money to help McVicker win an election, and now his business was being raided anyway.

The Storm October 2016

Ain't nothing but a bunch of crooks. They've been crooks the whole time.
ETHEL HESTER, BLADENBORO RESIDENT

The banks of the mighty Cape Fear River couldn't hold. More than a foot of rain had fallen on October 8 and 9, a Saturday and Sunday in 2016. The dirty brown water, the color of sweet tea, spilled into roadways and crawled into homes and businesses.

The same thing happened with the Black River. And the South River. And smaller tributaries like Beaverdam Creek and Plummers Run, which twist and turn through Bladen County like veins. The waterways that helped make this the Mother County, a center of trade and commerce centuries earlier, were now betraying the poor and desperate people still hanging on to the land.

Days earlier, Hurricane Matthew had made landfall along the South Carolina coast. As hurricanes go, the winds were relatively calm by the time they reached the U.S. mainland. What had been a Category 5 storm in the Caribbean had faded to a Category 1 by the time its eyewall peeked over the marshlands of McClellanville, South Carolina, just north of Charleston.

But with the wind came the rain. Rain that poured for days. Rain that filled every river and stream. Rain that eventually made its way to Bladen County and other nearby towns, where life once depended on the water. It didn't take long for the water to wreak havoc on life.

Dams broke. Neighborhoods flooded. People were told to leave their homes, let them sink. County leaders and first responders huddled in a makeshift command post. They drew up a list of washed-out roads on long, torn-off sheets of white paper stuck to the wall. First one sheet. Then two. Then three. A steadily growing picture of devastation mapped out in black Sharpie.

In Elizabethtown, the floodwater washed out Martin Luther King Jr. Drive and exposed more than 100 feet of drainpipe the town didn't have the money to fix. The river knocked out the county's power supply, taking with it clean drinking water and other critical infrastructure. Without power, cell towers became useless.

The outage lasted so long the Smithfield hog-processing plant had to shut down, meaning the 5,000 people who depended on the building for a paycheck could no longer go to work.

In the aftermath of the storm, people went back to where they lived to survey what the water had left behind: in many cases, not much. Piles of debris dotted rural roads, a line of demarcation between life and destruction. With each hollowed-out home—drywall ripped from the studs, warped floor torn up—came a heap.

In Bladenboro, the swamps spilled into downtown. Water seeped into shops and residences where it wasn't welcome. A Black woman named Ethel Hester left for her sister's place and wouldn't return for three years. Her story was repeated throughout Bladen and Columbus and Robeson Counties. That one single weekend in October 2016 turned the poorest people in North Carolina out of their homes. Floorboards turned soft as wet tissue and were left to rot like that for years as residents waited on federal money to rebuild.

"That thing they call FEMA," Ethel told us, "it ain't nothing."

The rivers remained at flood stage for two weeks after the storm.

As people sought shelter and lost hope, National Guard soldiers drove around in lifted vehicles—the kind normally used at war—and worked with firemen to rescue people. Helicopters flew overhead. Sometimes they carried supplies; other times they ferried dignitaries overhead, where they could get a buzzard's view of the devastation.

To the people on the ground, people who already felt forgotten, the hurricane was just another bad month. In what just happened to be the final weeks of the Obama administration, places like Bladen County were starving, more than ever, for the one thing he'd promised: hope. Here they had none of it.

Many, like Ethel Hester, had come to believe that local politics, especially, were a lost cause. "Ain't nothing but a bunch of crooks," she told us. "They've been crooks the whole time. The sheriff's officers are all crooks. We got a new jail out here. All of 'em are crooks there, too."

Into that soggy, sad vacuum stepped the 2016 election. Early voting was scheduled to start less than two weeks after Matthew came through.

Donald Trump and Hillary Clinton were arguing over who belonged in the White House, but that contest seemed a million miles away to people in places like Bladenboro and Tar Heel. Believe it or not, the very same night

Matthew landed on the Carolinas' coast, the *Washington Post* broke the story of Trump's *Access Hollywood* tape.

Absentee ballots had already been mailed to voters, and before the flood had even backed down, the political operatives of Bladen County were out, meandering around the washed-out roads, walking up to doors of people who hadn't seen anyone in weeks, asking them if they'd turned in their ballots.

At that point, working elections was one of the most reliable sources of income in the county.

North Carolina was a swing state in 2016, same as it was in 2012 when Obama lost the state by 2 percentage points, same as it was in 2008 when he won here by a third of a percentage point. Now, when Obama endorsed Clinton, he did so at the convention center in Charlotte with a big show. Afterward they stopped at a Charlotte barbecue restaurant, which national politicians often do in an attempt to connect with North Carolina voters.

That October, images of flooding and disaster on the local newscasts were interspersed with ads from politicians and outside groups telling you how wonderful or terrible any given candidate was. Donald Trump. Hillary Clinton. Richard Burr. Deborah Ross. Pat McCrory. Roy Cooper.

Mailboxes in suburbs and affluent areas across the state were hit with a steady stream of pieces that complemented the TV ads. As old-school as mailers are, the process of targeting who receives them has become sophisticated in the era of social media. Operatives pulled data from Facebook showing how far right or left a home was. If a Facebook user reacted mostly to posts about guns, for instance, that home would receive mailers about the Second Amendment. If the "likes" went to posts about abortion, the mailers would stroke that nerve. Trash cans filled with the discarded mail almost as fast as the Cape Fear River had risen.

On November 7, the day before the election, Clinton and Trump each held rallies in Raleigh, hopping in and out one more time in hopes their victory would be clinched by North Carolina's Electoral College delegates. At one point, their planes crossed paths on the same tarmac. Trump packed an aging arena at the state fairgrounds, where just three weeks earlier thousands of people had lined up for deep-fried Oreos and Krispy Kreme burgers. He led chants of "Lock her up!" to a boisterous crowd decked out in MAGA red and waving American flags. Later that night, just before midnight, in a very different scene, Hillary Clinton made the very last appearance of her campaign at a basketball arena on the campus of North Carolina State

University. Lady Gaga opened, often ad-libbing her lyrics to take swipes at Trump or offer praise for Clinton.

About 100 miles away in Bladen County, McCrae Dowless sat in his kitchen poring over lists of early voters. For him and his opponents from the Bladen County Improvement Association, the election work was already over. Nothing left to do but wait.

On September 24, 2016, just weeks before the hurricane, a shaggy, struggling twenty-two-year-old man with drowsy eyes and a drug problem knocked on the door of one of his former teachers and held out a stack of absentee request forms.

Matthew Matthis was an innocent and easily influenced kid, the kind who posts emotional updates on Facebook about his search for true love. But he was hardly a political creature like McCrae. As was true of most young men his age in North Carolina, sports loomed large in his life. He was a big fan of the UNC Tar Heels basketball program. Alongside his lovelorn posts were memes about the 2016 election, including one that read: *Some People Hate Trump; Some People Hate Hillary; Everybody Hates Duke.*

Matthew told the woman at the door that his name was Josh. She stared back at him, confused and disappointed. She knew him from school, remembered his name being Matthew Matthis. Josh, or Matthew, looked shaky, with stringy black hair that ran down past his shoulders, and asked her and her three adult children to fill out the request forms. Matthew told his old teacher that he was being paid $120 each time he collected fourteen or fifteen forms. She agreed to return the request forms, but told Matthew that when her ballots came, she would return them herself.

Two days earlier, he'd knocked on another door. This time, he was accompanied by his fiancé, Caitlyn Croom. Caitlyn and Matthew started dating when they were teenagers. In most photos of her, he looks as if he's been dropped in like an ornament over her shoulder, sometimes with a pencil-thin mustache, sometimes with a scraggly chin beard and sometimes clean shaven under a moppy head of hair, but always there, one way or another. In one, from 2014, she's in a blue dress and he's in a white T-shirt, and they're standing behind a sign for Ripley's Believe It or Not. A caption is superimposed behind them in which she takes on his last name: The Love of City Life. Since April 1, 2014. Matthew and Caitlyn Matthis.

Typical teen love stuff.

Now they were working as a pair, a modern-day, less-thrilling Bonnie and Clyde, chasing down ballot request forms for ten dollars a pop in the heat of the late southern summer. Heather Register, the home-owner behind one door, recognized Caitlyn as the girl who used to date her son. So she listened to them a few moments as they explained their work—that they were being paid to get people to request absentee ballots. Heather Register and her husband agreed to fill out the forms, just trying to help.

But they never received their ballot. Worse, Register would later tell investigators that when she tried to vote on Election Day a few weeks later, the elections official told her she'd already voted.

An absentee ballot is just a piece of paper, with words and places to sign your name. It's a simple method of voting that went on relatively quietly until 2018 and then, of course, beyond. Some people want it to be the future of American elections; other people believe it's the worst thing to happen to democracy. It's proven to be mostly secure. But in places like Bladen County, despite any laws to prevent such activity, the ballots have been known to pass through the hands of friends and family who should never touch them. The instances, taken on their own, seem so small. What's the harm, if you're in the middle of a television show, of having your nephew carry your ballot down to the post office with the rest of your mail? What's the harm in handing it to an old student, or your son's old girlfriend? What's the harm in witnessing something you didn't witness, if it's for a friend?

Any person in North Carolina who wants to vote by mail can do so through a fairly simple three-step process. First, at some point between the primary and the general, they send in their official request for an absentee ballot. Then, in the weeks leading up to the election, the state sends the ballots to those voters. Finally, voters must fill out the ballot themselves, sign it themselves, and put it back in the mail themselves. Up until 2020, the state required two witness signatures on the front of the ballot. (After 2020, it dropped that number to one.) A voter who is physically unable to perform any of those tasks can have a family member assist.

The definition of family is often left up to the individual. The state outlines a list of family members who are eligible—children and parents, for example—but well short of second cousin from your husband's brother's side, which in Bladen County might very well cause an argument. "Do you realize how many people I'm kin to in this county?" McCrae Dowless told us once. Indeed, most any cemetery in Bladen County has a Dowless headstone. McCrae was joking, but there's a grain of truth to it: he's always, always, looking for a crack in the rules. For vote collectors like him and the Improvement PAC, these cracks are where they can shimmy into the process and bend the election whichever way they want it to go.

They start by carving out the universe of people who are likely to vote for their candidate. The reason behind their vote—they may truly believe in the candidate; they may just be willing to do what you tell them—matters very little to the vote collectors.

Next comes a lot of walking. A small battalion of people goes door to door, knocking and asking residents to request an absentee ballot. The workers take those forms and drop them off at the county board of elections. In Bladen County in 2016, so many people were dropping off so many forms that office staff started a logbook.

The second crack in the system is that it was possible to see which voters had requested ballots. McCrae and the Improvement PAC both kept track of which forms had been turned in, too. McCrae printed out lists almost daily, to follow which voters were in the game and who still needed to enter. The list helped him keep an eye on the universe of voters in the county, and he marked off the ones he knew his team needed to chase down after the ballots were mailed.

The third crack in the system was in the requirement for witness signatures. To get the two witness signatures required in 2016, McCrae and the Improvement PAC would send workers out in pairs, visiting the same doors they visited months earlier and asking voters to be sure to fill out ballots and return them. The pair of workers can also serve as the two witnesses required to sign the ballot envelope.

This is where the vote collectors approach the line between legal and illegal. Reminding people to vote is not a crime. But taking a person's ballot and mailing it in for them is. So is filling out a ballot for someone else, unless they have a specific disability, in which case you have to disclose that you helped the voter by signing a different part of the envelope. Ensuring that each absentee ballot is signed, sealed, and delivered is tedious, careful work that constantly risks crossing the line into fraud, and it needs to be done hundreds of times over to gather votes from people who live sprawled across one of the state's largest counties by land mass.

But that's how people vote in Bladen County. Of the nearly 9,000 people who turned in ballots for the Bladen County at-large commissioner race in 2016, more than two-thirds did so early or by absentee.

The practice is so common, in fact, that in 2016 a voter in East Arcadia filed a complaint with the county elections board that the Bladen Improvement Association PAC never came by to pick up his ballot. Just to say that again: someone was so conditioned to having their ballot illegally picked up that they filed an official complaint when it wasn't.

During the fall of 2016, McCrae was working for a slate of several candidates that included himself in the Soil and Water Conservation Board race, Ray Britt of Ray's furniture store in the at-large commissioner's race, and a first-time candidate named Ashley Trivette, who was running for a seat on the county commission. Trivette was in her early thirties, blonde, fit, with pageant-ready makeup and sculpted eyebrows on a face that had none of the wrinkles and worry that warp most other faces in the county.

Trivette's seat was easy. She was running in District Two, which covers White Lake, a body of water dotted with vacation homes owned by people from other cities. According to the map that hangs on the wall in McCrae's office, White Lake has enough white voters that a white candidate of either party can expect to perform well. "You don't have a Black county commissioner in District Two and District Three," McCrae once explained to us, as he traced the outlines of the county's three commissioner districts, drawn by the U.S. Department of Justice years ago as part of a settlement in a lawsuit brought to enforce the Voting Rights Act.

McCrae was running unopposed for his Soil and Water seat. But late in the election cycle, the Bladen County Improvement Association PAC—the organization with which McCrae launched his career as a political hack two decades earlier—mounted a write-in campaign against him.

If the eight ballots in the nursing home started McCrae's small-town feud with the Improvement PAC, this write-in campaign was the thing that set him off so much he'd take it national.

On election night 2016, state Democrats gathered at the Marriott in downtown Raleigh were stunned and silent as they watched state after state fall to Trump. Many clasped their hands against their chins as their eyes stared at the screens. Others downed beers. By the time North Carolina joined the red list around 11 P.M., they knew they'd lost.

Some stood up and left, heading quietly into the night. Others said soft goodbyes and patted each other on the shoulders. Just then, though, small consolation appeared on the screens. Cable news anchors blasted word that their party's nominee for governor, Roy Cooper, had a chance to take down incumbent Republican Pat McCrory. Cooper soon took the stage to spirited applause. Democratic lawyers began to mobilize across the state to make sure a network was in place to defend the victory.

On the other side of town, at an Embassy Suites across from the mall, Republicans were in full-on party mode. Nobody seemed to care that their incumbent governor had lost. Instead, College Republicans and party operatives who wished they were still in college ordered rounds of drinks as they awaited their soon-to-be president on the big screens. Meanwhile, McCrory and his lawyers were already plotting ways to challenge his loss.

Less than 5,000 votes separated Cooper and McCrory on election night. It was enough that McCrory couldn't demand a recount, but still, in the grand scheme of an election where 4.5 million people cast a ballot, this was a very close race.

That night, the biggest scandal appeared to be a technology glitch in Durham County that locked poll workers out of the electronic register of voters. It prompted hours-long lines at some precincts that were known to be Democratic strongholds. There would later be suspicion that the problems were the work of Russian hackers, a theory that ultimately went unproven.

For the Republicans, the trouble was, given the demographics of the Durham precincts impacted by the glitch, the McCrory team couldn't rely on that as a basis to challenge the results. Most of those voters were Cooper voters.

Instead, his legal team sought another way to question the election's legitimacy. They set out to prove voter fraud. To do it, they needed a willing chess piece, somewhere in the state's 100 counties. The sitting governor and his team turned to little Bladen County and its best-known political operative, who was hopping mad that night about the antics of his rivals.

★ ★ ★

The Hearing That Went Haywire
December 3, 2016

They may be illogical. But they're not my rules.
IRVING JOYNER, CIVIL RIGHTS ATTORNEY

McCrae Dowless easily won reelection to the Soil and Water Conservation Board. But for someone running unopposed, it was surprisingly close. A single write-in opponent amassed 3,356 votes, nearly half of Dowless's 7,786. The write-in candidate even won two precincts outright.

The write-in candidate's name? Franklin Graham.

Now, there is a man in his seventies in Bladen County named Franklin Graham. But if you were to mention the name to anyone else, anywhere else in North Carolina, you'd stir up images of the fiery, far-right conservative son of evangelical icon Billy Graham.

In this case, the Bladen County version of Franklin Graham won an inconceivable amount of support in the election, courtesy of the Bladen County Improvement Association PAC. The name was written over and over on ballots.

McCrae was beside himself. Meanwhile, McCrory and his lawyers were seeking any avenue they could find to overturn the governor's election. McCrae figured he had information they'd want to see, so he told them about Franklin Graham. On inspection, Governor McCrory's team claimed that many of the write-ins looked like they had the same handwriting. "Overtly similar," the governor said.

Bladen Improvement denied the allegations. Horace Munn, the group's president, told reporters that Bladen County's Black voters often believed they had no choice but to vote absentee, out of fears of intimidation by white people at the polls. He told a local television station that some voters had asked his volunteers to help them write in the name Franklin Graham, but he denied doing anything illegal.

McCrory pressed on. His lawyers knew that in order to challenge the results of the narrow gubernatorial election in court, they needed a local candidate to make the first move. McCrae Dowless was a willing wagon horse. McCrory's lawyers convinced McCrae to formally challenge the results of his election—an election which, remember, he *won*.

Essentially, McCrae's complaint alleged that too many of the Franklin Graham write-in entries were in the same handwriting. "Upon in-person visual review of mail-in absentee ballots by a forensic handwriting expert, it appears that literally hundreds of fraudulent ballots were cast," the complaint read. It was hilariously formal language for a guy who simply calls the controversy *bullsheeit*. "These ballots all appear to have been cast in support of a ticket of candidates, but in particular for a write-in candidate for the Bladen County Soil and Water Conservation District Supervisor."

That, the complaint alleged, was evidence of fraud.

On December 3, 2016, McCrae drove from Bladen County toward the state board of elections building in Raleigh. It was a warm winter day, with temperatures in the mid-fifties, and the parking lot was unusually full for a Saturday at a state office building.

The room wasn't made for a crowd, at least not as large as the group gathered that day. The board was here to decide whether McCrae's complaint about the Bladen County Improvement Association PAC merited further investigation, and whether that investigation would mean the county's election results should be thrown out, and whether that would be enough to change the results of the governor's race. McCrory's campaign had spent $260,000 through a legal defense fund to challenge absentee ballots throughout the state—this was their last moonshot.

The board chairman called the meeting to order at 1:30 P.M. Immediately, Democratic board member Joshua Malcolm, from Lumberton, spoke up. "I'd like to hear from Dowless," Malcolm said.

Malcolm, a powerful Democrat in a county where there still wasn't any other party, lived just thirty miles away from McCrae, knew him personally, and had a history with him. Malcolm had spent years on the state elections board but had been sidelined from the majority when McCrory was governor. In North Carolina, the governor's party controls the state's elections. Still, Malcolm sat in his big swivel chair with his fellow board members, sporting a shaved bald head and chiseled jaw, and shaping the board's agenda with the confidence of a man who believed he was the smartest person in the room.

"Where is Mr. Dowless?" Malcolm asked again.

McCrae walked toward the front and, before the chairman or anyone else had even brought the room to order, blurted out that he was prepared to testify truthfully. The board's lawyer stopped the proceedings to ask whether McCrae had been called to testify, or whether he was just up here swearing an oath nobody'd asked him to take. The other members whispered.

Just then a deep, slow, soft voice rose in the room. "Mr. Chairman?" The voice belonged to Irving Joyner, a North Carolina civil rights era icon and law professor at North Carolina Central University who made a name for himself representing the state chapter of the NAACP in the second half of the twentieth century. By now he was in his seventies, with gray scruff for facial hair and eyeglasses that moved when he wrinkled his nose. Still, every time he spoke, the low tones almost forced the audience to lean in and listen.

He was there on behalf of the Bladen Improvement Association. Joyner asked for the opportunity to cross-examine McCrae. The chairman allowed for it, and Joyner and his associate took a seat at the cramped table for lawyers at the front. Joining him were two attorneys from McCrory's Republican camp who were representing McCrae, and one sent by Cooper and the Democrats.

Five lawyers and McCrae Dowless, packed around a table.

For the next hour, the lawyers volleyed shots back and forth. McCrae's attorney outlined the complaint: the similar handwriting on many of the written-in votes for Franklin Graham, the apparent coordinated effort by the Bladen County Improvement Association PAC, and some problems with witness signatures on ballots.

"It appears that this organization incentivizes obtaining absentee ballots," the McCrory attorney said of the Improvement PAC.

Irv Joyner called the complaint "creative storytelling."

"In my community," he said, referring to Black eastern North Carolinians, "GOTV [get-out-the-vote] is not a crime."

A Republican board member asked Joyner whether it was legal for someone other than the person casting an absentee ballot to write the name of a write-in candidate, as appeared to have happened with Franklin Graham.

It was legal, Joyner argued. Under the law, the professor said, anyone could assist a voter. And they wouldn't have to declare they assisted unless they actually filled in a circle on the ballot. He homed in on this point. It was only illegal to *bubble in* next to a candidate's name, Joyner said. But writing out a name for a voter was a different story.

"But that's totally illogical," the board member said.

"Well, they may be illogical. But they're not my rules," Joyner responded. "I didn't write this."

Things seemed to be going well for the Democrats. But squabbling between Roy Cooper and Pat McCrory wasn't the real story. All the while, Malcolm, the board member from Lumberton, was waiting for the perfect moment to bury his neighbor and nemesis, McCrae Dowless, once and for all.

After a half-hour break, the hearing resumed with an agreement that McCrae would testify, but if he didn't want to answer a question, he could simply invoke his Fifth Amendment right against self-incrimination.

On the stand, McCrae started by explaining why he'd filed a protest in an election he won. "I'm not saying there's any wrongdoing here," he explained. "I just wanted it investigated because it was a high volume of write-ins." From his swivel chair up front, Malcolm pounced. He asked McCrae how he came to file the protest, who put him up to it. He and everybody in the room knew McCrae was a pawn for the McCrory campaign, but they needed McCrae to say it on the record.

McCrae stammered at first, saying that he called the local Republican Party chairman the day after the election to talk about the thousands of write-in candidates against him. McCrae testified that the county party boss promised to make a phone call. Then McCrae said under oath that a few days after the promised phone call, a lawyer for the McCrory campaign asked him to sign this protest.

At that, his own attorney cut him off. "Objection," the attorney said, then turned to his client. "Mr. Dowless, do not reveal the contents of your conversations with [the McCrory attorneys]."

Malcolm continued to press McCrae for details. It quickly became apparent that McCrae didn't actually know the facts behind the allegations he'd made. Had read some in the paper, maybe. Had heard others at the hearing earlier that day. But the facts he swore to in the complaint as being based on his own personal knowledge? Under oath, that didn't seem to be the case.

In the written complaint, McCrae had said he knew how much the Bladen Improvement Association paid its workers for the GOTV efforts. At the hearing, Malcolm asked him how he knew that. "I've seen that, yes," McCrae said confidently. "I didn't actually get that, but somebody else had it and I seen it."

"Someone gave that to you?" Malcolm asked.

"Yes," McCrae replied.

"Who?"

Dowless didn't want to say. "I'd rather take the Fifth on that, who gave it to me."

By now it was clear that McCrae didn't actually write any of the complaint. The entire basis for the hearing that day seemed to have been written by lawyers who had very little interaction with McCrae Dowless. The lawyers sitting in the room that afternoon certainly didn't care about the outcome of the Soil and Water Conservation Board race. McCrae Dowless was a means to a much more consequential end.

Then the questions shifted again. Suddenly the hearing was no longer about the Bladen Improvement PAC. Suddenly Dowless was facing questions about his own vote-collection scheme.

And they came from all directions. How many people worked for him? What were their names? How much did they get paid? What did they get paid for?

The barrage continued for more than an hour. First from Malcolm. Then from Irv Joyner. Then from other board members. McCrae grew defensive under the onslaught.

Finally Joyner asked for the complaint against his clients to be dismissed. Malcolm made the motion, and it passed three votes to two. The Bladen Improvement PAC was cleared of any wrongdoing.

Then Malcolm made a second motion: that the state board forward the findings of its investigation into the 2016 election in Bladen County to the U.S. Attorney for the Eastern District of North Carolina.

That passed unanimously.

In about a month's time, McCrae had gone from winning an election to filing a complaint about that victory to becoming the subject of a new investigation.

★ ★ ★

The Vampire Beast April 7, 2017

★ ★ ★

This is not legal advice.

JOHN HARRIS, ATTORNEY AND MARK HARRIS'S SON

On the night of January 4, 1954, a man named Johnny Vause walked out of his Bladenboro house and found his new puppy dead, its nose chewed off. Six other dogs had been killed in the weeks around the new year, all with similar wounds. And when police opened their bodies, they contained only a few drops of blood.

The next morning, the local news ran the story that gave birth to a legend. "A 'vampire beast' that sucks blood from its victims had Bladenboro citizens up in arms," the *Robesonian* wrote.

The police chief called on hunters to look for it. They spent all night out near Cotton Mill Hill, a village where lintheads lived, looking for something that was "like a cat." Reporters around the region and country picked up on the story. A *Charlotte News* writer noted that the dog death total would almost certainly be higher, but that "many, many others have whimpered and drawn closer to the fire, displaying the extra-sensory perception which traditionally comes to the fore in animals when vampires are abroad in the land."

A cotton mill worker named Lloyd Clemmons said he saw the animal skulking in his yard. Three feet long. Twenty inches high. A tail fourteen inches long. It left him "plumb spellbound." Another resident, Mrs. C. E. Kinlaw heard a noise on her porch. When she went to investigate, the beast charged her. She screamed. Her husband ran in behind her. The beast split.

By the third night, 600 hunters joined the rally, bringing dog decoys and guns to Cotton Mill Hill to find and kill the beast.

"There's not much sleep for anybody in Bladenboro," the police chief told the paper.

People all over North Carolina waited for news that the beast had been caught or killed. In Charlotte, folks remembered the "Beast of Briar Creek" from the 1930s. Four young men from a fraternity from Chapel Hill actually traveled to Bladen County to slog through the swamps along Highway 211. But soon, with no evidence that a beast even existed, the police chief and mayor declared that it was gone.

It was a swift and unsatisfying end, but in the state and national press, it made for a lovely metaphor. For several years after, out-of-towners who stopped in Bladen County would claim to have seen it. The following winter in Lumberton, five pigs and three chickens were killed on a tenant farm. No blood was evident, and rumors began to fly that the vampire beast had crossed the county line.

All around the state, the beast of Bladenboro became a legend.

"The Beast of Bladenboro, we suppose, has gone back to wherever beasts come from, and all is quiet in the swamp country of Bladen pending the next senatorial primary, which brings out the b - - - t in folk," the *Asheville Citizen-Times* editorial staff wrote. "It is safe to predict, however, that the Beast will reappear in some guise and rend the Tar Heel night with horrible cries. The power of suggestion, you know. Or to quote Lord Acton, 'All power tends to corrupt, and the power of suggestion makes headlines.'"

The first time McCrae Dowless called Mark Harris, it was late at night.

It was 11:25 P.M. on April 6, 2017, just hours after their meeting at Ray Britt's furniture store, and a handful of months after the state board had forwarded their concerns about McCrae's 2016 work to the U.S. Attorney. The two talked for seven minutes and twenty seconds. Over the next eighteen months, they'd contact each other hundreds of times, according to phone records.

From the jump, Harris couldn't get enough of the relationship. McCrae is easy to like. He carries himself like a humble Bladen County tour guide. Understated, soft-spoken, yet aware of every turn in the road. If you didn't know about his past, didn't know about the hearings from just five months earlier, you might think his plan for boosting Republican votes was foolproof. And lawful.

Harris woke up the next morning still turning their first date over in his head. The pastor had heard the speculation of foul play in eastern North Carolina elections, sure. To this day he swears that the last thing he'd want to do is sign on with someone who was breaking the law. The morning after the meeting, he called his son, John, a young lawyer who was on his way to work at a law office in Raleigh.

An idealist with a straight jaw and classic All-American boy haircut, John wouldn't know how to get in trouble if he was dropped into a bucket of it.

As a high schooler at the century-old McCallie School in Tennessee, he was president of the student Senate, an honor council designed to regulate truth and fairness among students. He was also president of the Young Republicans. From there he went to UNC and Duke as a Robertson Scholar. While in law school at UNC he proposed to a young woman who was a Morehead Scholar and doctor's daughter. His father officiated at their wedding, and afterward everybody partied at a reception at a country club in New Bern.

It was John who first thought his father had a shot to win the Ninth District. When the congressional maps were redrawn before the 2016 primary, it was John who saw how much more rural and less affluent the Ninth was than it had been. The new district was set up nicely for a man of faith who had happened to take a political lead against same-sex marriage that rural, conservative voters overwhelmingly favored.

John had been a law clerk in Washington during that 2016 campaign. He wasn't involved day to day in his father's run, but he supported from afar by analyzing data and giving his parents advice. Many nights after his wife and young child were asleep, John called his mom, Beth.

In the union between Mark and Beth Harris, Beth is the strategist. She is also the technologically savvy one. Until the late 2000s, Mark didn't even have an email address. He hired a secretary who handled his church correspondence by printing out emails and stacking them on his desk. He'd handwrite his responses on the printouts, then hand them back to his secretary for the response. But Beth, she was up on everything.

During the 2016 primary campaign, she and John went on for hours about the numbers and polls and early voting tallies he pulled from the board of elections. On the night of the March primary, as Mark Harris conceded victory to incumbent Robert Pittenger, John clicked through the results. He sent his mom a few text messages. It was late, 11 P.M., when he shot both of his parents an email:

"I mentioned by text that things looked strange coming out of Bladen County. I've taken another look, and can confirm that the absentee by mail votes look very strange."

The results were close enough that Harris and his campaign team considered calling for a recount. Any wrongdoing they could find, they figured, would only bolster their argument. In his email, John Harris highlighted the wild mail-in ballot numbers in Bladen County:

- 221 votes for Todd Johnson, who most voters wouldn't notice in a lineup

- 4 votes for Mark Harris, who nearly won the election
- 1 (one) vote for Robert Pittenger, the sitting damn congressman

How the heck? John wondered. He went on in his email, "The irregularity suggests perhaps there is a more systemic error, and given that you outperformed Pittenger in both early voting and on Election Day in Bladen County, it may be worth investigating. This smacks of something gone awry."

John had a hunch that the man behind the margin, McCrae Dowless, did it by collecting absentee ballots and bringing them to the board of elections. That would be a crime. Still, in a move that was either polite or weak or both, the Harris campaign didn't mount a challenge. Pittenger walked away with the party nod and sailed on to another term in Congress. But even in victory, Pittenger was a wreck. That fall, in September 2016, the city of Charlotte erupted into protests after the police shooting of a Black man. During the uprising, Pittenger appeared on CNN and said that the violence in Charlotte's streets was mostly caused by Black protesters who "hate white people because white people are successful and they're not."

The comment rallied the powerful Democrats to find a strong candidate who could contend with Pittenger. But in a way it motivated Harris as well.

Mark and Beth saw Pittenger as a congressman who sat in an ivory tower looking down. Mark had gone down to the protests in Charlotte with a group of faith leaders from different backgrounds. He didn't agree with the window-shattering portions of the demonstrations, but he did believe that politicians like Pittenger had forgotten about large swaths of the population.

He also saw parallels between the protesters in the city and the poor people of rural North Carolina. Beth described Pittenger's approach to Bladen County as "They don't matter. There's not enough of them to matter." Her husband, she says, believed those people do matter.

Now in the spring of 2017, a more motivated Mark Harris considered a second challenge. And this time he meant to hire the same Bladen County operative who'd appeared to be the secret weapon the last time around.

That morning after the meeting at Ray's furniture store, Mark called John. He walked his son through what Dowless had told him about his two-step process. How Dowless sent workers to collect the absentee ballot request forms but not the absentee ballots themselves. How Dowless sent a team of two people to witness absentee ballots but not collect them. How Dowless swore to him he wouldn't even take a ninety-year-old woman's ballot to the mailbox if she asked. Based on McCrae's presentation the day before, the elder Harris said, the operation seemed to be legal.

John didn't believe it.

He tried to convince his father to stay away. Their conversation stretched on through his twenty-minute drive into downtown Raleigh, as he sat in his car in the parking garage, and as he walked across the street and sat on a bench outside of his office. John told his dad that McCrae was a convicted felon. The young man who was president of his high school honors council said he worried McCrae would do something illegal. And even if he didn't, he still might do something that would stain the victory.

"You better believe that Robert Pittenger, if it's a close race, he's going to send everything after you to determine, you know, whether or not anything had gone on," John told his dad.

John, by now pacing outside his office, said he had to go to work. But the conversation continued via email. The first note from John simply quoted the North Carolina statute that made it a felony to collect someone's absentee ballot.

Mark responded half an hour later. "So you found no problem in handling 'request forms'? I am certain they have them mailed in then!"

John replied right away in an email that began with a cold admonition: "This is not legal advice." It was as though he was talking to a would-be client whose case he knew was bad, a case he didn't want to take. It was also as if he knew that one day his emails would be made public. "The key thing that I am fairly certain they do that is illegal is that they collect the completed absentee ballots and mail them at once," he wrote. "The way they pop up in batches at the board of elections makes me believe that. But if they simply leave the ballot with the voter and say be sure to mail this in, then that's not illegal."

Mark remained unconvinced. His next response pushed back on his scholar son's well-reasoned, well-researched advice. "Mom brought up a good point," Mark wrote. "Maybe they just go with the person to their personal mailbox and put it in, and raise the flag for the mailman to pick up. Since the ballot is already sealed and signed over the seal, they don't pick them up, to my understanding, but rather encourage them to mail it that day by putting it in their mailbox and raising the flag."

John, in disbelief, flung back one last reply. "Good test is if you're comfortable with the full process he uses being broadcast on the news."

Mark Harris didn't respond. His answer came two weeks later when he started writing checks to McCrae to secure his service for the 2018 election.

Had he listened to his son, there's no telling who'd hold the office of the Ninth Congressional District today, or who'd have his reputation smeared. Because unbeknownst to the Harrises, or to anybody else in the state, was that in that same space of time when Mark and John were arguing about whether to hire McCrae Dowless, another candidate was also courting McCrae Dowless.

Congressman Robert Pittenger.

The steakhouse sits in a row of chain restaurants in Lumberton. To a long-haul trucker on I-95, it would make for a hearty meal and night out after a long trip. For McCrae Dowless, it seemed like a good place to talk about winning elections.

During that month of April 2017, while McCrae was texting and calling Mark Harris, one of Pittenger's young staffers called. He, too, had noticed the outsized results from 2016, and he wanted to know more. He asked McCrae if he'd meet with the congressman. Sure, McCrae said, and they arranged to break bread at the steakhouse.

They would've made quite a pair. McCrae Dowless, coming from a wood-paneled kitchen in a one-story brick ranch with cigarette smoke stuck to everything. Pittenger, coming from a 13,898-square-foot mansion that was on the market for nearly $7 million at the time. Pittenger told the *Washington Post* that it was McCrae who was the salesman. Said that McCrae came to him, not the other way around. He told the paper he didn't want to be involved with McCrae and said he declined to hire him.

McCrae has a different story. He says he was the one being courted by Pittenger. Says that they were set to meet, just the two of them in the steakhouse. Says he was the one who had second thoughts, not the congressman. "Well, I got to thinking about that thing," McCrae told us one afternoon in his office in August 2019. "I says, 'Shit, I ain't gonna do it.'"

And he didn't. On the day of their scheduled meeting, Robert Pittenger drove across the state to Lumberton.

And McCrae just didn't show up. No calls or texts. He just left a sitting congressman alone at a restaurant in Lumberton.

McCrae didn't stand him up on principle alone, of course. Like most things in his life, the decision was motivated by money. Both Harris and Pittenger wanted him to work three counties—Bladen, Robeson, and Cumberland. And the modern-day flim-flam man wanted to hear the best offer. "I knew Pittenger wouldn't have paid that much," McCrae tells us. "He'd have said $3,000 or $4,000. You can't do three damn counties for $3,000 or $4,000. You can't do it. And I said, 'Hey, I'm not gonna do it.'"

Harris, meanwhile, had started writing checks. McCrae told his intermediaries that he'd need $30,000 to work through the primary and $90,000 to win the general. He would need a total of $120,000 for GOTV efforts in three mostly rural counties on the forgotten and flooded east end of the Ninth Congressional District.

Exactly three weeks after his meeting at the furniture store, Mark Harris pulled into a hotel parking lot off Highway 74 in Monroe, a Charlotte suburb. McCrae Dowless pulled into the same parking lot. Harris handed over a personal check for $450 made out to Patriots for Progress, a political action committee McCrae and some others had created years earlier. That check was the official down payment for the genius of McCrae Dowless in 2018.

Two weeks later, Harris wrote a second check, this time for $2,890.

Together now, Mark and McCrae circled the most important date of the year in Bladenboro: the annual October Beast Fest.

About a dozen years earlier, a few organizations in Bladen County came together to start a new fall festival that might bring little attention to their little slice of the world. Every small town worth its salt in North Carolina has one; the biggest is the barbecue festival in Lexington. They're particularly popular among politicians looking to meet potential voters. Around the state you can find festivals for collards, grapes, yams. Just about anything that can be harvested goes good with a handshake with a local politician.

Bladenboro folks dedicated their fall festival to the blood-sucking cat from the 1950s. Each year the event grows a little larger. They add a parade, maybe a show from some up-and-coming gospel artist. But always, there are politicians, and sometimes the politicking gets rowdy.

In 2016, the candidates for state House of Representatives met here face to face. Flyers had been circulating around the county that year that the Democratic candidate was a white supremacist. That candidate believed his opponent, a funeral home director, was the bastard circulating them. The Democrat chose the Beast Fest as the place to make things right. During their shouting match, the funeral home director suggested they take it across the street, away from the crowd and collards. As they walked across the road, the Democrat shouldered the Republican a few times, then "stepped back a little and coldcocked him," a witness told the *Bladen Journal.*

Usually the Beast Fest is friendly, though. A big reason is a shared love of collard sandwiches, made here and almost nowhere else in the world. The Lumbee natives from neighboring Robeson County have made them for generations, though they've never really taken off as a regional delicacy. Their secret—their joy—is that all of the ingredients are from this place and of this place: collards, cornbread, fatback, and chowchow. Most members of the Lumbee tribe can't even say, much less eat, collards without cornbread.

You can find them at one of about a half-dozen booths at the Beast Fest. You can also find muscadine slushies, a personal favorite of Mark Harris's.

Mark and Beth Harris love the Beast Fest. It's where their campaign truly took off in October 2017. Just a month earlier, they'd been snubbed at the Dublin Peanut Festival just up the road. They'd rented a truck and waved during the peanut parade, but at the grand opening ceremony, when the emcee asked elected officials and preachers to come to the stage for introductions, Mark wasn't invited. He was a challenger, the organizers said, not yet elected.

The next month, for Beast Fest, McCrae Dowless had an idea: the campaign would raffle off a boy's bike and girl's bike. No cost to enter, just your name, phone number, and email address. Vital data to a new campaign looking to build supporters.

It worked. Harris spent the day shaking hands. He had a muscadine slushie. He gave away the two bikes. These are campaign tactics more often seen in races for a seat on county commission than for an office in Washington.

"That's all they wanted," Beth Harris told us. "They wanted someone who would remember them when they went to Congress."

While Mark and Beth Harris were parading and handshaking, the state board of elections continued its probe of McCrae Dowless. Many of their findings from the previous fall had already been turned over to federal prosecutors. Those files, though, sat unopened.

The elections officials made repeated calls to the prosecutors, begging to look at them. They sent emails. They requested meetings. But nobody at interim U.S. Attorney John Bruce's office responded. It's not clear whether the messages never made it to Bruce's desk, or whether he simply ignored them. A string of national news events in early 2017 hint at an even larger reason.

For starters, on January 20 that year, Donald Trump was inaugurated. He signed a series of executive orders in his first month in office to let people know his priority was immigration. That focus seeped into all areas of the administration, from elections to border patrol. That spring, the administration turned its attention away from coordinated election fraud schemes to a more symbolic, and less prevalent, form of election tampering: they homed in on undocumented immigrants voting illegally.

This was, in a more accurate use of the term, a witch hunt, and one that only a truly devoted U.S. Attorney could handle. So North Carolina's two Republican senators nominated Bobby Higdon, a conservative Sunday school teacher who had unsuccessfully prosecuted former vice presidential nominee John Edwards in a federal case just a few years earlier. The files on McCrae Dowless were sitting in Higdon's office ready to be reviewed, but instead Higdon got right to work carrying out the orders of the president and Attorney General Jeff Sessions: he was to find the illegal votes from undocumented citizens.

In one sweep, Higdon's office rounded up twenty immigrants in eastern North Carolina. All but one were legal residents of the United States. Among them was a seventy-year-old woman from South Korea who'd lived in Columbus County for more than two decades, arrested while she fed her rabbits and chickens. She received a fine of $100. Meanwhile, the Bladen County elections file remained unopened by any holder of the office of the U.S. Attorney for the Eastern District of North Carolina.

One lower-level prosecutor, however, was very damn interested in the board's findings. Jon David, the state district attorney whose territory included Bladen County, made repeated overtures to election staff, asking for updates. His concern, though, was hardly wholesome.

His requests started back after the 2016 hearing. He'd called state elections officials and asked them to come to Bladen County, but they scheduled a quick phone call instead. For months, David didn't hear anything. In August 2017, the same month as the roundup of the twenty immigrants by federal prosecutors, David, the top state prosecutor for southeastern North Carolina, emailed the elections staff for an update: "I'm interested in knowing the findings of your investigation and what steps can be taken to prevent future irregularities in the process."

Two weeks passed before the state elections director sent a quick three lines promising an answer soon. Another shove-off. Then more nothing, right up until late October 2017, just before municipal elections. David's emails were more impatient by this point. A lengthy missive from late October ended with a plea: "Ultimately, my office is responsible to the citizens of Bladen County and we need better collaboration with your office in order to best serve the citizens. Please contact me as soon as possible regarding these issues," David wrote.

Finally, in late November 2017, the elections board invited David and his staff to Raleigh to review their findings. Investigators were writing a warning letter to the Bladen County Improvement Association PAC, telling them to stop illegally witnessing ballots and engaging in other behavior. But they told David they had no plans to issue a criminal referral for the PAC.

They were, however, sending the case of McCrae Dowless and the Republicans to the feds. David's office was happy to be included. Happy to see an early draft of the letter to the PAC. Grateful to get a heads-up on the plans to pursue a federal criminal investigation against McCrae.

But what David hadn't told anyone in Raleigh was that his interest was at least partially personal. He was having a secret affair with Ashley Trivette, the Bladen County commissioner whom McCrae helped get elected in 2016.

Turns out, the elections staff knew about the relationship and considered it a conflict of interest. That's why they hadn't shared details of their investigation with his office. That's why they hadn't been quick to respond to his calls and emails.

And there, in short, are the two reasons no prosecutor ran with the findings from the 2016 election. The federal prosecutor was too busy chasing voter fraud that was nonexistent, and the state prosecutor was deemed a compromised adulterer and frozen out of the investigation.

Hard to believe people think the justice system's broken.

★ ★ ★

The Boss Man February 1, 2018

Yo, do u care who u vote for?
MATTHEW MATTHIS

On February 1, 2018, thirty-three-year-old Josh Lawson, general counsel for the state elections board, walked alongside his boss, state elections director Kim Strach, into the towering Wells Fargo building on Fayetteville Street in downtown Raleigh. Just steps from the state capitol, the building is stacked with bankers and floor after floor of white-shoe law firms. At the top of the building is the Capitol Club, a member's-only breakfast and lunch spot frequented by the genteel businessmen and women who work nearby.

Lawson and Strach weren't heading to lunch, though. They were on their way to the twenty-first floor to see the U.S. Attorney for the Eastern District of North Carolina, Bobby Higdon. After more than a year of trying to get the attention of federal prosecutors, they'd finally landed a meeting. And not just with Higdon. The newly minted head of the Public Integrity Section at the Department of Justice also flew in for the discussion. There were not two better people to whom you'd want to pitch a case on election fraud in eastern North Carolina. Fifteen months after the 2016 election, it looked like the state board's investigation might finally yield results.

A week earlier, Lawson and Strach sent Higdon an eight-page letter, attaching 270 pages of evidence. Higdon had been working in private practice immediately before his appointment but had previously spent more than a decade as a federal prosecutor. Though his biggest brush with headlines was the prosecution of John Edwards that ended in his acquittal, Higdon was a serious lawyer whose appointment had been well received by the local legal community.

By the time Lawson and Strach walked into his office, Higdon's staff had already spent countless hours tracking down the few individuals in eastern North Carolina, most of them immigrants, who were voting illegally.

Lawson and Strach now warned him of fraud of a different kind. "The facts . . . demonstrate efforts to impact the process by which ballots in a federal and state election were obtained, cast, and counted," the letter to Higdon concluded. "Therefore, the results of the investigation to date are being presented for review by appropriate prosecutors."

That was about as far as Lawson and Strach, the state board of elections officials, could go. They didn't have the power to file criminal charges themselves. They needed a prosecutor.

Lawson took out his notepad at the start of the meeting. During his time as chief counsel with the elections board, he made sure to document everything related to Bladen County. He always figured someone would come behind him and question him, or potentially cast doubt on the work. He even recorded his phone calls with people in the county. A meeting with the U.S. Attorney and a senior DOJ official was no different.

One of the key points Lawson wanted to make to Higdon was that the evidence gathered by investigators with the elections board suggested both sides—the McCrae Dowless side and the Bladen Improvement side—were cheating. "Bladen. Both sides. Both sides. Both sides," Lawson wrote in his notes.

In other words, this wasn't just a Republican or Democrat problem. This was a democracy problem. That meant this case was ideal for a federal prosecutor hoping to carve out a serious, headline-making name for himself. Already, the North Carolina State Bureau of Investigation had opened a case. The FBI had assigned an agent, too, a woman who was part of the team that brought down Bernie Madoff.

Now Strach and Lawson appealed to the egos of the men in the room. They believed this case could snag national attention for them. They left the meeting with a sense that something would happen—that after years of speculation and accusations and finger pointing, someone would protect the rural county's election.

Then three months passed, and another primary season was upon eastern North Carolina.

"Mark, I'd like you to meet some folks," McCrae Dowless told Mark Harris.

Early voting was underway across the state. They were standing outside the Bladen County Board of Elections on a cool spring day, almost in the same spot where a board member tried to run McCrae over with a motorcycle a few years earlier. By now the elections were running together. What would later be talked about as an extraordinary plot against American democracy was just another work year for McCrae Dowless. Maybe with a little more cash.

Mark Harris and his campaign were on their way to paying McCrae about $130,000 over the course of the 2018 election. McCrae used the cash on various campaign expenses, including payments to workers on the ground.

The playbook was as it ever was. McCrae sent a small army of people out across the county to knock on doors, convince people to fill out an absentee ballot request form, and then follow up after the ballots arrived to make sure they actually voted. The workers drove down dirt roads and knocked on doors, not out of a love of politics or a sense of civic engagement. They did it for the cash. McCrae paid roughly $200 per stack of request forms.

By 2018, the opioid crisis was part of the fabric of Bladen County. The rate of unintentional deaths due to drugs was about 29 percent higher than anywhere else in North Carolina. Wilmington, just forty-five miles east, had become a hub; by the mid-2010s, it ranked number one in the country in opioid abuse. The crisis then slipped into neighboring Brunswick County. The sheriff there instituted something called an Anchor Initiative, in which addicts can contact the sheriff's office and be put into a recovery program without being charged for the drugs in their possession. It worked so well that drugs became taboo in Brunswick County, pushing many of the steadfast dealers and users into the swampy forests of Bladen and Columbus Counties.

McCrae and many of his non-user friends have a name for these addicts. Harking back to the days when people who worked in cotton mills were called lintheads, he calls them pillheads. People like that were always looking for quick work for cash, and McCrae Dowless had stacks of it.

He was willing to hire them, but he gave them no leeway: payment on receipt of the ballot request forms. No exceptions. "These people, if you don't pay them to do something," McCrae says, "if you pay them an hourly rate, they'll go sit under a tree."

So these workers, these "pillheads" to McCrae, collected the request forms and brought them back to him. They would either return them to his house, where he'd look them over sitting in his swivel chair at his kitchen table, or to his office a few miles away, where he'd hold court from a different swivel chair behind an old desk with a full ashtray in a different wood-paneled room.

He'd look over the forms, then put the initials of the person who collected it in the top right corner. That way, if the board of elections had any questions about the ballot request form, he knew which worker to call. He made a copy of each form before turning it in. This way, he'd have the voters' information when the actual ballots went out, and he could send workers back to their houses to make sure they voted.

McCrae was confident going into the primary. In fact, he was so confident that on that day during early voting outside the board of elections office, he had Harris take a little walk with him. They went over to the tent being run by the Bladen Improvement PAC. Inside the tent were Democrats, most of them Black. On their list of preferred candidates was a young Marine Corps veteran named Dan McCready in the Ninth District. Their most important, though, was an even younger man, a Bladen County native named Hakeem Brown, a Black man who was running for sheriff.

Mark Harris looked at each of the people in the tent and shook their hands and said it was nice to meet them. He had no idea that they had received word that, going forward in 2018, they should tamp down their get-out-the-vote efforts. It's unclear whether they were told about an ongoing investigation, but the people Harris met in that tent were surely aware that this cycle would not feature the usual widespread vote-rallying campaign.

Harris was also unaware that investigators were watching and snapping pictures of his campaign's visits to Bladen County.

The next week, on May 8, primary day broke with temperatures in the upper seventies. Sunny, no clouds. The humidity was low enough that your shirt didn't stick to your back when you stepped outside. A great day for people to show up to the polls. That is, if they hadn't already voted.

The county saw 647 absentee ballots cast in the 2018 primary. McCrae couldn't claim credit for all of them, but many of them came from people in and around Bladenboro, near his house. These were votes from people he knew, and people he was certain would bubble in the circle he wanted them to bubble. They were people who'd been voting with McCrae so long that, by that point, they didn't even have to ask anymore.

The primary ended with Mark Harris taking the Republican nomination that had eluded him two years earlier. And a big reason was Bladen County. He'd won nearly 70 percent of the votes in that county others forgot. He received 437 absentee votes; Pittenger got 17. It's a difference of 420 absentee votes. But if you take into account that had McCrae been working for Pittenger, nearly all of them would've gone to the incumbent, it's a 840-vote flip in little ol' Bladen County.

Harris's overall margin, after all the votes in the Ninth District were counted from Charlotte to Bladenboro, was 828 votes. Bladen County was the difference. And McCrae Dowless was the difference in Bladen County.

It was time now for McCrae and his operation to finish out the election and send Harris to Washington.

As McCrae and Harris celebrated, so too did McCready on the Democratic side. He gathered more than 80 percent of the vote in his primary. The national Democratic Party was poised to inject millions into the campaign in its mission to take back the U.S. House.

Meanwhile, the nearly 300-page investigative report from the state board of elections still sat in Higdon's U.S. Attorney's office in Raleigh.

With just six months until the general election, Lawson still waited for some word, some update, some recognition of their personal appeal to Higdon's office. Part of the disconnect was that Lawson's job is to protect elections; a prosecutor's job is to build a case. One demands urgency; the other, patience.

Included in the findings on Higdon's desk was evidence that the people working for McCrae were doing more than just collecting absentee ballot request forms and making sure those same voters put their completed ballots in the mail. The findings included proof of election fraud.

Investigators zeroed in on a couple named Caitlyn Croom and Matthew Matthis, who for some reason was still telling people his name was Josh. Of the report's 279 pages, 22 chronicled the work Croom and Matthis had done over the course of gathering votes for McCrae, who was saved in Matthis's phone as "McCrae Boss Man." Included in the report were handwritten statements from Croom and Matthis detailing how they came to work for McCrae, what they did, and why they thought they were doing it: money.

Croom wrote that McCrae would pay them half of $225 for collecting twenty absentee ballot request forms and the other half after they collected twenty signed and witnessed ballots. She said McCrae instructed them not to tell people they were getting paid by the ballot. And that she knew what she was doing was wrong.

But that didn't come through in other pages. One document details a text-message conversation between Matthis and a friend from Bladen County who was living in Ohio at the time of the election. Matthis asked for his friend's date of birth and the last four of his Social Security number so he could request a ballot in his name.

A few weeks later, the texts show, Matthis filled it out. "Yo, do u care who u vote for?" he asked. "I got ur ballot in the mail. Who u want for president?"

The friend didn't care. Neither did Matthis.

"I was just trying to survive and make money," he wrote in his statement, which sat in the U.S. Attorney's office, a handwritten siren of what could become of the 2018 election, if only anyone in a position of authority cared to intervene.

The ballot-harvest season runs along the same timeline as beans in eastern North Carolina. Planting starts in late July but mostly in August and early September, in order to have a crop by the first frost in early November.

In early August 2018, a woman who was paid by the Bladen County Improvement Association PAC dropped off 184 request forms at the county board of elections. This, perhaps more than any other event, marked the unofficial start of the 2018 general election between Mark Harris and Dan McCready.

A few weeks later, on August 22, another big batch of ballot request forms showed up, filled out and signed, more than 100 in all. McCrae Dowless's signature is hard to miss: a big *M*, then an underlined small *c*, then the uppercase *C*, followed by some squiggles. Then a big, loopy *D*, followed by an *o*, and one clear cursive *l* that gives way to more squiggles.

That signature was next to a line declaring those 128 ballots had been dropped off. The first seeds of the 2018 general election harvest were planted, and the rain was on its way.

★ ★ ★

Like the Rapture August 2018

You can't tell us that and us not do something with it.
ELECTIONS ATTORNEY JOSH LAWSON

After 2016, scientists said Hurricane Matthew and its flooding were 500-year events. But just two years later, in late summer 2018, a behemoth hurricane named Florence tore a path through the Atlantic, headed straight toward southeastern North Carolina.

By the second week in September, as elections officials were preparing to send out absentee ballots, forecasters were comparing Florence to the mother of all North Carolina hurricanes, the only storm to make landfall on the state as a Category 4, Hurricane Hazel. In October 1954, Hazel's eye came ashore just south of Wilmington on a full-moon high tide, the worst morning for a storm landfall all year. Hazel transitioned boats into firewood and tossed recently harvested cotton into the air like snow. It turned the barrier islands into the ocean floor.

Folks in eastern North Carolina have endured many a storm—Fran and Floyd and Bertha are always on the tongue—but when people start bringing up Hazel, they actually listen. They boarded up and fled as Florence approached. Nursing homes evacuated rows and rows of people in wheelchairs. Michael's father, then in the last months of life, was one of them, lifted in his wheelchair into a twelve-person shuttle van, headed to another home he wouldn't remember. Animal shelters moved dogs and cats. In Southport, as has been tradition since 1900, the appointed voluntary weather observer raised two red-and-black hurricane flags on the pole at Fort Johnston. On the night before Florence landed, the few living souls who remained on the coast gathered in bars, and the bars felt like the inside of mausoleums.

Florence's winds were gracious, dipping to Category 2 and 1 range. But the storm unleashed hell in rain. Florence officially made landfall in Wilmington, sending 100-year-old oaks onto houses, killing a mother and baby in one. Then it hung out for more than a day, right there off the coast. In

Southport, workers at a nuclear power plant were stranded for a week, sleeping on cots. Farther north in New Bern, rescue missions were underway. With each hour and rain band, the rivers in eastern North Carolina swelled. Bridges that on dry days crossed unnoticeable streams were now cracking under the weight of water. Inland sounds that usually smell of saltwater filled with freshwater and runoff from upstream. Counties like Bladen were divided into new, if temporary, peninsulas, as creeks you could holler across on a normal day raged.

The storm dumped feet of rain on eastern North Carolina—between twenty-four and thirty inches, depending on where you were standing. It was like the sequel to a bad movie, flooding out some of the same houses that were still rotting from Matthew.

The Cape Fear River crested at more than sixty feet. More than 5,500 hogs and 3.4 million chickens drowned on farms, many of their limp bodies making their way downriver. Swift rescue boats looking for signs of life cruised on water surfaces that, in some places, were up above the tops of cornstalks.

One good thing, if you can call it that, is that there weren't as many people to evacuate this time. The state had been so slow to start the recovery process after Matthew that many of the homes damaged two years earlier were still empty. In some places, debris still dotted the road when the second round of floodwaters came to reclaim its territory.

Families that were still relegated to "temporary" FEMA trailers stood, once again, in line for free food, water, and cleaning supplies from the Baptist Men and other aid groups. First responders and volunteers handed out 20,000 bottles of water and 1,000 prepackaged military meals in Bladen County alone.

This time, the storm hit about a week before absentee ballots were set to be mailed out.

State elections officials sent a memo to county boards days before the hurricane, telling them what to do if floodwaters meant they couldn't mail ballots. The memo also reminded staff to move voting equipment and paperwork to higher ground where possible.

For Bladen County and surrounding areas, an emergency order extended the voter registration deadline by three days. Officials also gave an extra week for absentee ballots to reach the boards of elections. The state board of elections dumped nearly half a million dollars into an ad campaign in the weeks between the hurricane and Election Day to tell voters they still had options.

Not only did the 2018 election bring the federal midterms; it was also a sheriff's race year. Jim McVicker was up for reelection after his first term.

And Hakeem Brown, a young and popular Black lawman who worked as a license and theft inspector with the DMV, was hoping to unseat McVicker. Brown, a Democrat, had the full support of the Bladen Improvement PAC, and McVicker, a Republican, had McCrae Dowless. If the people of Bladen County would traverse washed-out roads and around downed trees to vote for anything that year, it would be the sheriff's race. And if they happened to vote for a congressional candidate in the process, so be it.

Mark Harris was preparing to deliver a sermon in Uptown Charlotte on Sunday morning, two days after landfall, when his phone rang.

"We need you down here," Bladen County commissioner Charles Ray Peterson said. A fire truck in Bladenboro had been swept away by the river. Was there anything, Peterson asked, Harris could do to help them get a new one?

Harris had promised Peterson that if he needed anything, he should just ask. Thirty inches of rain meets the qualifications for "anything." Power needs power to make progress, though. Harris had received a similar promise from Mark Meadows, the North Carolina congressman and chairman of the House Freedom Caucus who would later become President Trump's chief of staff. Meadows had told Harris that if he could ever be of help to the people of the Ninth District during the campaign, to simply let him know.

A promise on a promise, now being called in.

The next morning, Harris and Meadows went east to Bladen County. They crossed the Pee Dee River as its milk-chocolate-colored water was still rising. Hours earlier in the same area, a creek that drains into the Pee Dee burst over a roadway. A young mother in a Hyundai Elantra tried to drive through the water. The creek picked up the car and dropped it against a tree downstream. She reached over to unhook her fourteen-month-old son from his car seat. But she needed both hands to push the door open. As she tried to do both—get out and hold him—she lost her grip, and the water carried the little boy away toward the Pee Dee, making Kaiden Lee-Welch one of the storm's youngest victims.

About an hour east of the Pee Dee crossing, Harris and Meadows came to another river, the Lumber, which had made a lake out of land right along the interchange with Interstate 95, perhaps the most important highway in the United States. I-95 was closed for nearly sixty miles along the North Carolina–South Carolina border. Harris and Meadows called their best source in Bladen County, Sheriff Jim McVicker.

McVicker arranged for an escort to take them the final thirty or so miles, snaking along backroads through the swampy forests. "It felt like the rapture must've occurred and I was left behind," Harris told us of the landscape he saw during the police escort. "There was no sign of life. I mean, it was like everything was just gone."

A flood is a narcissist on arrival and long after departure, leaving marks everywhere. On Interstate 40, which runs northeast of Bladen County, thousands of fish glimmered, dead on the highway after the big draining. Weeks and months later, tall grass and shrubs leaned toward the river, paying tribute to the water's exit path. Tree trunks wore rings. Furniture piled up alongside roadways. People begged for help.

Elections, though, go on.

The first person to turn absentee ballot request forms in to the Bladen County Board of Elections after the storm was McCrae Dowless. Logs show that he dropped off 123 forms on September 21, just one week after the hurricane. Elections in Bladen County are won not in the voting booth but at the mailbox, and so McCrae kept at it, turning another thirty request forms in to the county board of elections four days later. And three more the next week.

But he wasn't alone. The drop-off log reads like a back-and-forth between him and people associated with the Improvement Association. Prentis Benston, the former sheriff, even dropped off a dozen request forms about a week before the election.

Sometimes they'd drop off a dozen or fewer. Other times it would be 100 or more. A total of 1,339 absentee ballots were requested in Bladen County. McCrae personally turned in 572 request forms, nearly half of the total.

The Improvement Association was working to try and put a Black man back in the sheriff's office. They'd had four years of McVicker. Many believed he and Dowless had stolen the 2014 election from Benston in the first place. More than that, they believed his tougher-on-crime initiatives were mostly just tougher on Black people. And in October 2018, when it surfaced that McVicker had hired his daughter-in-law to the department, it was all the evidence they needed to confirm their suspicions that he was in the job for personal gain. The county commission held a long public meeting to discuss that hiring and ultimately voted on party lines to approve the hire, 5–4.

The vote only added fire to an increasingly contentious election cycle.

In mid-October, McCrae prepared another list of folks who'd requested absentee ballots. It was time to make sure they voted. Now he needed the same workers to go out and nudge people. Or, if needed, maybe something a little more than a nudge.

He had no idea that in that same stretch of days, elections director Kim Strach and her lawyer Josh Lawson had another meeting with another prosecutor about the election from two years earlier. This time, Strach and Lawson met with Wake County district attorney Lorrin Freeman. By then, Freeman was coordinating the SBI's involvement in an investigation into Bladen County politics. Freeman's investigators were interviewing people about 2016 during the most heated part of the 2018 election. More than once, McCrae would be on his way to work on the campaign and pass a strange black vehicle with dark tinted windows, the kind frequently driven by undercover police officers.

Lawson and Strach say their goal for the meeting was simply to come up with a plan to protect the 2018 election. The elections investigator had heard rumblings of problems with the 2018 general. They were there in Freeman's office to ask the same question Charles Ray Peterson asked Mark Harris, the same question Mark Harris asked Mark Meadows: Anything you can do to help?

The meeting was on October 19. Early voting had already started. Lawson pulled out his notepad, as always, and recorded. He scribbled down a few notes early on, but nothing big, as they eased into the conversation. Then Freeman said something that stunned him.

Her office, she said, had evidence of significant fraudulent activity affecting the 2018 election. Lawson quickly wrote it down, word for word: "Significant fraudulent activity affecting the current election."

Then he spoke up: "You can't tell us that and us not do something with it."

Except there wasn't anything to do. Freeman's job was to catch people breaking the law and then to prove what they did in court. To do that, she needed evidence. She needed to build a case. She needed to catch people in the act. She actually *needed* them to commit fraud in the current election.

Lawson and Strach, on the other hand, were charged with protecting the state's elections. They needed to keep the act from happening.

There was the disconnect again. How could they protect the integrity of an election and give Freeman the evidence she needed to catch the bad guys?

In the end, Strach and Lawson determined that all they could do was send a letter to Bladen County voters telling them to not let anyone else fill out their absentee ballots. And that was it. The letter was the only legitimate measure anyone in any official role took to save an election that was already almost certainly rotten.

★ ★ ★

Election Night November 6, 2018

★ ★ ★

I've never seen rain in North Carolina.

DONALD TRUMP

McCrae stayed up until after 4 A.M. the night before the election, sending text messages and making calls. He talked to Mark Harris for about twenty minutes at 10:30 P.M., phone records show. Harris told him the watch party would be on the other side of the district in Monroe, but he'd try to get back to Bladen that weekend.

Just after 9 A.M. the next morning McCrae was back up again, calling and texting. After nineteen months, it would be his last day on the payroll for Red Dome, the group that funded him with money from people who funded the Mark Harris campaign.

Political campaigns alter economies in places like Bladen. Harris had paid out $130,000 to McCrae over the previous nineteen months, and McCrae had disbursed that throughout the county in five-dollar bills. But even that was nothing compared to what Harris's Democratic opponent shelled out.

Dan McCready had entered the Ninth District race in the spring of 2017 as a response to Trump's election just a few months earlier. A U.S. Marine Corps veteran, McCready shook at the core when he saw Trump criticize Khizr and Ghazala Khan, the parents of an American Muslim soldier who died in Iraq in 2004. "In my view," McCready, then thirty-three, told the *Guardian*, "Trump is the greatest threat to our constitution and our democracy of my lifetime, and people must view this as a final straw."

McCready grew up the son of a prominent lawyer in Charlotte, measures five foot eight or so when he stands on his toes, and dresses like any senior bank vice president in the skyscrapers in Uptown Charlotte—blue button-downs, collar always open, tucked into jeans or khakis. But McCready was no banker. After serving in Iraq in the Marine Corps, he came home and cofounded a clean-energy investment firm that helped fund solar farms. By November 2015, that firm, known as Double Time, had raised close to $40 million in capital. As business took off, though, McCready visited Kentucky for a family wedding. Driving through the rolling hills, he marveled at the craftsmanship of the homes and barns. The trip made him reconsider meaningless possessions. "I didn't own a single thing made in the U.S. that was worth passing on to my kids," he told the *Charlotte Business Journal* in 2014. He started an e-commerce site called ThisLand.com, aimed at buying and selling and promoting American-made goods.

The 2016 election had stirred a national movement of opposition to Trump and the Republican Congress, and by the fall of 2018, pundits were predicting a "blue wave" in the midterms. It would be fueled by young Democrats ranging from the far-left Alexandria Ocasio-Cortez from Queens to the scruffy-faced moderate Joe Cunningham from the South Carolina Lowcountry, and in North Carolina their guy would be McCready, the idealistic Marine Corps veteran and dad romping through the state's southern skirt with the campaign slogan "Country over Party." He was a moderate by any measure, and his instinctive conservativism sometimes frustrated a campaign team that wanted him to attack Harris more aggressively.

What McCready wouldn't do himself, though, the party would do for him. National liberal groups pumped $6 million into McCready's run. They studied several decades of Harris's sermons and pulled the lines that worked for them. Some of the most memorable audio featured Harris suggesting that women should "submit" to their husbands and that careers might not be the "healthiest pursuit" for them.

The resulting ad landed just weeks after accusations of sexual assault dominated the bitter confirmation of Supreme Court Justice Brett Kavanaugh. "There was a narrative that they were establishing and wanted to push from day one—this was to be the year of the women," Harris responded in the *Charlotte Observer*. "So why don't we somehow try to create a wedge between Harris and women? And that is what you've seen take place."

Harris didn't have the money to combat McCready on the airwaves. His campaign raised about a third of what his Democratic opponents did. But he had history on his side. No Democrat had won the Ninth since the 1960s, and Trump owned the district by 12 percentage points in 2016.

More than that, Harris had the support of the Trump message machine. In early October, Donald Trump Jr. visited Charlotte to attend a rally for Harris, put on by Republican women at a gun range. Among the women in attendance was Beth Harris, Mark's wife and the unquestioned pilot of his political career. During a photo op with about a dozen of the female attendees, Don Jr. said, "Can I say that I'm gonna like taking this picture, or am

I gonna get Me Too'd?" The joke infuriated Democratic women and made the Republican women in the room laugh.

Tension around gender and race ramped up as the election drew closer. On October 19, a white woman named Susan Westwood came home drunk to her apartment complex in the upscale SouthPark neighborhood in Charlotte, in the heart of McCready territory. She saw two Black women in the parking lot and asked them if they lived there. One of the women pulled out her phone, and Westwood pulled out hers, and the result was the latest viral video. "I make $125,000 a year and I want to make sure you're all up in here," Westwood, who soon earned the nickname "SouthPark Susan," said in the video. "Girl, girl, I got you girl, girl. Girl, I'm white! Girl, I'm white! . . . I'm white and I'm hot, so what are you doing here?"

Into all of that, the very next week, stepped Donald Trump.

He announced a rally at Bojangles Coliseum in east Charlotte, hoping to boost support for Harris. It was at once a chance to stump for his preferred congressional candidate and a chance to offer a visible reply to Democrats, to show that for all the momentum liberals believed they might have following the Kavanaugh hearings, and the Don Jr. "Me Too" comments, and the SouthPark Susan videos all around the world, he was still the president. And people still loved him.

Loyalists lined up outside the arena days before the rally. They stayed through heavy rain that afternoon, smiling and eager. Once inside that evening, they stood for Trump and the pastor while Guns N' Roses' "Knockin' on Heaven's Door" blared over the loudspeakers.

Just forty-three days after Hurricane Florence came ashore, Trump started his speech with the sentences, "Thank you very much. I've never seen rain in North Carolina. It's raining, but we're gonna start." Then he went on, "In just eleven days the people of this state are going to elect Mark Harris."

With Election Day looming, the opening frost of the season was looming too, and farmers rushed to harvest the last of the bean crops. The ballot harvest was over, too. Matthew Matthis, still spooked over being questioned about his involvement in the 2016 election, shut his Facebook account down. His high school sweetheart, Caitlyn Croom, was posting as often as ever. That week Caitlyn asked people to share a post to honor people with autism, and she shared a quiz that determines whether your profile picture makes you an asshole (she laughed when hers came back 333% asshole), and she shared a picture of Denzel Washington with the words "If your absence doesn't affect them, then your presence never mattered."

McCrae Dowless was by now convinced his candidate would win. Never more so than the afternoon he opened his mailbox and saw a mailer for McCready. Most people would see an image that couldn't be more wholesome: a young man with his pregnant wife and three young kids—a girl and two boys—and two curly-haired labradoodles, one white and one Black, all looking at the camera. The only thing you could fault them for was being perfect.

And that was the problem. McCrae pulled his phone from his breast pocket and called Mark Harris. "Mark, we got that McCready mailer down here in Bladen today," he said. "That dog's been to a groomer. That ain't gonna fly in Bladen County. You're gonna win."

McCready spent $6.3 million on the campaign; Harris spent $2.1 million. Together they could've funded 400 jobs at Bladen County's per capita income of about $20,000 in 2018. They could've purchased 3 million Melvin's cheeseburgers.

Still, it may as well have come down to whether a dog looked too fancy for rural North Carolina.

On election night, the meatballs were warm in the chafing dishes, next to small plastic plates and pitchers of sweet tea. Jazz played over the ballroom sound system. Harris supporters arrived at Rolling Hills Country Club well before 7. Built in 1963, the club now sits in a developed part of the heavily Republican Union County, right between Chick-fil-A and Olive Garden on Andrew Jackson Highway. It was just a few blocks from the motel parking where Harris first handed McCrae Dowless a check some nineteen months earlier.

McCready's team tied blue and green and white balloons together in a Marriott in the upscale SouthPark neighborhood in Charlotte, next door to a Williams Sonoma. Both were worlds away from Bladen County, but Harris was at least a few degrees closer.

McCrae Dowless spent the night in the shadows. Perched in his chair at the head of his kitchen table, surrounded by those wood-paneled walls and pillows of smoke, calling and texting, calling and texting. He would place more than 250 phone calls that day before going to bed around 6 A.M. the next morning.

In a sign of things to come, at 6:30 P.M., about an hour before the polls closed, the state board of elections inadvertently posted incomplete absentee vote totals. The wrong information sat there for ten minutes on the biggest night of the year for the board's website.

At the McCready party, where they were handing out blue and white buttons with his picture and the words "Country over Party" written around the arc, the early news looked good. After votes from Mecklenburg and Cumberland Counties were mostly in, he had a 4,000-vote edge. But still Robeson and Bladen were unreported, as was much of Union. At the very least, he would make it a close race, something no Democrat had been able to say in the Ninth District for decades.

But then more Union County votes came through, and McCready's lead fell below 1,000. Then, at around 9:15, Bladen County's results were posted, and they helped push Harris to the top for the first time all night. People cheered at the country club. They moaned at the Marriott. At about 10:45, only a few precincts remained and Harris was still up by more than 1,000, so McCrae decided to call Beth Harris. They talked for about a minute, offering tempered congratulations to each other, then went back to where they were.

At 11:30, McCrae Dowless was steadily on his phone, crunching on data. He'd done his job. Not only did things look good for Harris, but McCrae's sheriff's candidate was rolling too. McVicker, the white incumbent, took to social media and said, "I just wanted to thank each and every person that has supported me during this election. I absolutely could not have done it without the support of the amazing people of The Mother County!"

The congressional contest wasn't even close in that Mother County: Harris collected 5,413 votes to McCready's 3,856. Of those who voted for Harris, 420 were by absentee ballot. That was a pretty healthy return on the 572 request forms McCrae's team planted and picked up earlier in the election season.

Just before midnight, former Arkansas governor Mike Huckabee sent a video message that was played on the big screen at the Harris rally. "I can't wait for you to represent all of us," Huckabee said.

The crowd started chanting, "MARK, MARK, MARK," and soon Mark Harris walked out to greet his supporters wearing the uniform of a Republican member of Congress: dark navy suit, white shirt, and red-and-blue striped tie. His white hair was, as always, neatly shaped, with a stark part on the left side. An American flag pin was on his right lapel.

Across the city in SouthPark, the 300 people at the Marriott for McCready slowly departed. They'd had one good cheer on the evening when they learned Democrats would retake the House. But would *their* Democrat be there? Probably not. On the podium in the ballroom, a blue poster carried the slogan in all caps—COUNTRY OVER PARTY. McCready's campaign manager made a brief appearance to thank everyone for their support. But they made no concessions.

Nearly 280,000 people cast votes throughout the district that year, and Harris was on his way to what would eventually be called a 905-vote edge. Less than half a percent. While McCrae sat at home with a satisfied smoke, and while McCready stayed in a Marriott room with his campaign team, Harris took the stage next to his wife, Beth, in front of a blue and white backdrop that read "MarkHarrisForCongress.com."

"We understand from our opponent that he does not intend to make a statement tonight, but is going to sleep on it. I guess and we will wait and see what the days ahead hold," Harris began. "But as you can see, tonight Mark Harris has been elected to the Ninth Congressional District. I am so thankful that all of you are here."

At midnight at the Marriott, the room was almost empty. A few McCready team members took out knives and popped the green and blue and white balloons. Two sheets of paper were left on the stage. One contained text for a victory speech; the other, text for a concession speech. McCready wouldn't be giving either.

Harris, meanwhile, looked back and forth across the room, his voice projecting excitement. He held a microphone in his left hand, and with his right he waved and pointed his index finger to emphasize his points, as if he were giving a Sunday sermon.

As he looked into the crowd, the previous nineteen months flashed before him. He knew which places had propelled him to victory. He knew that the meeting at the furniture store, the hundreds of calls and texts to McCrae Dowless, the Beast Fest and the peanut festival, the muscadine slushies and the collard sandwiches, they were all wrapped up in those 900 or so votes that separated him from McCready. They were the reason this room at the country club was full and McCready's room at the Marriott was empty.

As he continued with his victory speech, the pastor with the good hair made sure to mention the places that made the difference and praise the Lord for them.

"And I have to say, as I look at that map tonight," Harris said, "thank God for Bladen and Union Counties!"

PART II

And So Do We

★ ★ ★

Broken Men April 10, 1865

★ ★ ★

*There are some colored men in this hall who could vote now
with quite as intelligent a conception of what they were doing
as many white men. But I believe, also, that a large percentage of
the colored people are not yet qualified to exercise this privilege.*

ALFRED WADDELL

Hours after Robert E. Lee surrendered at Appomattox, Neill McGill went out into the Bladen County night seeking vengeance. McGill was a farmer in Elizabethtown and the leader of the local Confederate Home Guard squad that policed the Cape Fear region, terrorizing Blacks and white southerners sympathetic to the Union cause.

The new order of things signaled by Lincoln's victory offended McGill's view of the world. He had come into his fortune of land and human property like many white people in Bladen County did—it was passed down to him. His grandfather had received ninety-two acres of family land in a grant in 1786. In the eyes of people like McGill, the roles of the races had been well established for more than a century in eastern North Carolina. The rules were clear to people like him, made sense to people like him, because they benefited people like him.

North Carolina can be sliced up many ways, but its two overarching personalities were established in the early days of European settlement. The western half of the state became home to settlers who came down from western Pennsylvania along the Great Wagon Road. They were rugged outlaws driven by a desire to be left the hell alone. Still today many of their descendants prefer the whims of the woods, getting by on deer and bear in winter and rainbow trout in summer. Survive a year with them and you've earned your place, no questions asked.

In eastern North Carolina, though, you could spend years in a community and still they'd ask for your last name, or who your "people" are. The wealthy and more noteworthy residents from the flat coastal plain were historically an entitled lot who believed in hierarchies, ownership, and passing down plantations and people.

The oldest preserved tax list of Bladen County residents, from 1763, includes parts of what would later become four other counties. The official population was 3,000, but a note on the list makes an important distinction: "2,000 Negroes would bring the grand total to near 5,000."

Property records from the era include transfers of enslaved people. Musgrove Jones was a planter who had 920 acres that he worked with slave hands. He also ran the river ferry. On November 6, 1798, Jones sold "a negro wench named Phiby, 30 years of age & her child named Amy about 3 yrs." Perhaps it says a little about modern Bladen County that one of Jones's descendants is Pat Melvin.

Perhaps it says everything you need to know.

Still, despite the powerful generational legacy of the enslavers of the eighteenth and nineteenth centuries, it's just as important to know that some of the most prominent and defiant Black citizens in America emerged from bondage in eastern North Carolina. One Black man from Wilmington, David Walker, fled for the North in the early 1800s. In 1829, he was in Boston when he issued his *Appeal*, a famous document that urged enslaved people to rise up against their masters. Walker sewed the pamphlet into clothing sold to sailors, who smuggled it into the Cape Fear region. "The whites have always been an unjust, jealous, unmerciful, avaricious and blood-thirsty set of beings, always seeking after power and authority," Walker wrote. "America is more our country than it is the whites'—we have enriched it with our blood and tears."

Walker's call to revolt enraged plantation owners, and he died a year later, presumably poisoned by wealthy whites. His words, though, carried on like a bloodline through the generations of eastern North Carolina men and women who looked like him. Abraham Galloway was one of them. During the Civil War, he organized 5,000 Black people in New Bern to join the United States Colored Troops, which helped turn the war. For his efforts, in April 1864, Galloway was granted the opportunity to meet Abraham Lincoln. He and four others were the first Black men to walk through the front door of the White House. And when they did, they didn't sip tea and celebrate. They thanked Lincoln for the Emancipation Proclamation and then handed him a petition, signed first by Galloway. It demanded the right to vote.

These were all preposterous wishes in the eyes of people like McGill. As of 1860, the forty-year-old held thirteen people—eight women, five men—enslaved as property. When one would flee his farm, he'd post descriptions in the *Wilmington Journal* along with rewards—one cent for a man named John in 1845; twenty dollars for Isaac in 1850.

To McGill, a runaway slave was a financial setback. But a white man who dared to help a slave? A white man who defied the very system that kept them in power? That man, to McGill, was an even lower human form. "I will pay the above reward of Twenty Dollars for his delivery to me, tied," McGill wrote in the advertisement for Isaac. "And a reward of Fifty Dollars for proof sufficient to convict any white person of harboring him."

No man, Black or white, disgusted McGill more than Matthew Sykes, a lifelong Union sympathizer who lived in a rough and swampy community known as the Piney Woods, about ten miles east of Elizabethtown along the Cape Fear River. That night after Lee's surrender, McGill went out to find Sykes, and what transpired in those woods along the river would open a new era of white retaliation, the effects of which still linger.

The Cape Fear starts as a brown strip of freshwater surrounded by walls of green forest, hardly noticeable to modern road travelers. From here it becomes a 191-mile-long machine and cultural icon that powers thousands of homes today, threading through towns named Lillington and Fayetteville before reaching Elizabethtown.

The river stripes across Bladen County like a sash from the county's northwestern corner to its southeastern. Here is where it becomes a force, with the power you can feel from the banks. It continues to widen as it travels the forty-some miles southeast from Elizabethtown to Wilmington, the port city, where it is a reckless wonder, choppy and silver like the sea.

About twenty miles south of Wilmington, the Cape Fear rushes past the waterfront community of Southport, first discovered by Spanish explorers in the 1500s. In the 1700s, the British named the town Smithville, and it became a quiet fishing village with a small military fort. The air is salty there as the river makes a Z shape—south, then north, then back south, and into the Atlantic.

Every other river in North Carolina stops short of the ocean. Protected by the Outer Banks, the estuaries are ecological marvels and ideal mixtures for vulnerable populations of oysters and blue crabs. But the Cape Fear skips all that mingling and plunges into the horizon.

This unimpeded exit, you can understand, would be a key characteristic for people seeking freedom. And a key hindrance for people trying to keep them shackled.

Late in the Civil War, Union ships navigated the shallow shoals off the North Carolina coast to seal off the mouth of the Cape Fear. Here was one of the most important entry points of Lee's Confederacy, now unavailable to him. Without it he couldn't get supplies to Wilmington, where they would be put on the Wilmington & Weldon Railroad and sent inland to other Confederate units. Lee's armies responded by conscripting hundreds of slaves to help turn one of the barrier islands into the well-armed Fort Fisher.

To overtake the fort, the Union needed the help of people who knew the region. Few were better suited than the enslaved who worked the land.

For decades, Black men and women roamed across and along the Cape Fear to visit with family and friends when their plantation owners weren't looking. The river's harsh characteristics—bogs and marsh, along with the sharp, jagged knees of cypress trees poking up from the water—demanded a certain degree of trust between owners and slaves. No way could an owner oversee everyone at all times in terrain like that.

Slaves became virtuosos of the river, memorizing its every contour, and at night they slipped from plantation to plantation to commiserate and form alliances.

One autumn evening in 1862, a twenty-four-year-old brickmason named William Gould organized seven other slaves and quietly called them to a wharf near Wilmington. The city was in the throes of a yellow fever outbreak that year. Wealthy people fled and left their homesteads in the hands of their slaves, who in turn took off. Gould and his crew boarded a small boat with oars and a sail, but they left the sail down to keep from being noticed: from Wilmington to the Atlantic, those crucial twenty miles, they would have to pass nine Confederate forts.

It took all night, but Gould and his men slid down the river unnoticed, then around the Z-shaped exit, and into the saltwater sunrise. There they raised the sail, which soon was seen by Union forces aboard the USS *Cambridge*.

Once on a Union ship, the slaves had freedom and a purpose: they were to tell the Union everything they knew about the landscape, the forts, and the weaknesses of the Confederacy. An enslaved man named Charles Wesley helped build Fort Fisher. Once aboard a Union blockade ship, Wesley wasted little time outlining the details of the fort, from cannons to bunkers to soldiers' stations.

The information helped the Union develop detailed maps. To this day, there are more maps of Fort Fisher in library archives than of just about any other North Carolina landmark from that time. The information eventually helped the Union take Fort Fisher in January 1865. After that they secured the Wilmington port, choking the last breaths out of Lee.

The Yankees then pushed northeast up the river, into those brown and swampy waters of Bladen County, where dragonflies and mosquitoes and snakes had as much influence as people. Here the Union pulled in more slaves and white southern allies.

In the Piney Woods area along the river, Matthew Sykes couldn't wait to join them. Sykes had served two years in the Confederacy, succumbing to the pressure of the era, but he hated every minute. "He was as strong a Union man as any I ever saw," his father-in-law later said.

In March 1865, about nine months after his Confederate service ended, Matthew secretly joined the Union forces. But he quickly grew concerned about his wife, Catharine. He requested leave to spend time with her and told his unit he'd rejoin them when they came back down the river. They let him off at the Piney Woods and carried on to Elizabethtown. There they found an old homestead occupied by a leader of the so-called Home Guard. The Union soldiers looted Neill McGill's home and several others. It was a message to the rebels in Elizabethtown that a new day was dawning in America. It was a death sentence for Sykes.

By the time Sykes's leave was up in early April, the Union forces had already passed him by on their way back down the river toward the Atlantic, the war firmly in their grasp. Sykes and his family were left unprotected from the Confederates whose pride had been shattered and whose homes had been looted.

McGill rounded up two friends around midnight on April 10. The defeat in war combined with the disloyalty of neighbors was too much for him. With rain falling from the night sky and the ground soggy under their feet, McGill and his men set out to find Sykes.

Matthew Sykes had hid out in the woods for most of his leave, but the rain and chilly weather pushed him and Catharine indoors on the night of April 9. Matthew had gone to bed early that evening, and he was certain he'd wake up and chase down the Union troops before they left him behind. Catharine stayed up into the morning by the fireplace. Two hours before dawn on April 10, 1865, Palm Sunday, Catharine heard noises outside. She ran to wake her husband.

McGill and two Home Guardsmen knocked on the door. Each had a pistol. They pushed past Catharine's father and wasted little time finding Matthew, hiding in a pile of raw cotton inside a storeroom.

McGill's brash accomplice, J. L. McMillan, pulled a cotton rope from his pocket and tied it around Matthew. Rain fell harder against the roof of the double-frame house. The Home Guardsmen waited for an hour for the storm to pass, during which they berated Matthew and accused him of piloting the Yankees to their houses.

When a family member asked what they intended to do with Matthew, McGill gave a chilling reply: "He lies between two big fires: the North, or Yankees, ought to kill him for deserting their army. And the South will kill him."

As the rain slowed, the men instructed Matthew to tell his family good-bye because he'd never see them again. Then they took him into the damp woods. Ten minutes passed before Catharine sprinted into the darkness to wake her mother-in-law, Minty Sykes, who lived about two miles away. The two women hurried out to try to find signs of Matthew on a main road.

They came to the road's eight-mile post, about a mile from Minty's house, and saw tracks: two men and one horse. They followed the prints to a farm, where a Black man met them and said they were mistaken—these tracks belonged to people who lived on the farm.

Catharine and Minty turned around and soon found another set of impressions in the earth. They followed them about three miles before running into another road. By now they'd traveled so far and in such a roundabout pattern that they were almost back at Catharine's family's house. The tracks they'd been following were the ones McGill and the Home Guardsmen made earlier that morning.

Defeated and frustrated, they went to the house, where thirty people were waiting to help.

In daylight, the search party scattered on the main road again. Catharine again passed the eight-mile post. This time, she followed another set of tracks through a field, where she saw a horse tied to an ash heap, a mere hundred yards from the tracks she'd followed earlier that morning.

She and her group kept going alongside a juniper bay. About another hundred yards from the horse, Catharine Sykes saw her husband's body swinging from a sapling.

Other members of her group took him down. She examined his body. Matthew had been "tremendously hacked up," Catharine's father would later testify. He had gashes on his face, stomach, breast, and legs. "The body looked as though it had been violently stamped."

It was a grisly crime worthy of a death sentence. But when the trial for McGill and McMillan began the following October, their defense attorney was a sharp, manipulative lawyer who would become the most influential racist in the postwar South.

A failed Confederate soldier whose bitterness and hatred toward Black people would one day inspire an uprising that reshaped a region and brought an unofficial end to Reconstruction. A thick-bearded thirty-year-old with dark, deep-set eyes who served as a lieutenant colonel in the Confederate army but still demanded that everyone, even his wife, address him as "Colonel": Alfred Moore Waddell.

Waddell was a self-described "broken man" after the war, an "invalid" who returned home to Wilmington struggling to find his place. Lucky for him, his home city and state, too, were searching for their identities.

North Carolina was home to more than 360,000 freed slaves after the war, many of them in eastern North Carolina. The state had a progressive Republican governor, William Holden, who launched a campaign against the Ku Klux Klan and a mission to make Reconstruction work. But true equality—including voting rights—was inconceivable to many whites.

Wilmington was a growing city that had been a heartbeat of the Confederacy. The white leadership fumbled through Reconstruction reluctantly, while a motivated Black population pursued freedom and political status.

The city's uncertainty was a fine example. A line from George W. S. Trow, written a century later: "Democracy opens up the possibility of 'abandonment,' and creates opportunities for men and women who understand how to play to or on that feeling."

Waddell was such an opportunist. The great-grandson of a U.S. Supreme Court Justice, he'd been raised on a plantation in the Piedmont, near what's now Durham. He'd been a Whig, a party that served as a nest for many old-money aristocrats in the nineteenth century. More than love or money, though, he craved respect and admiration. His idol was Robert E. Lee. Even as late as the early 1900s, Waddell and his widow continued to teach Lee's writings in North Carolina's public schools, as though Lee were the crowned king of a generation of southerners.

Waddell emerged in early 1865 and filled a void, capturing the enthusiasm of the white supremacists in southeastern North Carolina who believed they'd been left for dead. He wrote a searing letter to Congress and published it in the *Wilmington Journal*, a paper whose editor was the state's Ku Klux Klan leader:

> Stripped of all false names, the fact is, we are a conquered, humiliated
> people, helpless in the hands of the victors. Some of the officers of the
> Freedmen's Bureau are deadly enemies of our people, and are doing

more to produce disaffection than any class of men among us. They write, and publish at the North, most villainous slanders concerning us, and still they expect social courtesies from us. If the South had overrun the North, would Confederate officers in gray uniforms have been welcomed into the bosoms of your families while they occupied your houses and insulted your people?

The newspaper later published Congress's response, which came from Philadelphia lawmaker W. D. Kelley, who wrote that the U.S. government could no longer "ignore the manhood of colored citizens of the country.... It is not our wish to control you on this subject. It is our hope that you will grapple with and solve the great problem submitted to you by the authors of the war." To Waddell and the editors at the *Journal*, the "great problem" wasn't theirs. To even view it that way was the mindset of Radicals with a capital *R*.

Two months after the Sykes murder in Bladen County, about forty miles from the sapling where he was hanged, a group of freedmen invited Waddell to speak to them, just to see if he had any room for them in his vision for the region.

They welcomed Waddell to the Wilmington Theatre. Waddell titled his speech "An Address Delivered to the Colored People by Their Request at the Wilmington Theatre." He talked down to his audience. He told them that one race was superior and one race was not. He told them, though, that white men had not suddenly turned into their enemies. He said they could live in harmony. But the harmony, of course, depended on their submission to the belief—or truth, to Waddell—that Blacks were inferior.

He then said that Black people were mistaken if they were under the impression they were free, before moving on to the most important and effective tool of white supremacy: elections.

Waddell told the men in that glimmering theater that a few of them might vote one day but that he favored an intelligence test first. "I believe that there are some colored men in this hall who could vote now with quite as intelligent a conception of what they were doing as many white men. But I believe, also, that a large percentage of the colored people are not yet qualified to exercise this privilege. . . . They would be mere tools in the hands of demagogues."

Four months later, Waddell was in the courtroom down the street, arguing on behalf of the men who'd hanged a Union sympathizer in Bladen County.

AND SO DO WE

The trial was a theatrical experience of its own, one that captured the attention of a region. The *Wilmington Daily Dispatch* ran Waddell's closing argument, word for word, across four columns on October 26, 1865.

Facing overwhelming evidence and witnesses, Waddell dug into a playbook he'd use throughout his career in military and law: he dehumanized the people who opposed him. He brought their character into question. With each witness, he worked to establish the murderous defendants as honorable citizens, and the deceased and his family as the opposite. One witness said Catharine Sykes was "one of the lowest women in the county." Meanwhile, of McGill and McMillan, the murderers: "Their character is as good as that of any man in Bladen County."

In his closing remarks, Waddell took aim at one family member who was "the mother of a colored child."

That defense—that a person who sides with Black people deserves to die—would serve Waddell later in life. But not this time. On October 30, 1865, the military court found McGill and McMillan guilty on charges of first- and second-degree murder and sentenced them "to be hanged by the neck until dead."

Conservatives throughout the region raced to campaign for them. They wrote letters to President Andrew Johnson, asking him to pardon them. Four months later, McGill and McMillan were in a brick jail in Wilmington when a mysterious man came to visit the sentinel guarding their cell. The man told the sentinel he was a friend of the prisoners and offered the guard $1,000 to smuggle in a jackknife.

The guard agreed to do that and to step out of the way while they escaped. He even used his military bayonet to start a hole in the brick wall for them behind a fireplace, at a point where the wall was only a foot thick. Then they used the jackknife to work their way through. Between 3 and 4 A.M. on a Friday in 1866, less than a year after they kidnapped Matthew Sykes at the same hour of a day, McGill and McMillan, along with another prisoner, squeezed through a fifteen-by-nineteen-inch hole and escaped.

There was no manhunt. The sentinel was arrested. McGill, who'd organized the murder plot, went back to Bladen County and farmed, hardly hampered by the charges or conviction. Johnson did indeed pardon both men. McGill filed for bankruptcy in 1873, but seven years later he'd rebounded and become chairman of the Democratic Party of Elizabethtown.

Over the years, it was a poorly held secret that the man who paid the $1,000 bribe to break the men out was none other than Waddell. Although that was never proven, the message was clear: in eastern North Carolina, sympathizing with Black causes could get you killed, and crimes carried out in the name of white supremacy would go unpunished, one way or another. And Waddell, as long as he was alive, would make sure of that.

Losing by traditional means, then overturning the decision with force, became the prescription for the (lieutenant) colonel's work for the next three decades, all the way through the fateful year of 1898, when Wilmington was the state's largest city and governed by a democratically elected, predominantly Black city council—and a seething Alfred Moore Waddell set out to take his city back.

★ ★ ★

The Spaulding Dynasty March 1868

We recognize the great issue before the people of this State to be the civil and political equality of all men before the law.

NEW NORTH CAROLINA CONSTITUTION, 1868

He was born in a pine cabin next to Slap Swamp, near Rosindale, an area of Bladen County named for the sticky substance harvested from the long-leaf forests. George Henry White was a free boy of color whose childhood spanned the war. In the spring of 1868, he'd just turned fifteen and the political world was opening up to young men who looked like him.

George's dad, Wiley, was part Black, part white, and part Native American. George's mom had been a slave who died not long after George was born. Wiley soon remarried, this time to a woman with the most significant maiden name of any Black family in eastern North Carolina: Mary Anna Spaulding.

Mary Anna's grandparents, Ben and Edith, were among the first free Black property owners in the state. Ben was born in 1773, the son of a slave owner and an enslaved woman. Edith, a Waccamaw Indian, inherited about 200 acres of land. Ben acquired much more on his own through the tar, pitch, and turpentine industry that drove the American economy.

It was messy work, performed mostly by enslaved people and other low-wage workers. To milk rosin from a pine tree, men swung axes to slash diagonal gashes in the bark. They'd put wooden bowls around the base, near the ground but not on it, and from the wounded tree the rosin dripped into those bowls. The men then transferred the smaller bowls to larger bowls to start the distillation process, turning it into turpentine. Meanwhile, they stuffed pine branches in a kiln and collected the black tar residue.

There were other crops—cotton, wheat, corn, and tobacco. But in eastern North Carolina during the eighteenth and nineteenth centuries, according to a biography of George White, "rosin was like liquid gold." Few things harvested from the colonies were more important to the British than tar

105

and turpentine. They used it to seal off their naval ships and waterproof ropes. People from the southern part of Bladen County, where George grew up, took wagons full of tar and turpentine up to the stores and docks along the Cape Fear River in Elizabethtown, where steamships and riverboats stopped once a week on their way back and forth between Fayetteville and Wilmington.

Ben never learned to sign his name, and simply wrote X on important documents, but even so, parcel by parcel, he and Edith managed to amass nearly 2,300 acres of soggy, fertile land in the early 1800s, all along the southern strip of Bladen County and the northern edge of Columbus County. They divided it up among their kids, who kept adding to it. Their head start on the rest of North Carolina's Black population is a case study in generational wealth. Today the descendants of Ben and Edith Spaulding continue to hold more than 10,000 acres across the two counties.

Being adopted by such a prominent family wasn't enough to put George Henry White on the path to becoming a politician on its own, but it didn't hurt. His father ran a farm on a humble chunk of family land that by 1860 was valued at $250, with personal property that came to $300, according to census records. That was far less than the other descendants of the Spauldings, but it wasn't bad.

George grew up learning how to raise crops and draw turpentine. He went to school two to three months of the year at most. But his parents helped educate him in the few hours they had free from work. Later in life he would credit them for helping him escape the stifling forest. "Boyhood was a struggle for bread and very little butter," he'd say.

Most of the South dipped into a depression during the Civil War. The Confederate dollar became worthless. But Wiley's business actually saw demand increase. Turpentine and lumber and wooden casks had become valuable for naval efforts.

George's family members worked six days a week, then gathered on Sundays to worship at Rehobeth Church. After the service each week, they'd get together to eat and gossip about the news in the community. "We looked forward to going to church," descendant Asa T. Spaulding would say in an oral history project years later. "Not only for spiritual reasons, but for social reasons."

George Henry White's great-uncle John Spaulding, thirty or so years older than George, started the Rehobeth Freedmen's School in Rosindale. George likely attended classes there during his teenage years. But the most impressionable moment came in the spring of 1868. That's when John Spaulding made a run at becoming the first Black man elected to the Bladen County Board of Commissioners.

At those Sunday gatherings after church, fifteen-year-old George would've undoubtedly heard firsthand accounts of John's rise in the local Republican Party. And he would've had an up-close view of the historic 1868 election—an election that, if just for a blink in time, gave Black men of the United States hope that they were on their way to something that looked like equality.

The courthouse was rowdy. White men and Black men filled the building in downtown Elizabethtown on a March evening in 1868. It was a year like no other for the Republican Party in Bladen County. Never before had southern Black men been able to run for office. Never before had an election included the votes of southern people who had been slaves.

One hundred forty years before the United States would choose its first Black president, and 150 years before the election fraud scandal of 2018, John Spaulding, George's great-uncle, sat in that Bladen County courthouse and watched as the men of his party, white and Black, nominated him for office.

The fifth of Ben and Edith's ten children, John was a light-skinned Black man who was born free in 1817. As an adult, John bought his own property and farmed it, much like his siblings did. He built a business around the naval stores industry. He knew the joy of owning property, and knew the best way to ensure other Black people would enjoy the same freedoms was to gain political power. He was sharp, a school administrator who knew agriculture and money. He was such a loyal reader of the *Wilmington Daily Star* that the paper recognized him for being a "worthy and industrious colored man" who "pays promptly."

The history of the United States is a string of pivot points, and 1868 is one of the most critical. In North Carolina, more than 73,000 Black men registered to vote for the first time, creating an unprecedented wave in a state with 116,000 white voters.

The top order of business at the county convention was to build support for a draft of the new state constitution, written as an endorsement of Reconstruction and a guarantee for voting rights for Black men, no matter their literacy level or whether they owned property. Each of North Carolina's county Republican parties was to read and adopt it, and then the state party would do the same before sending it to voters in April.

John Spaulding was in the Elizabethtown courthouse, some twenty miles north of the family homestead, and listened as the words were read aloud: "Whereas, the Constitution now offered to the people of the State recognizes that 'all men are created equal and are endowed by their Creator with certain unalienable rights, among which are life, liberty, the enjoyment of the fruits of their own labor, and the pursuit of happiness.'

"Resolved, that we recognize the great issue before the people of this State to be the civil and political equality of all men before the law."

Cheers echoed throughout the Elizabethtown courthouse after they unanimously adopted the resolution and nominated Spaulding for the commission. In a letter to the *Raleigh Daily Standard* announcing the results, the convention wrote: "It was one of the largest, most harmonious and enthusiastic meetings ever held in this County and we will roll up a Republican majority at the next election that will even astonish ourselves."

The letter was signed in all caps: "Yours truly, ONE OF THEM."

White conservatives were in a fit about "them." Whipped from war and resigned to defeat in 1868, they turned to their most enduring defenses: voter intimidation and accusations of voter fraud.

Say it way back then or say it this very minute, the two practices are used to justify the belief that some people in this democracy are not fit to vote. Even so, that year the momentum for Black suffrage overwhelmed the nonsense claims.

With every Black man on North Carolina soil ready to cast a historic ballot, they needed only a small assist from whites to get the new constitution passed, 93,086 to 74,086. The results were overwhelming in New Hanover County, home of Wilmington: 3,571 to 2,235. Just a few miles west of New Hanover, Bladen County voters passed the constitution, 1,276 in favor and 971 against.

The most significant local victor that night was John Spaulding, the fair-skinned farmer. He joined four white men to become the first Black commissioner in Bladen County history. "He kicked off a political wave for our family," Luke Alexander, the Spaulding family historian, told us from his home on the old family land. "He jumpstarted it in that era. And it was bookended with George Henry White."

Young George Henry White would have plenty to cheer for as the year 1868 continued. That November, voters throughout the United States gave an official endorsement of Reconstruction in the presidential contest: Ulysses S. Grant, the general behind the Union victory and a progressive living in the long shadow of Lincoln, won the White House. And William Holden, the outspoken opponent of the emerging Ku Klux Klan who was first appointed governor in 1865, retained the governor's mansion.

White southerners in eastern North Carolina faced a most unthinkable future. Black men would now be commissioners and postmasters and education leaders. They'd be former slaves in positions of authority, with the ability to say yes or no to requests from their former masters. They would be able to write laws and set ordinances at the structural level, and they could even choose the look of the mail carriers they hired.

The prospect of such good positions going to people who just a decade earlier had been their servants? Unthinkable. The former Confederates didn't mourn, though. They rallied. They planned revenge, physical and systemic. They used the word they'd spread throughout the next decade: redemption.

"Away with useless complaints," the *Wilmington Journal* editor wrote three days after Grant's election. "Rather let us renew our love to the South, and do all we can to lift up her drooping head. As others turn against her, let us cling more closely to our mother. By our devotion to duty and to principle, let us protect and shield her from the shafts of malice and falsehood directed at her name."

The progressive and Black newspapers took on a far cheerier tone: "The tearful prayers of the loyal millions have ascended to Heaven, and the good God has heard them," read an editorial in the *Wilmington Post*. "Now let thanksgiving and praise take the place of supplication, for the victory is won!"

Out near the Bladen-Columbus county line, George Henry White was soaking up the historic news. Reconstruction was here. Blacks were voting and winning. His own great-uncle John had made history in his home county.

George began to wonder how far he might be able to go.

The Black Congressman from Bladen
1870–1896

★ ★ ★

They have therefore commenced a system of disenfranchisement.
ADDRESS TO THE COLORED PEOPLE OF NORTH CAROLINA

When George Henry White was a young man, his father took a job in Washington and left the family behind in North Carolina. Family historians and writers who've studied George's life say the details of the move and job are unclear, but George remained close to Wiley. In the first year of his father's absence, George took care of the family cask-making business at his father's request.

When George graduated from the Whiten Normal School around 1872, he could speak passable Latin. He possessed a blend of gifts uncommon for any man at the time, let alone a Black man with fewer resources. He knew how to use language in ways to move people, both in written word and spoken. Meanwhile, his father's departure had also forced him to become an able businessman and farmer.

He saved up $1,000, equivalent to almost $20,000 today. And in 1874, after fulfilling his obligation to his father and the farm, George took the money with him on a two-day train ride to Washington. When he arrived, he handed the savings over to Howard University to cover his tuition.

George would now live with his dad in Washington and walk two miles to campus each day, eventually earning a normal certificate from Howard. His obituary would later state he also earned a law degree there, but that couldn't be true because the college didn't have a law school in the late 1870s.

By the time White finished at the university, he was a solid man in a suit. He stood five foot eleven and 245 pounds with a bushy mustache that flared out on either side. He would move back to his home state, but not to Bladen County. He took a position as a school principal in New Bern instead. He knew he wanted to enter politics eventually, but the political climate of

North Carolina had changed significantly just in the few years since he'd headed to Washington.

Two years after the historic election of 1868, the Ku Klux Klan rode through eastern North Carolina's towns on horseback at night, warning Black voters to stay away from the polls. The years since the Civil War had left white conservatives with worthless bonds and little political clout. They were enraged over an amnesty bill that allowed anybody to hold office in the South, with the exception of a few former Confederates. The swift shift in power was most evident in the eastern counties around Bladen, where a plantation economy had ruled for more than a century.

The Klan wanted to fill the state legislature with Democrats willing to overthrow Governor Holden. Male-pattern bald, with hair around the sides and back of his head, Holden was a longtime critic of the Confederacy and fierce anti-Klan lawmaker. His supporters were diverse—and his opponents saw that as a weakness.

The voter suppression campaign of 1870 worked. Democrats took a two-thirds majority in the legislature that year. They swallowed up congressional districts. One newly elected member of the House had a name that rang out in Bladen County and all across eastern North Carolina: Alfred M. Waddell.

The legislators immediately launched an impeachment of Holden. They succeeded, clipping the progress of 1868 by force and intimidation within just two years. On December 19, 1870, seventeen Black legislators representing counties mostly in eastern North Carolina delivered an "Address to the Colored People of North Carolina." It was the first of what would become a genre of farewell addresses by Black politicians over the next thirty years.

They are mad because their slave property is lost. They are mad because the Reconstruction measures have triumphed and we are permitted to represent you in this body. . . .

The only offence of Gov. Holden . . . is that he has thwarted the designs of a band of Assassins, who had prepared to saturate this State in the blood of poor people on the night of the last election. . . .

It avails nothing, that they have got control of the General Assembly, by deception, fraud, and intimidation; so long as the friend of the poor, and protector of the innocent and defenceless, occupies the Chair of State, and you have the right to go to the polls unmolested. They have therefore commenced a system of disenfranchisement, by amending the charters and towns, by allowing but one day for voting, by allowing voters to be challenged at the polls, and by requiring each to vote in the township in which he resides. They have thereby already disenfranchised thousands.

Black voters still had an ally in Washington, though. President Grant remained aligned with Radical Republicans. He was deliberate about protecting voting rights, in ways that few presidents before or after have been. He assigned federal troops to protect Black people at the polls, something white southerners said was an irresponsible waste of taxpayer money. And of course, it was mildly inconvenient to their suppression efforts.

But after the 1870 election, Grant's party—Lincoln's party—began to argue over just how liberal it would like to be. A senator from Missouri named Carl Schurz grew tired of Grant and the Radical policies. Schurz had helped end slavery, but he opposed the increased role of government in a formal Reconstruction, which he found tyrannical. So Shurz formed a more moderate party, the Liberal Republicans. The new party appealed to a class of southern whites who didn't want to be associated with white supremacists but also weren't crazy about formal Black equality.

The Republican cracks emboldened the conservatives, who were hardly conflicted on matters of race and rights: voting was a duty for whites, they believed. Holding office was a duty for whites. And here now Black people accounted for nearly 60 percent of North Carolina's population—and they were *voting*? For the Confederate whites, the path forward was to bond around a tight core of white supremacy while the liberals argued among themselves.

Klan numbers grew, and southern Democrats became an immovable, irrational force.

In May 1872, the Liberal Republicans nominated Horace Greeley to challenge Grant. Greeley lost badly, but the movement managed to spoil the overall image of Reconstruction in the country. Conservatives only needed a small window, and in 1876 the Conservative Party formally adopted the name Democrats, quickly crushing the last hopes of Reconstruction.

Republican Rutherford B. Hayes was awarded the presidency in a controversial election in 1876. Three states had been too close to call, and both sides claimed victory. A commission that included Supreme Court justices ultimately awarded the states to Hayes, leaving him with a narrow victory in the Electoral College. Even though he was a Republican, Hayes was a states' rights guy. He quickly withdrew federal troops from the South, leaving the elected state governments in control.

In North Carolina, Democrats pounced. They took aim at the Thirteenth, Fourteenth, and Fifteenth Amendments. They passed laws that stripped voters of the ability to choose county commissioners. Instead, the commissioners would be chosen by the justices of the peace—who were, of course, first selected by the legislature.

The political careers of the first Blacks to hold office, people like John Spaulding, came to quick and unceremonious ends.

John's great-nephew George Henry White moved back to his home state in the late 1870s, and he was getting real lessons in how this country that pledged equality and emancipation was shaping up for him. Over the next decade he'd take and pass the North Carolina Bar exam and become a successful lawyer.

In 1884 he was elected to the state senate from Craven County, a few counties northeast of Bladen. Eventually he settled in Tarboro, an old town surrounded by cotton plantations in Edgecombe County. Tarboro was situated in the Second Congressional District, known around the state as the Black Second, because of the number of Black voters there. Knowing the numbers were in his favor, George White set his sights on a political position that would've been unthinkable just a generation earlier.

U.S. Congress.

One truth has held up since the country's founding: racial divisions and economic prosperity are knotted together.

The post–Civil War investment boom that began in 1867, with railroads and westward expansion, came crashing down around 1873, in large part because of the passage of the Coinage Act, which reduced the value of silver. The first Great Depression, or Long Depression as it became known, lasted into the early 1890s.

Cotton prices that had been twenty-five cents a pound in 1868 were down to twelve cents a pound in 1890. Poor whites and poor Blacks were worn out and frustrated. They'd soon expose racial superiority for what it is in a capitalist country—a made-up idea that works to keep a lot of people of all races in poverty while a few get rich. The poor whites and poor Blacks banded together.

A new political party, the Populists, took root. They stole members of the still-progressive Republican Party, but their biggest draw was a solid group of white Democrats who'd come to realize their skin color wasn't doing them a whole hell of a lot of good.

Alone, Populists were no match for either party. But in 1892 they were participants in elections all the way up to the presidential contest, where Populist James B. Weaver won 8.5 percent of the popular vote. Many Republicans saw opportunity in the new party. If they could merge with them and form a so-called Fusion Party, perhaps they could shove aside the Democratic reign.

George Henry White, though, was opposed to fusion. He believed Blacks would benefit less than whites in a merger. He wanted to talk about anti-lynching bills; Populists wanted to talk about the economy. So when he decided to make his first run for Congress in 1894, he stuck with Republicans.

At the Republican state convention that year, attendance was abysmal. Some said they believed Republicans should just concede that year's elections and come back in 1896 with a better plan. One concern with that idea: they knew if they waited two years, Democrats would devise more ways to suppress the Black vote.

White was the solicitor in the Second District. He stood up and addressed those concerns by saying that for eighteen years in the Black Second, most of the votes had not been counted. White, hoping to prevent more rifts in the Republican Party, withdrew from consideration for Congress that year. But he returned two years later.

On September 10, 1896, the Republican and Populist Parties nominated White to Congress, a decision that caused great "dissatisfaction on the part of many Populists."

By November, White, the sticky-heeled farm boy from Bladen County, had become perhaps the most popular Black man in eastern North Carolina. In the general election, he marshaled support in the Black Second and won by 4,000 votes to become the only man of color elected to the Fifty-Fifth Congress.

He was as witty as Atticus, the *Colored American* declared, and sterner than Cato. He was the perfect model of private worth and public virtue. The daily newspapers in the state, by now mostly run by white supremacists, were less thrilled. The *Charlotte News* wrote that "the dark shadow has fallen upon the people of eastern North Carolina."

★ ★ ★
Sacred Texts July 1898
★ ★ ★

We are the modestest people in the world, and
don't hold as many offices as we will.

GEORGE HENRY WHITE

Thirty years after he freed the two Bladen County murderers from jail, Alfred Waddell was still going by "Colonel." But as of the mid-1890s, newspapers would sometimes switch it up by calling him the "Honorable" Alfred M. Waddell, a nod to his three terms in the U.S. Congress that started with the white supremacy campaign of 1870.

While in Washington, Waddell served on House committees dear to him: the Committee on Post Offices and Toll Roads and the Ku Klux Klan Committee.

The first one may seem insignificant to modern ears, but that wasn't the case in the late 1800s. In those years, postmaster was a prestigious job. In eastern North Carolina, men like Waddell became obsessed with the position, especially when they heard a Black man had the job. It was an injustice, they believed, to have to walk into the post office to ask a Black man for postage.

White leaders and opinion makers celebrated the progress of Black leaders, so long as those Black leaders didn't have power over them. "There is no doubt that the condition of the negro in the south is and has been steadily improving," the *Washington Post* wrote at the time. "It is only when he is placed in the position of authority over a white man, it is when he comes in close personal contact with citizens, male and female, of all classes, in the daily distribution of mail, for instance, that the pride of race asserts itself and deplorable events occur." Waddell believed his duty on Congress's post office committee was to prevent those deplorable events from happening by preventing Black people from landing in such powerful roles.

The Ku Klux Klan Committee, by contrast, was organized to investigate and prosecute members of the Klan—to hold accountable the white groups that committed murder and larceny and other crimes against the bodies of Black citizens. An intention, though, is only as convincing as the implementation.

Seating Alfred Waddell on the Ku Klux Klan Committee was like putting a coyote on a committee to investigate mysterious livestock deaths. At one point the committee called former Confederate general William L. Saunders to Washington under claims that he led the KKK movement in North Carolina. When Saunders arrived in the nation's capital, he had free lodging with one of the committee members whose job was to censure and punish him, Waddell.

In the hearing, Saunders declined to answer questions, even as he was "badgered and bullied," Waddell would later say. When the Ku Klux Klan Committee set Saunders free, Waddell cheered the decision, calling Saunders "as brave and true a man as ever lived."

Despite serving as a dutiful racist and Democrat and Confederate for most of his postwar life, Waddell was constantly plagued by insecurity. Waddell's insistence that people call him "Colonel" was a small lie, sure, but it was also a plea to be recognized and respected. Several leaders in his party mocked him in private. They rolled their eyes at his long-winded speeches full of exaggerations. Some even said they thought all Waddell ever did well was marry up, considering all three of his wives were from prominent Wilmington families. Two were sisters: Julia Savage and then, after Julia died, Ellen Savage. Ellen died in 1895, and within a year Waddell was married to Gabrielle DeRossett, who was twenty-nine years younger than Waddell and who'd just lost her mother to an opioid overdose.

Waddell was an opportunist, chiseling his way into rooms with important people at whatever cost. After losing in the 1878 election to Republican Daniel Russell, who'd go on to become governor, Waddell found a number of ways to remain in the public eye.

In 1882, Waddell announced a new Democratic newspaper in Charlotte. He called it the *Charlotte Journal* and declared that he would be the editor and publisher. The *News & Observer* of Raleigh praised Waddell for uniting "large experience" with "unusual brilliancy," though it seems he still lacked in commitment, because he resigned from the position a year later.

The *News & Observer*'s affection for Waddell only grew, though. In the 1890s, a new editor named Josephus Daniels shared quite a lot in common with Waddell. For starters, they were white supremacists of the most dangerous sort, meaning they were white supremacists in positions of power. And they were willing to use positions of power to bring harm to Black people in the state. Especially powerful Black people. While Waddell constantly undermined his Black counterparts in Congress, Daniels built a growing hatred for people like George Henry White, a Black man who dared to educate himself and walk with a dignified gait.

Their connection was even deeper. Like Waddell, Daniels had demons from his past to run from. And like Waddell, he coveted prestige and respect, earned or unearned.

Nearly thirty years younger than his friend Waddell and ten years younger than his nemesis George Henry White, Josephus Daniels was born in the town of Washington, known to many in North Carolina as Little Washington, a small community along the Pamlico River where on certain nights in spring and fall you can see the sun set over the river to the west and the moon rise over the river to east at the same time.

Daniels's father was a shipbuilder and a well-known Union sympathizer. Much like Matthew Sykes, the man murdered in the Bladen County woods the morning after the Civil War ended, Josephus Sr. served the Confederacy during the war, not because he wanted to but because he had to. He built ships to operate as Confederate blockade runners, nimble boats used to scurry around the Union blockade with supplies for the South.

Like Sykes, Josephus Sr. was vocal about his opposition to the war, and he was closely monitored by Confederates as he conducted his work. Also like Sykes, he feared for his life and the safety of his family. When his son was three, Josephus Sr. moved them to Ocracoke, a sixteen-mile-long island on the Outer Banks that remains one of the most isolated inhabited islands in the United States.

Josephus Sr. regularly traveled across the Pamlico Sound, the largest estuary south of the Chesapeake and a haven for shrimp and oysters, to take people and goods from Ocracoke inlet to Little Washington. On one of those trips, a Confederate sharpshooter picked him off and killed him. Josephus Daniels Sr. left a wife and three sons for Washington, including the three-year-old who carried on his name but not his ideas.

Josephus Daniels Jr. worked in a print shop when he was a teenager and spent most of the rest of his life working with ink. He became the editor of the *Wilson Advance* in 1880. Two years later, when he was just twenty, he and his brother Charles started the *Kinston Free Press*. Josephus was a skinny young man with narrow, eager eyes. He believed that a newspaper should have a point of view and that any editorial page that didn't make enemies also didn't have friends.

Had his father been around to read some of the things he wrote, the story of eastern North Carolina might've turned out differently.

The young Josephus Jr. started by ripping off columns in support of prohibition and Democratic policy. He ratcheted up the anti-Republican and anti-Black rhetoric when Republican James O'Hara won a seat in Congress out of the Black Second.

Caught in the clash between Daniels and O'Hara was Josephus's mother, Mary, who was the postmistress in Wilson. In one editorial, Daniels described a political meeting of O'Hara's Black supporters like this: "Think of five hundred perspiring Negroes packed into a courthouse, wrangling and near-fighting on a red-hot day! It was stifling and odors were rank."

O'Hara, in response, had Mary fired from her postmistress job. For Josephus, who still lived at home with his mother, the event only crystallized his racist editorial slant.

Daniels wrote and wrote, moving up the newspaper ranks as he did so. In 1894, at the urging of none other than William Saunders, the former Klan leader who'd made a mockery of the congressional committee several years earlier, Daniels took the position as editor of the *Raleigh News & Observer*, the biggest print pulpit in the state.

Here he could use the power of the press to transform failed leaders like Waddell into heroes again, and he could mock respected figures like George Henry White with impunity. The louder the headline, the better. "A very gentle man" is how Daniels's third son, Jonathan, once described him, yet "also a very violent man . . . editorially."

With each word Josephus seemed to grow more convinced that white supremacy was the key to power and prosperity and to a functioning society. There had to be an order, he believed, and he for sure wanted to be at the top of that order. He found people from eastern North Carolina who gladly agreed with him—most notably Furnifold Simmons, the leader of the Democratic Party. Together the two, along with people like Waddell, would start a friendship that altered the course of the state for more than a century.

The Fusion success of 1896, which delivered White to Washington as Congress's only Black representative and also ushered progressive white Daniel Russell into the governor's mansion, had left them embarrassed and angry. So in March 1898, Daniels and Simmons met in New Bern to discuss a plan for redemption. After the meeting, Simmons wrote a 200-page document he called the *Democratic Party Hand Book*. It outlined what he formally called "the White Supremacy Campaign."

The playbook may have been new, but the strategy was merely refurbished from previous generations. Simmons and Daniels knew there was one never-fail tool to drive a wedge between poor white men and poor Black men: white women.

Despite the reality that for decades white slave owners ravaged and raped and fathered children with Black women they enslaved, there persisted an image of the "Black beast."

He was big. He was dangerous. And he was exactly what the white supremacists needed him to be: a myth.

Whites may have been the ruling race for most of the first century of the United States, but deep within them was a fear of a Black uprising. Nat Turner's rebellion in the mid-1830s in Virginia lived on in white memory as a historical marker of what was possible when Blacks pulled together.

In 1898, Daniels and Simmons launched a modern white supremacist campaign leveraging the full power of Daniels's newspaper. Simmons sent the 200-page handbook out to white homes, but for those who couldn't read or write, Daniels had another idea: he hired a young cartoonist from Sampson County, a sweeping county that shares a border with Bladen. The cartoonist, Norman Ethre Jennett, was known as "Sampson Huckleberry."

In 1898, the state Democratic Party offered to pay Jennett's salary, so long as he could produce cartoons that effectively took the idea of minstrel shows and drew them on paper to be circulated all around the state. He started in August of that year, and he would have a cartoon on the front page of the paper nearly every day through the election.

The first came on August 12, during the Republican judicial convention. It was an image of Republican solicitor Oliver Dockery surrounded by men with long faces colored dark around wide, white lips, titled "Dockery and His Supporters."

The next day, stretching across four columns at the top of the paper of record for North Carolina, Sampson Huckleberry drew the ankle of a giant person with "The Negro" written on the pants leg, his boot holding down a small person with his arms flailed with "White Man" written on his pants.

The caption: "A Serious Question—How Long Will This Last?"

George Henry White was a keynote speaker at the North Carolina Republican Convention that summer of 1898. He was up for reelection that fall. The growing white supremacist campaign was weighing on him.

Escalating hostility toward Blacks in Wilmington was spilling out into the rural areas that surrounded it. George White may have left the area where he grew up to run for Congress in another district, but Wilmington and nearby Bladen County remained home.

Wilmington was the closest city to his relatives, and the place that supplied news about the areas where he grew up and had those Sunday after-church lunches.

That summer at the convention, he stood in front of the crowd of Republicans in Raleigh and delivered an address that, according to Benjamin Justesen's biography, would haunt him throughout the rest of his career in eastern North Carolina. It was a speech that became "sacred text to white supremacists across the Tar Heel State."

The *News & Observer*'s account of the speech was spliced and twisted for the sake of the white supremacy campaign, Justesen concluded. White himself even said he was misquoted. Still, the *N&O*'s reporting on his words became the definitive account. Whether he said them or not, these are the sentences that ricocheted around the state, framing George White to white voters for the rest of his political career.

And it was picked up by racist newspapers across the state, including the *Wilmington Morning Star*, which called White a "malicious windbag."

"I am not the only negro who holds office," White said in the *N&O*'s version. "There are others. There are plenty more being made to order to hold office. We are the modestest people in the world, and don't hold as many offices as we will. I invite the issue."

And then the fateful line.

"We imitate white men. You steal and so do we. You commit crimes and so do we."

★ ★ ★
The Editorial That Shook the Old North State
August 1898
★ ★ ★

You sow the seed—the harvest will come in due time.
ALEX MANLY, NEWSPAPER EDITOR

One month after White's convention speech, his old friend Alex Manly, a Black newspaper editor in Wilmington, picked up a white competitor's newspaper and read another column aimed to inspire fear among white women—this time from a white woman.

On page 2 of the *Wilmington Morning Star*, the paper republished a speech from a prominent Georgia woman named Rebecca Felton. She'd actually delivered the words one year earlier, in 1897, as an address to farmers' wives in Tybee Island, Georgia. Papers in other parts of North Carolina ran it as news in 1897, but for some reason it never made its way to Wilmington until the following year. The *Star*, an open supporter of the white supremacy campaign, didn't bother to make the distinction in its 1898 reprinting. If you were Manly or any other resident of eastern North Carolina that morning, you'd have read the words as if Felton had said them yesterday. They struck like a hammer against iron in the 1898 white supremacy campaign.

Felton's family home had been destroyed by Union soldiers in the Civil War. Her livelihood had changed when they could no longer own slaves. The emancipation left her working in the fields again. Her frustration came through in her words. In her letter, she suggested that courthouses were shams and frauds. She mocked white liberals who were "honey-snuggling" with Black men at the polls while white women on farms throughout the South were "scared to death if left alone" with a Black man. She said that if the arms of government wouldn't protect those white women, the white men of the region must stand up and "lynch, a thousand times a week, if necessary."

Manly, the newspaper editor, would have known a thing or two about women being taken advantage of on farms. His grandmother was an enslaved woman who worked for former North Carolina governor Charles Manly. They had a son, Alex's father. The governor kept his two families—his white family and his slave family—separate. Alex's dad went on to work as a railroad fireman.

Alex and his brother Frank began publishing Wilmington's Black newspaper, the *Record*, around 1893. Alex's skin was so light that he could, if needed, pass for white. But Alex owned his Blackness. He made a point of correcting people and insisting that they acknowledge that he was a Black man.

He focused his newspaper work on civil rights. He exposed poor working conditions in the Black wards of the Wilmington hospital, and it actually led to improvements there. White leaders and even some Black leaders bristled at his "aggressiveness." But he eventually gained strains of respect from his counterparts at white-owned newspapers.

By the time he read Felton's words in the *Star* that morning, Manly had grown tired of images of the "black beast" who terrorizes white women. So on August 18, 1898, he countered. It was, as some historians would later write, the editorial "that shook the Old North State."

In North Carolina's 330 years as a state, no single act of journalism has done as much to change its course:

A Mrs. Felton from Georgia, made a speech before the Agricultural Society at Tybee, GA, in which she advocates lynching as an extreme measure. This woman makes a strong plea for womanhood and if the alleged crimes of rape were half so frequent as oft times reported, her plea would be worthy of consideration. . . .

If the papers and speakers of the other race would condemn the commission of crime because it is crime and not try to make it appear that the Negroes were the only criminals, they would find their strongest allies in the intelligent Negroes themselves; and together the whites and blacks would root the evil out of both races.

We suggest that the whites guard their women more closely, as Mrs. Felton says, thus giving no opportunity for the human fiend be he white or black. You leave your goods out of doors and then complain because they are taken away. Poor white men are careless in the matter of protecting their women, especially on farms. They are careless of their conduct toward them, and our experience among poor white people in the country teaches us that the women of that race are not any more particular in the matter of clandestine meetings with colored men than are the white men with colored women. Meetings of this kind go on for some time until the woman's infatuation or the man's boldness brings attention to them and the man is lynched for rape.

Every Negro lynched is called a "big, burly, black brute," when in fact many of those who have thus been dealt with had white men for their fathers, and were not only not "black" and "burly" but were sufficiently attractive for white girls of culture and refinement to fall in love with them as is very well known to all. Mrs. Felton must begin at the fountain head if she wishes to purify the stream.

Teach your men purity. Let virtue be something more than an excuse for them to intimidate and torture a helpless people. Tell your men that it is no worse for a black to be intimate with a white woman, than for a white man to be intimate with a colored woman.

You set yourselves down as a lot of carping hypocrites in that you cry aloud for the virtue of your women while you seek to destroy the morality of ours.

Don't think ever that your women will remain pure while you are debauching ours. You sow the seed—the harvest will come in due time.

Never before had a Black man so publicly confronted the narrative of the "burly, black brute." Never before had a leader said that white women were actually attracted to Black men instead of white men.

White men throughout the state boiled. They called Manly's words vile. In houses and halls around eastern North Carolina, men talked of killing him. A terrorist militia called the Red Shirts saw its numbers spike. South Carolina Senator Ben Tillman came to Fayetteville and spoke to the white supremacist leaders. On the surface, his words were meant to demean them. But the obvious aim was to rally them.

"Why didn't you kill that damn nigger editor who wrote that?" Tillman taunted a crowd of Democrats. "Send him to South Carolina and let him publish any such offensive stuff, and he will be killed."

That Manly was correct didn't seem to make much difference. That he was himself was biracial didn't, either. The truth is, there was no rape epidemic. Even the newspaper editors printing story after story at the time would later admit that they inflated the numbers. In New Hanover County, "just one rape and one 'seduction' were reported between July 1896 and July 1898," David Zucchino writes in his book *Wilmington's Lie*.

Facts aside, the mere suggestion that white men were anywhere near as violent as Black men was ammunition for the white supremacy campaign.

In Wilmington, men clamored to retaliate, threatening to burn down the *Record*'s offices and lynch Manly that week. But Simmons, the campaign's leader, raised a calming hand. He told his constituents that retribution would come, but first they must vote Democratic in November. Simmons knew the editorial would galvanize people at the polls. There were only a few weeks till Election Day, so they waited.

With the print campaign in full swing at white newspapers across the state, Simmons and his editor friend Daniels figured they should contribute a live-event component to stoke momentum. They went around the state looking for orators willing to stand in front of hungry audiences and spit red meat and lies.

Nobody was more ready for the task than Alfred Waddell.

In October 1898, two events drew headlines. In one, the white press pounced on a story about George Henry White and a train. White apparently had gone to a circus and sat in seats reserved for white people. As a congressman, he wasn't immediately ejected for sitting there. Instead, a larger problem emerged: other Black members of the crowd tried to join him. They were removed. Afterward, they were angry with him "insulting every respectable negro at the show."

Also that month, Waddell gave a speech at Thalian Hall, a prestigious theater with balconies for the elite. Delivered to a gathering of about a thousand men, many of them Red Shirts, and their wives, on October 24, 1898, it proved to be the most effective address of Waddell's life. "Shall we surrender to a ragged rabble of Negroes, led by a handful of white cowards, who at the first sound of conflict will seek to hide themselves from the righteous vengeance which they shall not escape? No! A thousand times no!" he said.

And then Waddell shouted the lines that still rumble throughout eastern North Carolina like aftershocks more than a century later. "Let them understand once [and] for all that we will have no more of the intolerable conditions under which we live. We are resolved to change them if we have to choke the Cape Fear with carcasses."

The crowd roared, one of the most deafening cheers in the history of the city, the papers would say. "The time for smooth words has gone by," Waddell said.

The *Wilmington Messenger* said the speech "electrified his hearers. It was the most remarkable delivery ever heard in a campaign here in the memory of this generation. It was . . . a speech that will ring for all time in the ears of all who heard it."

Waddell, never too successful to fish for more compliments, sent a copy of the speech to his cousin, the acclaimed novelist Rebecca Cameron. She replied with the rousing affirmation he craved.

"We have been amazed, confounded, and bitterly ashamed of the acquiescence, and quiescence of the men of North Carolina at the existing conditions; and more than once have we asked rather simply: Where are the white men and the shotguns?" Later in the letter, she wrote, "I hope it will not come to this last resort, but when it does let it be Winchester and buckshot at close range."

The weekend before the election, the *New York Times* printed a list of the number of Black elected officials in each North Carolina county. Bladen had ten school board members, one county commissioner, and four postmasters.

Following the list, the *Times*, which just two years earlier had adopted the motto "All the News That's Fit to Print," added a few editorial thoughts about the statistics. "The number of negro office holders in some of these counties is small, and they are nearly all east of the centre line, but they give a pretty strong indication of what we may expect if the mongrel party which has put these negroes in office wins. If they make such a showing in a few years, what may we not look for if their party triumphs and they get on top again?"

The day before the vote, Alfred Waddell excited a large crowd at Thalian Hall again, this time telling them: "You are Anglo-Saxons. You are armed and prepared and you will do your duty. . . . Go to the polls tomorrow, and if you find the negro out voting, tell him to leave the polls and if he refuses, kill him, shoot him down in his tracks. We shall win tomorrow if we have to do it with guns."

For Manly, the editor of the *Record*, the situation was deadly. He knew he would be a hunted man no matter which way the election went. His family had begged him to leave Wilmington. So the night before the election, he did. He gathered his belongings in a horse and buggy and dressed in a dark suit and hat. Given his light skin color, he probably looked like any of the town's white merchants as he rode through the streets.

Out at the edge of Wilmington, Manly came up on a checkpoint being manned by Red Shirts, the unruly white militia. They asked for a secret password for the checkpoint. Manly had obtained the password through a German grocer who made him swear he wouldn't tell it. He recited the word and the men asked where he was headed. To an auction to buy some horses, he told them. "If you see that nigger Manly up there, shoot him," the white men said. And they handed him two rifles.

Manly ordered the horses to move, and he carried on from there on a slow march up the East Coast. Behind him, the city he'd covered in his famous Black newspaper was about to be torn down. Defeated and dejected, he kept pointed toward Washington, where he would seek out work from an old friend from Bladen County, George Henry White.

★ ★ ★

The Rigged Election and the Massacre
November 10, 1898

★ ★ ★

The Republicans are hacked, and know they are defeated.

FURNIFOLD SIMMONS

Election Day 1898 broke in eastern North Carolina with temperatures in the forties. A chilly breeze cut through the cypresses and towns along the Cape Fear.

WHAT WILL YOU BE? asked the top headline on the *Wilmington Messenger*, followed by the subhead "Today White Men of North Carolina Must Declare Where They Stand."

Under the bold text was a letter from George Henry White's Democratic opponent, W. E. Fountain. The *Messenger* printed it word for word. Fountain issued an urgent appeal to the white Populists who'd merged with the Black Republicans to bring Fusion victory to the state two years earlier. On this much, believe it or not, Fountain and George White agreed, if for different reasons: Fusion could not last. A man must choose where he stands on the matter of race. Would he strive for equality for the Black man? Or would he cast a vote for Simmons's campaign?

"THERE IS NO ISSUE BUT THE SUPREMACY OF THE WHITE RACE OVER THE NEGRO RACE," Fountain wrote in all caps.

In the *News & Observer*, Jennett, or "Sampson Huckleberry," created a cartoon for the front page that depicted a white woman standing like a soldier on guard next to a ballot box, her shoulders back and arms straight down to the side while her chin holds strong. Her shirt has puffy shoulders and her dress is long, and they meet at an impossibly small waist, which has a belt around it with a barely visible "US" written on it. The caption under the cartoon on the front page of the state's most important newspaper read "Good Morning! Have you voted the White Man's Ticket?"

In the bottom right corner of the same front page, the paper did print one small box, perhaps to give the appearance of balance. The headline read "The Black Man's Ticket." And the story quoted a Black man with his own passionate appeal: "White men are going to the polls tomorrow to vote the white man's ticket. I appeal to you negroes to go to the polls and vote the black man's ticket."

Despite the fact that many Black people made up their minds not to vote out of sheer self-preservation, the news in eastern North Carolina was rife with fabricated stories about Republican and Black shenanigans throughout the region. Furnifold Simmons's words ran far and wide: "Republicans are sending out lying telegrams, falsely saying Democrats concede defeat. We will carry the State and elect the Legislature. The Republicans are hacked, and know they are defeated." The *Wilmington Morning Star* ramped up the fear with a report, possibly true, of a "dastardly outrage" in which a Black boy threw a rock at a gray-haired woman.

For anyone with white supremacist leanings, the message was crisp: it was time to reclaim North Carolina and rid the state of "negro domination," of "mongrel rule."

"The young man who comes of age this year and casts his first vote for the restoration of white supremacy in this State starts life as a voter well and honorably," wrote the *Star*.

Many voters feared violence at the polls. So they went early. By the 5 P.M. deadline, the white supremacists had essentially free pass to the precincts and their chairmen.

Around 9 that night, about 150 white men surrounded one precinct in a stable on Tenth and Princess Streets in Wilmington. The precinct had ten Black voters for every white voter registered, making it an almost certain Democratic loss in a fair election.

The men, with white handkerchiefs around their arms, entered the precinct where vote counters were adding up the results. The white men knocked over an oil lamp and pulled guns. The Black election officials hid in the back room and ran out the door. William Harriss, a former Wilmington mayor who had lost the job the previous March, stuffed Democratic ballots into the ballot boxes. They stayed there while the remaining precinct judges, two white Democrats and a Populist Democrat, counted the tally. When they posted the results, one Democratic candidate had received 456 votes in a precinct with only 343 total registered voters.

Similar stories played out throughout the region. By the next morning, Democrats owned ninety-four seats in the state House, compared to just twenty-three for Republicans and three for Populists. The state Senate now was forty Democrats, seven Republicans, and three Populists. The sweep carried on through the local races, where Democrats reclaimed sheriffs' jobs and solicitor positions and judgeships. For the white supremacists, it was the successful completion of their first step in the playbook to taking back power.

There was one Black eastern North Carolina politician they couldn't take down, though. George Henry White won the Black Second with 49.5 percent of the vote. But the overall turnout was down significantly. In Halifax County, for instance, the white supremacy campaign pushed turnout down to 3,951 total votes, four votes fewer than White himself received two years earlier.

George White, from Bladen County, had become North Carolina's last political survivor of a wave of white supremacists in red shirts. Now he would be their only target. After the election, the *Wilmington Messenger* described him as "a saucy, bitter nigger with the strange name of White, as if a nigger was ever white."

The next day, Wednesday, November 9, Alfred Waddell met with a group of white men to issue a set of demands for Wilmington's Black population, which he said he wanted met by 7:30 A.M. Thursday, November 10. They were to resign from any job of significance, including those at the post office. Now that white supremacy had carried the state, they wanted Wilmington's Fusionist mayor and police chief to step down immediately, even though their jobs weren't up for a vote for another year.

One problem with the demands is that there was no centralized group of Black people in Wilmington, no one body that represented every person with brown skin in town. The white supremacy campaign had painted the battle as two sides, but in fact there was no other side. There was no Black supremacy campaign, no appointed leaders to send to Waddell's house to hash out the details of a concession.

The next morning, Waddell waited until 7:30 A.M. When no response arrived, he walked out into the cool November air, just a few blocks from the Cape Fear. Near the river, his followers were gathered, waiting for the response.

He asked 75 white men to go with him to the *Record* office and carry out the last order of business—to ask for Alexander Manly. Instead of 75 men, though, 500 lined up behind him. Now in his midsixties, Waddell had a long coat wrapped around a growing belly and his boots crunching against the dirt streets. This was, finally, his moment. After all the years being pushed aside by the establishment Democrats, Waddell was no longer the butt of jokes but the leader of men, the author of a coup.

They marched five blocks south to the offices of the *Record*. Along the way, Black people ducked inside their windows and homes. The 500 angry white men stood outside and called for Manly. The paper hadn't published that day, a decision made by Alex's brother Frank. Alex was probably somewhere in Virginia by now.

Soon the whites were in the building, tearing it apart, tossing Manly's pictures and papers into the street like Frisbees. Then someone lit a match and the building went up in flames. The Black fire department rushed to the scene, but they were held up along the way by white city leaders who told them to stay back. Eventually, they got through, and put the fire out before it could take down a nearby church.

The entire second floor of the *Record* was charred when the white men stood out front and took pictures with it later that morning. Many wore suits and hats and held rifles, proud and accomplished as if they'd just built something.

News of the fire traveled fast and inconsistently. At a cotton mill near the Cape Fear River, Black workers heard whispers and worried. Many ran home, defying a plea by the mill's managers to stay and work. The sight of Black men running through the streets to protect their houses was seen as a threat to the white leaders. They described the Blacks' frightened sprint as an act of aggression. Surely, they said, soon the Black residents of the city would start shooting.

Around lunchtime, Governor Russell in Raleigh started to receive telegraphs filtered through coup leaders' fingers. As far as Russell knew, the riot was started by Black men. He organized a state militia from men freshly returned home from the Spanish-American War.

Meanwhile, the first gunshot rang out at North Fourth and Harnett Streets, near the cotton compress. One account said that a "half-grown negro boy" fired it; a police officer later reported that the shooter was a white man. Regardless, twelve Black men and three white men were soon bleeding on the dirt streets of Wilmington. Medics rushed fourteen of the fifteen—one white man chose not to go—to the hospital. When the emergency doctor, who was white, filed his report from the day, he determined that "all but the two white men" had been shot in the back.

Still, reports of a Black uprising churned throughout the state. Men in Fayetteville boarded a train to offer armed support. The false narrative of the day had confirmed the false fear peddled for months in false stories in white newspapers such as the *N&O*. The militia mobilized. White leaders pulled out military-grade weapons that hadn't been seen by most citizens in city streets before. By early afternoon on November 10, 1,500 white men were armed and walking through Wilmington's streets. Several years later, one of them would write, "It is doubtful if there ever was a community in the United States that had as many lethal weapons per capita at that time."

On one block they forced a Black postman to his knees to beg for his life. On another, two fifteen-year-old white boys left a Black man whimpering. Out near Third and Harnett Streets, where the first shots were fired, the white men were giving the boulevard a repugnant nickname that would be passed down through generations in the city: "Niggerhead Road."

By day's end, a number of people were killed, but nobody knows the number for sure. At the National Lynching Memorial in Montgomery, Alabama, today, twenty-two names are listed on the weathered-steel box for New Hanover County. Some accounts list many more, in the hundreds. The white newspapers list far less, as few as a couple.

Regardless, dozens more were now on a list to be targeted for removal or death over the next several days. The men on the list were not ordinary citizens. They were leaders. Barbers, butchers, lawyers. The educated and the employed were most dangerous to the myth of the unintelligent Black brute.

Waddell forced the Fusionist mayor to step down and, after a haphazard same-day election, stepped into the old mayor's vacant position. He appointed a new police force, much of which was made up of the same rebels who'd run roughshod through the city that afternoon. Many were drunk by the time Waddell promoted them.

Countless Black wives and children fled Wilmington that night and week. Hoping to avoid the checkpoints, they dove into the Cape Fear and trekked through the swamps to the west and north. They traveled along the banks of the river into neighboring communities like Bladen County. An uncounted number of them would die before finding their next bed.

It was an earth-shifting day for Black residents across the region.

George Henry White had practiced law in New Hanover County courts, and he'd received a hero's welcome from the citizens there after his election in 1896. Relying on reports from family and friends in the area, he described the Wilmington massacre as "the miserable butchery of men, women, and children."

Later, White said it was, "the horrible scene of aged and infirm, male and female, women in bed from childbirth, driven from their homes to the woods, with no shelter, save the protecting branches of the trees of the forest, where many died from exposure, privation, and disease contracted while exposed to the merciless weather."

★ ★ ★

The Last Black Congressman March 4, 1901

★ ★ ★

Phoenix-like he will rise up again some day and come again.
GEORGE HENRY WHITE, BLADEN COUNTY NATIVE

In his final year in Congress, George Henry White introduced a bill that would make lynching a treasonable offense.

In a speech to the House, White's words echoed Alexander Manly's controversial editorial. White said that rape and assault of any woman should be punishable by the courts, not by mobs. And he declared that Black women were just as endangered by white men as white women were by Black men.

"I am prepared to state that not more than 15 per cent of the lynchings are traceable to that crime," White said. "And there are more outrages against colored women by white men than there are by colored men against white women."

From his newspaper office in Raleigh, Josephus Daniels read White's words and fumed, same as he had two years earlier about Manly's editorial. Any statement that a Black woman in North Carolina was just as threatened as a white woman in North Carolina, the paper argued, was not only false but a danger to North Carolina.

Later, George White even made a point to distinguish between "some white people" and "all white people," saying, "No better people live anywhere on God's green earth than some of them."

But White specifically said that the "fellow who edits the *News & Observer*" was not among those people. And he said that "unfortunately, men of the type of him . . . are now in the ascendency."

The baseless fears of white folks have a long history of obscuring the very real and documented dangers for Black people. There were 4,743 documented lynching victims in the United States in the late 1800s and early 1900s. But as long as newspapers had editors such as Daniels, and as long as towns had mayors such as Waddell, the story of threat in the South was that white citizens, specifically women, were in far greater danger than the Black men and women who were being shot, hanged, and fed to alligators.

White's antilynching bill, of course, died in committee.

White began to lose support among Republicans in his district. Local powerbrokers and supporters claimed that he had gotten a little too connected in Washington, a little too distant from them. A prominent white Republican wrote to the Goldsboro newspaper to say that the Black people in the Second District had, under the direction of White, become "so 'uppish' that we can't make them stay in the background." The same white supremacy that had powered the Democrats was now infecting White's own party. They were just using different language.

The *News & Observer* was hardly discreet. The paper printed a cartoon depicting White as a Black face with white lips atop the body of an elephant labeled "GOP." The cartoon figure's trunk slurps a money jug that reads "Term in Congress Worth $5,000 a Year." The text under the caption reads, "But most people think our only negro congressman has had it about long enough."

Even with White's political career all but over, and his lifelong mission of passing laws to protect Black citizens and Black voters thwarted, Daniels wasn't satisfied. "He must be made an impossibility for the future," the editor wrote of White. "And he will be."

What Daniels had in mind wasn't another Wilmington, nor any physical harm to White personally. This time the Democrats were after something far more sweeping and conclusive than even to mount a campaign against a single Black congressman. This time they sought to eliminate the need for armed white rebellions altogether by rigging the voting process.

They floated the idea of a poll tax and literacy test. Constitutionally, the U.S. Supreme Court had ruled that poll taxes and literacy tests were legal because they, at least on the face of it, applied equally to white and Black voters. Generational poverty and systemic education gaps were social issues, not constitutional ones, the Court had essentially ruled.

But at the turn of the century, nearly a quarter of North Carolina's white population was illiterate. Thousands were poor. Any sweeping barriers to voting would do just as much harm to the white Democrats as it did the Black voters.

They found a solution in Louisiana, another southern state with a large Black population. Louisiana had instituted a loophole to the poll tax and literacy test: a grandfather clause. It stated that any man who voted before

1867—or whose *father or grandfather* voted before 1867—would be exempt from the new standards. The clause was creative, if diabolical: no Black man in the United States could vote before 1868.

North Carolina's state legislature drafted an amendment and put it on the ballot as a referendum in 1900. They could've passed something similar themselves, but they figured a statewide vote would give it more credence and lasting value, and they were confident that existing voter suppression efforts would ensure its passing.

In 1899, Josephus Daniels, the *N&O* editor, traveled to Louisiana to "report" on the grandfather clause there. He didn't tell his readers, of course, that his trip was paid for by the state's Democratic Party.

Over the course of a few days, Daniels went from town to town, sending back cheerful stories, all public relations messages masked as objective dispatches. "CREOLES LIKE THE AMENDMENT," read one headline.

The Louisianans he interviewed raved about the clause, he told his readers back home. He depicted a state with a cleaner, fairer government that was doing things the right way, free of corruption. He interviewed a state senator named C. C. Cordill, who said that before Louisiana's amendment, 3,000 Blacks and 380 whites were registered in a local parish in 1896. Two years later, after the amendment had passed, in the same parish the white voters outnumbered Blacks 369 to 14.

On August 2, 1900, the voters of North Carolina, or at least those who dared go to the polls, passed the suffrage amendment, 60 percent to 40 percent. That's if you believe the Democratic poll officers in charge of the election. In the areas around George White's Black Second, where Black people made up 68 percent of the population, the amendment somehow passed.

Marion Butler, the Populist senator from North Carolina, wrote a letter in the *Washington Post* asking for an investigation into fraud in North Carolina. But it would find no traction. "Butler's telegram will receive no attention in North Carolina," Furnifold Simmons confirmed.

Three weeks later, George Henry White sat down with a reporter for the *New York Times* and confirmed that he wouldn't run for office in the next election. How could he? The suffrage amendment would essentially leave the Black Second with no Black voters.

In the long interview, White was reflective and frustrated. He said he had three reasons for leaving political life. For one, he knew he couldn't win. Also, he needed work. And then there was his wife, now ill in New Jersey after spending years enduring the attacks on her husband. "I cannot live in

North Carolina and be treated as a man," White told the newspaper. "I have been made the target for those who have been fighting against the negro race in North Carolina, and nothing has been too hard to say of me."

White said he would move to New York, or somewhere in the vicinity. He predicted that at least 50,000 Black North Carolinians would move either north or west. White would be in the north, but he recommended the west to as many as could take it. He painted a life of owning land and building a farm for themselves.

Much of his frustration was directed toward the overt racists who'd stripped voting rights of the majority of people in his district. But at the end of the interview, he tossed a sharp axe at the Republican Party that had fueled his career. His words echo those of civil rights leaders throughout time who say that the complacent white moderate can be as dangerous to Black causes as any unabashed racist.

"The fact is, the white Republicans of North Carolina are Republicans in order to get the negro vote to maintain them in office," he said, "but they do not want the negroes to hold office."

That November, Black candidates lost in every contest in the Black Second. The *Tarboro Southerner* declared that the "George H. White supremacy no longer reigneth."

As a lame duck congressman, White tried to push one more bill, an appropriation to fund "a home for the aged and infirm colored people." The bill passed the House rather easily, and eventually he was able to get the Senate on board.

Eight days later, on January 29, 1901, the last Black man in Congress for many years to come stood on the House floor and delivered his final speech. It would be his longest. At the heart of it he said it was a plea for colored people of the country, but it was also a speech about stolen votes. White pointed out that in Scotland Neck, the total registered vote that year was 539, but somehow, miraculously, 831 people voted. And Democrats—can you believe it—won eleven of every twelve of those mysterious votes.

At the end of his speech, he laid out practical ways for Black citizens to stand on equal ground as their white counterparts.

And then George Henry White, now a tired man pushing fifty, his hair starting to recede and his dark mustache growing ever bushier, delivered the last words any Black person would speak in Congress for three decades.

You may tie us and then taunt us for a lack of bravery, but one day we will break the bonds. You may use our labor for two and a half centuries and then taunt us for our poverty, but let me remind you we will not always remain poor. You may withhold even the knowledge of how to read God's word and learn the way from earth to glory and then taunt us for our ignorance, but we would remind you that there is plenty of room at the top, and we are climbing.

This, Mr. Chairman, is perhaps the negroes' temporary farewell to the American Congress; but let me say, Phoenix-like he will rise up some day and come again.

These parting words are on behalf of an outraged, heartbroken, bruised, and bleeding, but God-fearing people, faithful, industrious, loyal people—rising people, full of potential force.

Then came his last words, which actually drew applause.

The only apology I have to make for the earnestness with which I have spoken is that I am pleading for the life, the liberty, the future happiness, and manhood suffrage for one-eighth of the entire population of the United States.

On March 4, 1901, as the clock struck noon in the capitol building in Raleigh, the very moment when White's term in Congress ended, Democratic legislators stood and announced the historic moment to cheers.

"George H. White, the insolent negro . . . has retired from office forever," said Alston Watts. "And from this hour on, no negro will again disgrace the old State in the council of chambers of the nation. For these mercies, thank God."

George White followed through and moved to New Jersey, where he founded the town of Whitesboro. Historians generally count the Great Migration as starting in the mid-1910s. But in North Carolina, White's move kicked it off in earnest.

It's impossible to overstate the damage the 1898 insurrection and voter suppression campaign that followed did to eastern North Carolina. Many of the Black families that fled Wilmington landed in Columbus and Bladen Counties at first, then moved on to Durham. Others just went north to Maryland and New Jersey and Pennsylvania.

Over the next generation, while scores of other southern Blacks migrated to the Midwest, those from eastern North Carolina around Wilmington took a straight line north. Many of White's own family members would move to

Whitesboro, leaving the sweeping farms in Bladen and Columbus founded by their Spaulding ancestors a century earlier. Among his descendants who were born in Whitesboro is Stedman Graham, the longtime partner of Oprah Winfrey.

After White's last speech in Congress, twenty-eight years passed before another Black person was elected to the body. For North Carolina, it took far longer—ninety-two years.

If not for the events of the last three years of the 1800s, eastern North Carolina would be an almost unimaginably different place. Before the white supremacy campaign, Wilmington was the largest city in North Carolina, and 56 percent of its 20,000 citizens were Black. Black businesspeople owned ten of Wilmington's eleven restaurants, it was home to one of the country's few Black-owned newspapers, and the Black male literacy rate was higher than that of white males. If left to prosper without political interference, Wilmington might have grown into the largest metro area in the South, with Bladen County as its sprawling bedroom community.

But that's not what happened.

White and his prosperous family members had sensed that southeastern North Carolina wasn't the place to set up a future. His uncle, Aaron McDuffie Moore, had gone to Durham. So had his cousin, CC Spaulding. Indeed, in 1898, one of the most tumultuous years of White's life, McDuffie Moore cofounded the North Carolina Mutual Life Insurance Company, kicking off an era where that city developed Black Wall Street. "Wilmington became an incredibly hostile environment, but Durham at that time was a new city, basically," Luke Alexander, the Spaulding family historian, told us. "Wilmington stunted its own growth. It would've been the magnet. And it imploded. Durham was one of those places where the energy transferred."

During the Great Migration, while Black people in Mississippi and Alabama took trains to Chicago and other midwestern cities, eastern North Carolina's highway and train lines took them directly north, to Washington and Baltimore and Philadelphia, much the same as George Henry White's family did. Then, though, an interesting thing happened. When their children became college age, many came back south to the state's ribbon of Black colleges. Schools such as N.C. A&T and N.C. Central attracted some of the brightest young minds in the country, and they were the heartbeat of the civil rights movement. The sit-ins, the freedom rides, the marches to Washington—the overturning of literacy tests and the passing of voting rights act. No doubt George Henry White would've loved to see how his grandchildren's generation came back to his home state to reverse the laws that forced him out.

The white supremacy campaign's lasting effects can be measured in census numbers, too. Black residents peaked at 61 percent of North Carolina's population in the 1880 census. By 1910, it was 55 percent, and it would continue to drop from there. Today Black people make up less than 30 percent of the state.

Meanwhile, the white people who drove them out were hailed as heroes during the early twentieth century. After Waddell died in 1912, Wilmington's city council signed an official proclamation of appreciation, saying it was "mindful of his service to the people of this community in a time when courage and determination and wisdom were tried to the uttermost, and of his subsequent service as mayor during the period of reorganization and ensuing prosperity."

The next year, Josephus Daniels, the racist newspaper owner, became the secretary of the navy for Woodrow Wilson. Eight years after that, in 1920, Rebecca Felton, whose speech calling for a thousand lynchings a week lit the fire for the Wilmington coup, became the first woman to serve in the U.S. Senate. She was eighty-seven years old and served for twenty-four hours. The historical marker in DeKalb County, Georgia, that celebrates that accomplishment says nothing of her beliefs on slave ownership or lynching.

When George Henry White died on December 28, 1918, the *Wilmington Morning Star* and the *News & Observer* ran just three paragraphs. His funeral was held on Lombard Street in the center of Philadelphia, and he was buried at Eden Cemetery, one of that city's first African American cemeteries. Engraved on his modest headstone are the climactic words of his final speech in Congress, topped with the gold outline of a phoenix, wings spread wide.

It's some 500 miles from where he was born, in that pine cabin on Slap Swamp in Bladen County. His decision to choose that as his final resting place was a continuation of what's no doubt his lasting statement on his home state, written down by family late in his life:

"May God damn North Carolina, the state of my birth."

★ ★ ★

The Carnival Worker September 13, 1953

★ ★ ★

This is my payback. You know, I want payback.
IRVING JOYNER, CIVIL RIGHTS ATTORNEY

She was a young mother, just nineteen, with a two-month-old in the crib. Thay Lewis White, a white woman, was doing housework on a Saturday morning in the home she shared with her husband along a state road about five miles south of Elizabethtown. It was September 13, 1952, and Milton was at work at the hog market.

The ironing board was upright when someone broke in through the back door and hit her over the head with the iron, leaving it bloody and with her hair sticking to it. She was raped there. Her blood splashed on the walls and doors, and it inked a path to a cornfield about fifty feet from her home. There, Thay Lewis White was raped again and left to die in the late summer sun.

At 11 A.M., a witness saw a Black man washing his hands near an old mill, about a mile and a half up the state road from White's home. Douglas Grayson was nineteen, though court records and police reports and newspaper articles would say he was twenty-three or twenty-four. He was raised in Virginia and never learned to read. "Illiterate," the court would call him. When he became a teenager, his mother had committed him to the State Hospital for the Insane. The hospital discharged him on March 31, 1949, declaring him sick but well enough. A psychometric test found him to have the mental capacity of someone who was four years, eleven months old.

Grayson found work with a traveling carnival as a dishwasher. That September, the carnival had a stop in Elizabethtown. He attended the show, which actual court documents describe as featuring "naked women" who "excited his lust." His boss fired him that night. He had no ride home, no family around. He wandered in the woods of Bladen County until sunrise.

He was seen late the next day, the same Saturday of Thay Lewis White's death. He was washing his hands there at the mill. And the next time anyone saw him he had dripping-wet jeans and was at a fruit stand in Elizabethtown.

He tried to steal the stand's cigar box full of cash. Someone called the police, and when an officer arrived, Grayson ran. The officer caught him and flung a fist into his face, knocking him down. While in the officer's grasp, Grayson, who also went by Grisson, offered a strange piece of information: he mentioned the White murder and said he "knew who did it."

He said he was there, and blamed it on a person named "Jean." He described the kitchen, the iron, and the cornfield, and even showed his hand to compare it to the size of the baby's head, but he insisted the killer wasn't him.

That afternoon White's husband, Milton, came home from a day's work at the hog market and surveyed the scene, the blood, the sleeping baby in the crib. He followed the trail left by his lifeless wife into the yard. He heard a scream from the cornfield. It was his mother-in-law, Thay's mother, who'd come by to visit and followed the same bloody path. There Milton found his wife, head split open with a bloody two-by-four in the harvested cornstalks next to her.

Officers grilled Grayson for hours, and he admitted to the murder around 2 A.M. the next day. Grayson would later go back on his confession and say he didn't murder the woman. But it was already too late for that to make any difference.

The papers called her pretty; they called him an imbecile and a Negro. The next day the *News & Observer* ran a photo of one of the investigators pointing to the bloody iron. By now, a half century after the reign of Josephus Daniels, the *N&O* was moving toward becoming a progressive newspaper. But still it saw the world through white eyes, and the image of the "Negro beast" still leaped from the words on its pages.

The next day, a Sunday, the sheriff wanted to bring the confessed murderer back to the scene so that he could reenact his every step. A mob gathered at the White home. First a few, then dozens, then more than 500, many of them armed.

The sheriff asked that they disperse. Most did, but several stayed on. A few banged on the police car's window as they drove the man up to the back door. Several gathered in the woods next to the cornfield, hoping to snatch Grayson if the deputies slipped up. God, they hoped he'd run.

But the walkthrough ended peaceably. The officers put Grayson back into the car and took him to Raleigh to Central Prison, where he would await trial. For a brief moment in Bladen County, white law enforcement had successfully saved a Black man from being lynched.

AND SO DO WE

At least 124 Black people were lynched in North Carolina during Jim Crow. Fifty-seven of those occurred in counties east of Interstate 95. But that number is surely too low. It doesn't account for the countless killings that fell within the boundaries of the law, or those carried out by officers.

It doesn't include, for instance, the name Bobby Joyner.

Bobby was walking home from choir practice on a Wednesday night in January 1951 in the town of La Grange. If you're looking at a map of eastern North Carolina, La Grange would be a dot in the middle, almost the same distance from Virginia as it is South Carolina, and as far from Raleigh as it is Wilmington. It's along a long, flat, hazy Highway 70.

Irv Joyner was seven years old that night. He looked up to his seventeen-year-old cousin, Bobby. They'd each watched their grandparents try to vote and be denied. They'd each been trained as boys to be careful with white officers. They'd each wanted a better future. Even so, that Wednesday night in January, at some point on his way home from choir practice, Bobby encountered two policemen, one of whom was Chief J. A. Wheeler. The officers said they'd received numerous tips and complaints about night prowlers. They'd even sicced a dog on one person, who'd got away.

The two white police officers stared down the Black boy. Whatever happened, they knew they could control the story. Which they did, in the next day's newspapers. They said Bobby was trying to break into a home, the home of John Mitchell, a white man. They said they'd been watching the home that night from the woods, which would be a strange thing to do, if you think about it at all: a police chief scoping out a single home on a winter night. They said they yelled at Bobby and told him to hold up his hands. Initially he did so, they said. But when they tried to detain him, they said, he wheeled and swiped a knife. It nicked Wheeler's coat.

The two officers fired eight bullets into Bobby's body. Six were in the boy's head.

Seven-year-old Irving Joyner watched as his family reeled and tried to stack evidence against the officers. Black people have never needed proof to believe that white officers could become murderers, but the Joyner family knew a jury would.

What actually happened that night, according to Irv Joyner and evidence his family gathered, was that his cousin Bobby was walking near the white school on the other side of the street from the Mitchell home. Police shot him there. Executed him. Then they carried his dead body across the street and put it outside the window where Mrs. Mitchell, a white woman, slept. A garbage collector admitted to the family that the officers had called him in the middle of the night and told him to help them dispose of the evidence. The officers then cut streaks in the screen of the bedroom window.

Irv's uncle was a mortician, and he took pictures showing where the body had been dragged across the street.

Even casual observers who were sympathetic to the police were livid. "'Tis a poor officer whose reflexes are so slow he can't tell when he has killed a man," R. C. Maynard Jr. wrote in a letter to the editor in the *N&O*.

The newspaper's editorial board wrote a scathing editorial of the cops' performance, saying, "The State of North Carolina imposes capital punishment, but it does not use executioners who fire upon a lifeless body."

Even so, the officers faced no punishment. They were never even charged with a crime.

But they did launch the career of one of the most influential civil rights attorneys in North Carolina history. Irv Joyner has represented the Wilmington Ten, the group of citizens wrongly convicted of arson and conspiracy. He's marched alongside William Barber, whose Poor People's Campaign of the 2010s has included battles against the North Carolina legislature over voting rights. And, of course, recently he's represented the Bladen County Improvement Association in its legal matters involving accusations from Republicans and McCrae Dowless.

"When I see police brutality, immediately, you know, the flashbacks," Irv Joyner told us in January 2020, sitting at a long table at the Campbell School of Law in Raleigh. "This is my payback. You know, I want payback."

White's Creek Missionary Baptist Church is a redbrick building with a white steeple and four white pillars. Across from it, in a small field that's a piece of a larger farm, surrounded by pine trees and a few oaks, is the small cemetery with a headstone for Thay Lewis White (4/4/1932–9/13/1952). Right next to her stone is one for her mother, Myrtice (10/31/1907–3/23/1990), and father, Berry (1/2/1904–6/4/1966).

Grayson was convicted of rape and murder, despite his insanity plea. But his trial was hardly fair. His attorneys appealed it, and the appeal went to the state Supreme Court.

That court found that the judge in the first case had led the jury to rule that Grayson was sane. Specifically, the judge told the jury that Grayson's insanity plea was "upon him and not upon the State, to satisfy you of its truth," a rather egregious slipup in this country of "innocent until proven guilty." The state Supreme Court ruled for a new trial.

It was of little consequence in the life of Grayson, though. He was convicted again in the new trial and sentenced to life in prison.

Thay Lewis White's husband, Milton, remarried within a couple of years and had another child. In September 1955, Hurricane Ione dumped seven inches of rain in just a few hours. A fishing pond near their home broke through a dam and came into the home. Milton's new wife grabbed their child, an infant girl, while Milton grabbed the three-year-old boy he'd fathered with Thay Lewis White. Milton climbed onto the roof with the toddler. But his wife and daughter were swept away by floodwaters. She lost her grip on the girl, who floated away and died. Mrs. White was rescued shortly after that by two men in a boat, who found her by following her cries.

Grayson served more than thirty years of his sentence before being paroled in 1982, a state prison official tells us. His parole ended three years later. A background check on Grayson doesn't list a death date, instead saying he's a man in his late eighties, last known address in Alamance County, not far from the prison. We tried to find him, but with no luck.

Perhaps the most peculiar takeaway from the incident came from the Bladen County police and officials.

Instead of questioning their interview tactics, or wondering whether the man they'd arrested was in fact the murderer, they took the oddest step to prevent future attacks:

They banned carnivals and fairs.

Bladen County hasn't had a Ferris wheel or pig race since.

★ ★ ★

The Firebombing at Fowler Simmons
April 27, 1971

★ ★ ★

*If whites are going to move on us offensively, then we're
going to move on them offensively.*

BEN CHAVIS

Six miles of country road separates Thay Lewis White's gravestone and Booker T. Washington School, which sprouts from a field near the tiny town of Clarkton. It looks like most other midcentury schools, one story and red-brick with a flat roof that's leaked a time or few during heavy rains. When Harold Ford first saw it in the 1950s, it looked like an opportunity.

Ford was a young Black man who'd grown up on a farm his grandparents ran near the South Carolina line. He rode mules to the store as a boy, harvested and hung tobacco every late summer day, then went to football practice in the evening, back at a time when most of North Carolina's coaches had to schedule practices around harvests.

Like Delilah Blanks, though, he was more interested in school than the farm. He was a student at the Laurinburg Institute, at the time one of the country's most prestigious schools for African Americans. It was founded in 1904 because Booker T. Washington himself asked a family in the area to do so.

Ford's grandparents didn't have an education, and they sure wanted to make sure he had his. Each evening, Ford's grandmother required him to give a report on what he'd learned that day. Sometimes he'd try to get off easy and list something from a few days earlier.

"You said that the other day," his grandmother would fire back.

"She never went to school, but she sure could remember what I'd done every day," Ford, now eighty-nine, told Michael in a July 2020 interview at his home.

Young Harold left the farm for Fayetteville State, a historically Black college. He finished one year there before being drafted into the army. He

144

suffered through basic training in the Georgia summer and promptly flew to Seattle, then to Japan, then Korea. He saw some of the worst of that war, including the Battle of Bloody Ridge, which left 500 dead just north of the 38th Parallel. To this day, he shakes his head when he talks about it, but his Korean veterans hat remains on the armrest, ready to go.

Explosions destroyed his hearing, but he came home better than most. He finished his career at Fayetteville State, where he played tackle on the football team. He's in the school's hall of fame. After college, a friend called to tell him to contact the principal in Clarkton about a job. Ford soon came here and started as a math teacher and coach. The principal owned the land across from the school. As part of Ford's recruitment package, the principal told him to walk off a piece of property from the land—just go mark it off—so that he could build his home on it.

Harold Ford raised four children in that home. When they became teenagers he told them to find jobs, too. His daughter Sheila worked in a nearby tobacco farm in the day and went to basketball workouts at night, much like her father did all those years ago.

For all the ways in which the rural South has struggled, and all the ways it's failed to take care of its most vulnerable, the supreme characteristic of the region is its work ethic. From the days of tar and turpentine in the eighteenth century, to the rise of King Tobacco in the nineteenth century, to the sprawling hog-slaughtering operations of the twentieth century, people in places like Bladen County have long supported the pleasures, guilty or otherwise, of the rest of the country. North Carolina has nearly 10 million hogs. For context, it also has 10 million people and ranks ninth in population among U.S. states. Want chicken? North Carolina harvests 830 million of those each year. It also produces 1.7 billion pounds of sweet potatoes, more than any other state in the land.

There are countless families like the Ford family in eastern North Carolina, folks who wouldn't know what to do if they weren't putting their hands to work. While he was coaching basketball and teaching math and raising children, Mr. Harold Ford also earned his electrician's license. That job, which he did at night, gave him access to nearly every home in Clarkton. White or Black, everybody needed an electrician, and Ford was there for them. He wired just about every house in town, and if he didn't, he'd been called out there.

So when Bladen County finally got around to integrating schools in 1970, merging the all-Black Booker T. Washington High School and the all-white Clarkton High School, the superintendent knew exactly who to hand the basketball team to. Ford became coach and assistant principal.

Tensions rose everywhere else during desegregation. White families throughout eastern North Carolina famously started private "Christian" schools so they could keep their kids in all-white classes. But the basketball program at Clarkton High was not one of those trouble spots. "I knew everybody," Ford says now. "Wired most of their houses."

Ford instituted a full-court-press style of play. His team never settled back into a half court, never stopped running. Ford's goal, he always said, was to prepare his players for the real world in whatever field they wanted to join. "There are no zone defenses in the NBA," he says, "and I figured, Why teach them something they couldn't use later?"

The philosophy led little Clarkton High to three state championship appearances in the 1970s, and a state championship victory in 1985. They were the biggest thing in the county some years, with people waiting outside the gym for seats on nights when rivals from East Bladen or Bladenboro were in town. Yearbooks from Ford's teaching days show senior classes with a mix of white kids and Black kids. Ford's children, who grew up in the 1970s and 1980s, say they never had a problem with race in school. Sports has a way of doing that, of insulating people from the trouble around them.

But Bladen County's troubles simmered.

School integration played out in different ways across different parts of the South. In eastern North Carolina, it happened late, and it came with violence.

In Bladen County, that violence took the form of dynamite, blasting caps, and a detonator wire attached to flashlight batteries inside a shoebox. In late January 1971, sheriff's deputies rushed to East Arcadia School, whose student population was about 96 percent Black. A bomb was waiting for them under the schoolhouse steps.

The U.S. Justice Department had previously ruled that some of the students from here would have to go halfway across the county to Elizabethtown High to comply with integration. In Elizabethtown, the white students won a court order that stopped them from being bused to East Arcadia. The Black students had called in a young civil rights activist and attorney named Ben Chavis to help them. Chavis, who'd grown up in Oxford, North Carolina, in the northern part of the state, was with the North Carolina–Virginia Council of Racial Justice. His activism began when he was an assistant to Martin Luther King Jr., but by the early 1970s he was starting to waver on the idea of civility as a tool for progress.

For several days he'd arranged peaceful protests outside the board of education in Bladen County. Then on that Tuesday morning, someone called the sheriff's department to say there was a bomb at the school. And it wasn't an idle threat. The sheriff's officers called in soldiers from nearby Fort Bragg, who flew in on a chopper and landed in the field. They poured acid on the shoebox to see what was inside and found the dynamite. Then they took it apart.

The next week, after the bomb scare at East Arcadia, Chavis went thirty miles east to Wilmington. There the city had three high schools during segregation—two white, one Black. The school board elected to close the Black school, Williston, to fulfill the court-ordered desegregation plan. This infuriated Black residents, who'd taken pride in the school. After all, Williston was the school where Martin Luther King Jr. had scheduled an April 4, 1968, speaking engagement. He canceled the trip to attend the sanitation workers' strike in Memphis. Yes, the day Martin Luther King was assassinated in west Tennessee, he'd planned to be in eastern North Carolina.

But now Williston, the school where he would've spoken, would be shut down. The idea of a decaying school with cobwebs left Black residents livid. They took to the streets in January 1971, and sixty-three years after the 1898 massacre, Wilmington was on fire again.

On February 6, 1971, a white-owned grocery store in a Black neighborhood of Wilmington was firebombed. The store, Mike's Grocery, was next to a church where protesters, including Chavis, had gathered. Authorities who rushed to the fire said they were met with gunfire. Their return fire killed a nineteen-year-old Black man named Stevenson Gibb Mitchell. The officers said he was carrying a shotgun. Chavis and his fellow activists argued that Mitchell was murdered by the cops. More than 1,000 people filed through Mitchell's funeral.

The day after Mitchell's death, a white man named Harvey Cumber was shot with a pistol, prompting the mobilization of the National Guard. For three nights, during which most national attention was turned to the Apollo 14 spacecraft's trip to the moon and back, and an earthquake in California that registered 6.6 on the Richter scale, 500 National Guardsmen stayed on standby around Wilmington as the protests and fires carried on.

Two months later, in April, Chavis led a march from Wilmington to Raleigh to protest the treatment of Blacks in Wilmington. As the marchers made their way through Elizabethtown, they were heckled by a group of workers in front of a Fowler Simmons, a department store in downtown owned by Bobby Simmons, a white man. The marchers carried on without incident, but Chavis didn't forget the insult.

Just a couple of weeks later, on a Saturday night one week to the day before Elizabethtown High's first integrated junior-senior prom, a group of young Black people were leaving the Chimney nightclub when shotgun blasts blew up the quiet night. One after the other, the sounds usually heard in the deep woods during deer season sent lead slugs knuckling toward the nightclub patrons. Six Black people were hurt in the incident. One died.

Ben Chavis rushed back to Bladen County to organize protests. He arranged for a march that Tuesday at 11 A.M. About fifty Black students were set to join him. Overnight from Monday into Tuesday, someone threw firebombs into Bobby Simmons's store. Molotov cocktails were nothing new in North Carolina by this point. Not only had they been used in Wilmington that February; white supremacists had also used them to bomb four civil rights leaders' houses in Charlotte just a few years earlier. But none of those had been as effective, from a destruction standpoint, as the ones that landed in Bobby Simmons's store.

One of Simmons's workers, a white woman, lived several miles away on Peanut Road. For weeks the woman had feared the trouble from Wilmington making its way to Bladen County. She'd heard rumors that Chavis and his Council of Racial Justice were actually doing the work of Black Panthers. Few things could frighten a white woman in rural America like the words *Black Panthers* in the 1970s.

The night of the fire, the woman had her granddaughter, a second-grader named Cindy, staying with her. Cindy remembers the sound of the fire engines screaming past the house.

Cindy Singletary, for what it's worth, would grow up to become an attorney, one of the most prominent ones in Bladen County, the one who represents McCrae Dowless. She remembers that night as one of the most important of her childhood, her grandmother screaming into the spring night, looking toward the orange glow above the pines: "They've done it! They've done it! I know that's what's happened!"

The blaze at Fowler Simmons did some $350,000 in damage to the store. Firefighters were still on the scene the next day at 11 A.M. when Chavis and the fifty students showed up for their march. While they did, parents looked on. A newspaper report says that "black and white adults spoke to each other in hushed voices on street corners."

Meanwhile, Chavis was unapologetic in his conversation with a *News & Observer* reporter that day: "White people killed those brothers," Chavis said of the nightclub shooting. "If whites are going to move on us offensively, then we're going to move on them offensively." He became a sizzling character in the desegregation efforts, feared by whites and conservative Blacks throughout eastern North Carolina. He was a regular in headlines.

Soon enough, his celebrity led him to a place familiar with many Black activists in American history. In the spring of 1972, the district attorney in Wilmington made that abundantly clear, announcing charges against Chavis and nine other people in the February 1971 Mike's Grocery incident. Chavis and the defendants hired two lawyers to help them: one, a civil rights attorney out of Charlotte named James Ferguson; the other, a young man who set out on a path as a civil rights attorney at a young age, back to when police in the small town of La Grange killed his older cousin while he walked home from choir practice—Irving Joyner.

Ferguson and Joyner would end up working the case for most of their careers. In 1978, Governor Jim Hunt reduced the sentences of the Wilmington Ten. In 1980, a circuit court judge ruled that the prosecutors in the first case had tampered with witnesses and suppressed testimony that would have set them free.

But it wasn't until 2012 that Ferguson and Joyner would find their most arresting evidence. They found handwritten notes from the white district attorney, Jay Stroud, which showed that during jury selection he'd worked to find jurors who were with the KKK or were "Uncle Toms."

In other words, a generation removed from the 1898 massacre when dozens of Black people were killed and no justice was ever served, a white prosecutor in the same city had knowingly thrown the wrong people in jail, in no small part because nine of the ten were Black. On the last day of 2012, New Year's Eve, North Carolina governor Beverly Perdue, in one of her final acts as governor, issued a full pardon of the Wilmington Ten, forty-one years after the desegregation confrontations that swept through eastern North Carolina in 1971.

For Joyner, it was another step toward payback. "It's not so much [a decision] that will vindicate members of the Wilmington Ten," he said that day, "but it says a lot about vindicating North Carolina."

★ ★ ★

The Gospel Song at the KKK Rally
December 18, 1994

★ ★ ★

*The man that's got his hopes up too high, he's
the one that's got a long way to fall.*
BYRON MCNEILL

In June 1978, a balding sixty-two-year-old man who owned a dry-cleaning business became the first Black person nominated to serve on the Bladen County Board of Commissioners since Reconstruction. He talked with a local reporter from the *Fayetteville Times* about it, and in a telling remark, the first quote in the first paragraph read like this: "'You know that's one thing about politics: You can't afford to put too much of your heart in it 'cause it'll sure get broke,' Byron McNeill said. 'The man that's got his hopes up too high, he's the one that's got a longer way to fall.'"

One hundred ten years had passed since John Spaulding became the first Black commissioner here, and seventy-eight had passed since Spaulding's nephew George White stepped down from Congress, ending Black representation in Washington for a generation.

Next in line was McNeill, a business owner in his sixties. "A fella one time asked me if I served white people here," McNeill told the newspaper. He looked around the dry-cleaning shop, with pressed clothes hanging next to baskets of plants. "I told them I sure did, and got along fine with them. I found out a long time ago, if you treat people nice, they're probably gonna treat you the same way. Ain't no trick to it.

"Few years back, when they were burning buildings and so on [in] other places we had the same tension. The difference here was we had people with guts enough to sit down and talk the whole thing over, really thrash it out."

That November, McNeill won the seat, joining the five-person board as the first Black person in recent memory.

Within the first week on the job, this humble small business owner proved to have some teeth. He helped start a conversation that would take more than a decade and dozens of court cases to complete, one that would completely change the future of Bladen County politics and would lead to the 2018 election fraud scandal: he moved to expand the board to seven members and create districts that would guarantee Black representation.

In 1985, seven years after McNeill's election to the board of commissioners, the U.S. Justice Department launched an investigation into whether the county was in compliance with the 1965 Voting Rights Act. In response, the white commissioners decided to start the process of understanding what the expanded board might look like, district lines and all.

They turned to a newly formed group of Black leaders based in East Arcadia. These leaders had formed an organization whose mission, like that of its predecessors from other parts of the state such as the Durham Committee for Negro Affairs, was to advance the interests of local Black people: the Bladen County Improvement Association.

The white leaders asked the Improvement Association to develop a plan for the expanding commission.

That February, the association proposed to move from five to seven members, all elected from districts. Their most forward-thinking ask was that three of the districts be made up of 55 percent minorities. In the meeting, though, the white commissioners chided the association for not coming with specific district boundaries outlined.

"If you want seven districts, then show us how to do it," commissioner John Shaw said. "We've asked you to come up with some workable ways to solve this problem." The commission eventually appointed a fifteen-member committee to study the future of elections.

But this time the Bladen Improvement Association wouldn't put it down. Early in 1987, they formally turned the organization into a political action committee.

The PAC's most dynamic leader was a woman from East Arcadia who as a young girl waited for books to be thrown off the train, a woman who had come back to her home county to teach its kids, and who now was a fifty-year-old college teacher carrying a new title—Dr. Delilah Blanks.

On April 10, 1987, a Friday night, Dr. Blanks was among 100 people gathered at the Bladen County Courthouse in Elizabethtown. The building was three generations removed from the courthouse building where John Spaulding celebrated his victory back in 1868. The enthusiasm and crowd size were similar. Blanks, now an associate professor of sociology at UNC Wilmington, was ready for a fight.

Twelve Black speakers and two attorneys lined up to speak. Each of them announced support for giving Black residents the chance to achieve a 40 percent share of the county commission—which matched Black residents' share of the population. They said that this time, if the board didn't expand to their liking, the Bladen Improvement Association PAC would file a lawsuit.

Three nights later, the commissioners met all day in a closed session and voted to increase the board to seven members. When they presented the districts, though, Black leaders shook their heads—two of the three had Black populations of less than 25 percent. In other words, the county commission was almost guaranteed to be six white commissioners and one Black commissioner for the foreseeable future.

"Let's go to court," one of the Bladen Improvement Association members said.

That summer they did. On July 29 they filed a lawsuit that asked a district court to order the county to adopt elections practices that "do not dilute minority representation." Still, the white commissioners moved forward and approved their proposal the following month—a decision that even pissed off white residents.

"I would hate to see a division between our people and that is what we certainly appear to be headed to," said a local white businessman told the newspaper. "They [Black people] have told me they don't want to run Bladen County, that they want the opportunity to be part of it."

Finally, that April 1988—ten years after Byron McNeill first planted the idea—the county and its Black leaders, along with the Justice Department, agreed to go even bigger, all the way to nine members. Six people would be elected from three districts, and three would be elected at large. It all but assured several Black members on the next commission.

As significant as it was from a policy standpoint, it was symbolic in another way: it was the Bladen Improvement Association PAC's first major victory.

Many more would come.

Just weeks after the Justice Department's decision, Dr. Delilah Blanks filed paperwork as a candidate for the newly created District One, Seat One slot. A special election was here, to fill the roles Delilah fought so hard for, and nobody was here to fight against her for it. On May 6, 1988, the filing period came and went and she was the only candidate for the board without an opponent. Not just in the Democratic primary, but also in the general.

She would become the first woman, white or Black, elected to the county's board of commissioners.

"We're elected by the people and they expect something of us," she told the paper later, adding that her goal was "to serve as a role model and a success story."

She concentrated on public schools and bringing services to people in her area of east Bladen County. She was a threatening combination for many members of the board: a Black woman, highly educated, and confident. Backlash came in waves, as it often does. The first major education controversy she stepped into came in the winter of 1992, when Christian groups demanded that the book *Heather Has Two Mommies* be removed from public libraries. In March 1993, commissioners met to talk about moving *Heather Has Two Mommies* and other books with homosexual characters to different sections of the library.

Dr. Blanks argued on the side of keeping them where they are—not because she agreed with the content of the books, she said, but because she believed in the right of access to the content.

"You're talking about this being the Bible Belt," she said in front of a packed meeting of people who'd hurled their frustrations at her and the board. "I want to know where all those parents are that's letting their children read these books.

"Regardless of where you put the books in the library, the user has to have the right of access."

Blanks lost this argument. The book and books like it were ordered to sit on the top shelves, out of the reach of children, in the adult section.

That was only the first controversy involving reading material in Bladen County schools.

Later that year, Blanks became the first woman and first Black person elected chair of the county board of commissioners. She won the position by a vote of five to four. She voted for herself, and her challenger voted for himself.

One year later, in 1994, not completely by coincidence, a new piece of literature made its way around Bladen County's schools: applications to join the Ku Klux Klan.

The Confederate flag decal was two inches by three inches and affixed to a toolbox.

A worker at Mayo Yarns, the old cotton mill, had been bringing the tool-box with the flag sticker for years to his job repairing spinning frames. But in August 1994, his bosses asked him to take it off. The worker went home and thought about it. The next week, the decal was gone. For one day. The next day he came back with a new Confederate sticker.

The plant manager called him in and asked him to write a statement about why he insisted on keeping the flag. The worker wrote the statement: it was part of his southern heritage, he scribbled, and he was proud of it. The plant manager told him to remove it. This time the worker refused. And he was fired.

North Carolina is a right-to-work state where employees have little protection in cases like this. But he filed the wrongful termination suit anyway, on principle. In November, 300 people gathered for a Sons of Confederate Veterans rally in Bladenboro.

Three weeks later, it escalated. Kids at Spaulding-Monroe Middle School and Bladenboro High came home with KKK applications. The students didn't know where they were from, but that mattered little to their parents.

At the next school board meeting about thirty-five Black people voiced their concerns. They focused on a physical education teacher at Spaulding-Monroe who openly supported the fired Mayo Yarns worker and the Confederate flag. The teacher denied distributing the literature, but still anxiety grew.

Now one organization had seen enough of this pushback against white people. The following Sunday, December 18, the KKK planned a rally in downtown Bladenboro, just down the street from the cotton mill.

In one part of town, thirty-two people in white robes shouted "White Power!"

In another, just half a mile away, about sixty others listened to gospel music. About 200 people filled the streets in between, spectators in the middle of a new white supremacist campaign aimed at taking back the power that Dr. Blanks and her fellow Black commissioners had suddenly grabbed. The flag on a toolbox was just one small example, the Klan argued, of a total takeover.

At the gospel sing, held at Bladenboro Farm Life School, a sixty-year-old retired truck driver named Dewey Dove greeted people. Two boys threw a football back and forth, and another rode a bike across the lawn while girls chased each other around the stage. Dove, a white man, organized the rally to let his Black neighbors know that many folks in town disagreed with the Klan.

The mayor watched the rally from the street, looking for anyone he knew under a hood, relatives or otherwise. He said he didn't, and was thankful for that.

Others shook their heads, and shooed the Klan away. The rally ended early, hate having found little fuel.

At the gospel meeting, a Black woman named Ernestine Singletary sang with her husband and daughter alongside the white people who'd gathered. Afterward, she told the newspaper, "We've always got along together. It's too late for mess like that."

Say His Name: Lennon Lacy August 29, 2014

It was a display. It was a message. It was a back-in-the-day lynching.
PIERRE LACY

"I need EMS."

The caller was distraught. She was on her way to work at her brother's Bladenboro diner when she passed the horrifying scene near the old cotton mill. The same cotton mill where generations of Bladenboro residents had worked. The same cotton mill where a white man got fired for having a Confederate flag sticker on his toolbox twenty years earlier. Now it was the cotton mill next to the mobile home park where Sarah stood, trembling, her cell phone against her ear. "I have a man hanging from a swing set," she said.

It was 7:25 A.M. on August 29, 2014. West Bladen High School was set to play West Columbus High that night in football, and one of West Bladen's offensive linemen was limp, a belt tied around his neck and around the crossbeam of a swing set, feet dangling over the white sandy soil.

When the dispatcher asked where she was located, Sarah vomited. Then she told her, Off of Mill Road, not far from the center of Bladenboro.

"It's a male subject hanging from the swing?" the dispatcher asked.

"It's a Black male subject hanging from the swing," Sarah replied. "He hung hisself."

Hold there, briefly. To understand what Sarah was seeing, and how others would come to see it, consider everything else that was going on in Bladen County that year.

A sheriff's race simmered, as always, but this time more than usual. This time the incumbent was Black. Prentis Benston, son-in-law of Delilah Blanks, had served four years as the top law enforcement official. His narrow victory in the brutal 2010 election had been the Bladen Improvement Association's crowning moment. They'd picked away at political power for twenty years. They'd expanded the board in the 1980s, elected Blanks as chairman in 1993, and successfully denounced a Klan rally in 1994, and over the past decade they had expanded the Black representation on the board until the county commission was majority Black. Throughout the 2000s, white commissioners stated publicly their frustrations about having less influence. But nothing in a rural county is more important than the sheriff's office. Nothing. And in that 2010 election the Bladen Improvement PAC won it. When Benston accepted the job, he was the Barack Obama of small-town politics and power.

But just like Obama's victory, Benston's brought a boomerang: white Democrats hurdled the political fence to become Republican. Some Black people, too. Mark Gillespie, a Black man who ran the county's ABC liquor store and was a widely respected Dixie Youth coach, had become a commissioner for Bladen County's First District in 2010, the same year Benston was elected. By 2014, though, Gillespie had fallen out of favor with the Bladen Improvement PAC. They ran another Black man against him, and Gillespie got crushed in the primary by thirty points. When we talked with Gillespie a few years later, he said of the Improvement PAC: "They've pretty much sold to the highest bidder. Whoever has the most money, they'll go out and collect absentee ballots for them."

Seeing the opportunity, McCrae Dowless had taken his little startup business the same way—hard right. He copied everything he learned while working with the Improvement PAC and offered it up to the growing constituency of Republicans. Now he was running the program for Benston's challenger, Jim McVicker.

Of all the elections in Bladen County history, the 2014 sheriff's race would be the clearest and most sophisticated showdown between a well-funded white absentee operation and a well-funded Black absentee operation. And that day in late August, when Sarah held the phone against her ear, absentee ballots were set to be mailed in just a couple of weeks.

"Do you have anyone with you where we can cut him down from the swing? We need to see if he's breathing."

"He's not breathing, Patty."

"He's not breathing?"

"Oh, God, I don't have anything to cut him down with."

Lennon Lacy was seventeen. He'd laid out his number 51 West Bladen football uniform the night before. At some point after that and before Sarah's drive in to work, he died from asphyxia. Strangulation. The Bladenboro police pulled up that morning and immediately worked the case as a suicide. It was Labor Day weekend, after all. No need to complicate things and mess up a holiday weekend.

The police chief went to the home of Claudia Lacy, about a quarter mile away. She was on the phone with her sister when he knocked. He said she needed to come with him. She followed him in her car. When she got to the field by the cotton mill, an investigator took her to the back of an ambulance.

She walked up the three steps.

She smelled him.

She put her hands on his face, on his chest.

She'd just seen him the night before, had kissed him on his forehead to say goodnight. She still remembers what he was wearing: dark blue sweatpants and size 12 neon-green tennis shoes.

Who, she wondered, *would want to kill Lennon?*

On April 28, 1892, a white man named Ed Cain had entered a barn in Elizabethtown, where he was surprised to encounter a Black man. Tymon Purdie was robbing the barn, the newspapers would say. Fearing prosecution, the papers wrote, Purdie had no choice but to dispose of Cain. He allegedly grabbed an axe and decapitated Cain, then put the axe back above the door. Purdie was arrested and taken to the jail in Elizabethtown.

The following Monday night a group of 150 white men stormed the jail and forced the guard to relinquish his keys. They dragged Purdie from his cell and carried him to the ferry landing on the Cape Fear River. The same ferry landing that George Henry White's dad used when selling his tar and turpentine. The same ferry landing that Musgrove Jones, the ancestor of the Melvin's hamburgers family, once managed. Bladen County's only documented lynching would occur on that very same ferry landing.

The mob pulled Tymon Purdie to a pine tree and hanged him by the neck, then watched him struggle and perish. One foot "was uncovered," the *News & Observer* wrote. "The murderer was a negro," the *N&O*'s account said, "and although all of his race believe him guilty they are very indignant about the lynching, and trouble may result."

One hundred twenty-two years later, here was Lennon Lacy, also with one shoe on and one off.

Only the shoes weren't his. They weren't even his size. They were size 10 Air Force Ones, all white—hardly the neon-green shoes that had blinded his mother the night before. As she ran her hands across his face that Friday morning, she knew it was murder.

Her oldest son, Pierre, rushed to Bladen County from his home in Virginia. The next day they went to the police department. It was closed for the Labor Day holiday. Same thing on Sunday. Same thing on Monday.

On Tuesday, the police department came to their door and called it suicide. Without going to Lennon's room. Without checking for signs of depression. Without even comparing shoe sizes.

"You're gonna force-feed a lie to my entire family and make *us* think *we're* crazy," Pierre later said in the documentary *Always in Season*. "It looked like honestly it was a display, like it was a message, like it was a back-in-the-day lynching. That's how it made me feel."

Two years earlier, Lennon was a young teenager fighting his mother about moving. He'd always challenged her and amazed her. He was a high-energy young boy who learned his ABCs by rapping. He'd spent all his life in Virginia and hated that she was taking him to North Carolina and a county called Bladen. But Pierre convinced him he'd make new friends.

He did. They moved to Spinners Court, a public housing complex on the grounds of the old Spinner Park, where Bladenboro's semipro mill-league baseball team played from the 1930s to the 1960s.

Lennon made fast and best friends with two boys in the neighborhood, one white and one Black. At night Lennon would slip out the back door and knock on their windows. They'd say later that Lennon never drank or took part in drugs, just water and Powerade. But drugs were all around him. So was hate.

From his back patio, Lennon could see the home of a man named Dewey and his wife, Carla, who had a Confederate flag draped over their fence. Lennon was actually friends with their son, so he'd stop by from time to time. Dewey and Carla moved pills through their home and bodies. When their son had trouble with other kids in class, they'd let him set up shirtless fistfights in their backyard, and they'd cheer him on as he rubbed other boys' faces in the sand and cockleburs.

Still Lennon visited. And one night they had a guest, a friend who'd moved back from the Midwest. Michelle was thirty-two and a mother of three children. She was also white. One night in February 2014, Lennon found himself with Michelle, the last two people awake in the home. As she tells it, he kissed her on the chin.

They started dating after that, this thirty-two-year-old white woman and this seventeen-year-old Black boy. They kept the affair secret for months, before it slipped to two people who immediately asked for it to stop.

Lennon's mother, Claudia, asked Michelle to cut it off. She appealed to her as a fellow mother, and asked her how she'd feel if one of her kids came home with a significant other who was twice their age. The other person who hated the relationship was Dewey, the pill dealer with the Rebel flag on the fence.

Dewey had a cousin, it seems worth saying, on the Bladenboro police force.

That summer, Claudia sent Lennon back to Virginia to spend time with his older brother. She figured it would do him some good to be away from Bladen County, and away from his older girlfriend.

When he came back before school started, he seemed cured of the crush. But then, in late August, Lennon spotted a new man going in and out of the home with Michelle. The hurt became an obsession. Lennon ran back and forth across the properties, about a quarter mile apart, jealousy fueling every step. One night he punched a hole in Dewey's fence.

On the last night of his life, Lennon seemed to have regained his focus. On Instagram, he posted a picture of himself in a West Bladen shirt, and the caption read, "Last night pic before the game." He couldn't wait to start against West Columbus.

But by 7:30 the next morning, this five-foot-nine, 200-pound boy was hanging from the beam, the wrong shoes underneath him. And four days later, his mother was being told that the official report was that he'd killed himself.

Claudia looked at that Instagram post and looked at the suicide claim. "Last night pic before the game," he'd said.

It didn't sound like someone who wanted to kill himself.

The Reverend William Barber is a big man. He engulfs pulpits, partially because of a permanent arch from an arthritic condition in his spine, and from bursitis in his knee. He was in his early fifties in 2014, and the head of the state NAACP. His "Moral Monday" campaign—weekly protests against the state's Republican-led legislature's decisions not to expand Medicaid and turn back voting rights—had earned him national attention. Soon Moral Mondays would morph into the Poor People's Campaign, a modern-day fight for economic justice for people in places just like Bladen County. Barber is the "closest person we have to Martin Luther King Jr. in our midst," Cornel West would say.

On September 29, 2014, one month to the day after Lacy died, Barber rose from a chair at First Baptist Church of Bladenboro, the Black church in the heart of town. He took a few rickety steps toward the pulpit and started to speak. The crowd of 200 filled each pew and lined the walls of the church, which, as it happens, was cofounded by Lennon Lacy's great-grandfather.

He was here at the request of Lacy's family, he said.

"This service is dedicated to the life of someone who has walked among us," Barber started, his voice low, his eyes buried deep into the audience. "Lennon Lee Lacy died sometime between 2 and 6 A.M. on August 29. His body was found hanging from a child's swing set in downtown Bladenboro in a mostly white trailer park. These are the truths we know. No one knows for sure what happened that night."

Sitting in the crowd was the Black sheriff, Prentis Benston, locked in a race against Jim McVicker. His presence was at once comforting and discouraging for the Black people there. They'd elected him to bring an end to their fear of these sorts of things. They'd elected him in a county where Klansmen once worked as deputies, a county white supremacists were still trying to infiltrate. But when a Black boy was found hanging from a swing set, the case wasn't in his jurisdiction; it was in the Bladenboro Police Department's jurisdiction. So their gathering here was proof that even after winning the most important law enforcement office in the county, they still weren't safe.

In fact, maybe they were less safe than ever. Maybe, they wondered, this was all tied together. A backlash to Benston's term as sheriff in the middle of a simmering sheriff's race between him and a white man. What if it was all knotted together?

"There remain many unanswered questions," Barber said from the pulpit. "If Lennon was white and found in a predominantly Black neighborhood, would there have been a rush to determine that the cause of death was suicide?"

To Jon David, though, there weren't questions. The district attorney—the same district attorney who two years later was found to be having an affair with a Bladen commissioner—said in a statement on the day of Barber's address that the investigation was ongoing. But, David said, his office had not received "any evidence of criminal wrongdoing."

Two weeks later, a gutting story in the *Guardian* brought international attention to the case. Still, most eyes in Bladen County were on the race between Benston and McVicker. McCrae Dowless and the Bladen Improvement PAC were everywhere that fall.

It would be the last election cycle in North Carolina in which the state board of elections didn't have an investigative unit. (The General Assembly approved the budget for the investigative team in 2013, and it was assembled in 2015.)

McCrae Dowless's side won, sending McVicker past Benston by a mere 349 votes. To the county's Black residents, it was another disheartening moment in a demoralizing year.

Lacy's family wasn't done, though. And neither was William Barber.

The NAACP leader came back to Bladenboro on December 13 to celebrate, in a way, a new break: the U.S. attorney had agreed to turn the case over to the FBI. Now there was hope that a small-town police force's bungled investigation could be overturned.

Hundreds of people, white and Black, gathered in downtown Bladenboro that bitter Saturday wearing wool hats and coats. They marched through town, singing and chanting about justice. The march had spectators, mostly white people, who stood on the sidewalks in flannel and took pictures. Barber stood on a stage with Claudia and Pierre. The preacher was in top form, words ringing out down the streets.

"Refuse to be comforted by easy answers," he said, starting his voice's march up toward the decibel mountaintop.

"This was, this is, her son. We want you to hear his name. Somebody say it: Lennon!" he shouted.

And the crowd responded: *Lennon!*

"Lacy!" Barber said.

Lacy! his followers echoed.

"Lennon!"

Lennon!

"Lacy!"

Lacy!

"Lennon!"

Lennon!

"Lacy!"

Lacy!

"Justice!" Barber roared, and the crowd switched with him.

Justice!

"Now!"

Now!

"Don't be calm. Be concerned. A *chiiiild* has died."

Then came silence. Eighteen months of it.

On the other side of that silence was the fiery summer of 2016. Donald Trump was soaring to the Republican presidential nomination. Forty-nine people were killed in a mass shooting in an Orlando nightclub. Police shootings of Black men in Minnesota and Louisiana sparked a summer of protests. And in Dallas, five officers were shot and killed at the end of a peaceful Black Lives Matter march. Race and elections and justice were up for debate everywhere, though not often in the same breath.

While the country stared at videos of public violence that summer, a federal appeals court issued a ruling that made a faint whisper compared to the other noise. The U.S. Court of Appeals for the Fourth Circuit ruled that a relatively new North Carolina voter ID law—written ostensibly to combat voter fraud—targeted Black voters "with almost surgical precision." The 485-page ruling showed how, 110 years after North Carolina mandated voter literacy tests that decimated the Black vote, the modern legislature passed laws that restricted the voting practices more often used by Black people.

It's trite to say we don't learn from our past, but in the story of eastern North Carolina a larger question often looms: What if the past hadn't happened the way it did? How would the world be different today if, for instance, George Henry White had been able to serve for forty years in Congress, as his fellow North Carolina native Jesse Helms, the famous segregationist, did in the Senate? How would eastern North Carolina look today if a generation of Black success had not been erased in Wilmington in 1898? Would the eastern half of Bladen County still be poor today if Delilah Blanks hadn't had to fight in court just to get Black people from the area some representation on the board of commissioners? And what would Lennon Lacy be doing today if he were still alive?

This history of white reactions to Black empowerment, from one generation to the next to the next, from George Henry White's "Phoenix" speech to the "surgical precision" ruling, continues to shape today's struggle for power at every level of the political process.

During that hot summer of 2016, three significant events occurred in Bladen County.

First, on June 7, McCrae Dowless's get-out-the-vote efforts led to a rather staggering result in the congressional primary. His candidate, Todd Johnson, who finished third in the district overall, received 67.5 percent of the vote here. Mark Harris got 25.7. And Robert Pittenger, the sitting congressman who actually won the primary overall, received just 6.8 percent. This was the primary that caused Harris's own son to call him and say something was fishy, something was wrong. This was the primary election whose suspicious numbers would ultimately trigger the investigation that gripped the nation two years later.

But hardly anybody noticed at the time. Because later that month, the FBI released its findings in the Lennon Lacy case.

They arrived at Spinners Court on one page.

"One page for seventeen years of a person's life," Claudia says in the documentary about her son's death, before her son Pierre reads the devastating words "No evidence to suggest Lacy's death was a homicide. Accordingly, the investigation into this incident has been closed."

That one-page note from the FBI came on June 17.

Less than a week earlier, on June 11, Claudia attended the other big event in her town that month—the graduation ceremony at West Bladen High. She dressed up and took a seat in the crowd that Saturday morning.

She watched the purple caps and gowns hop onto the stage one after the other to cheering family members, an entire graduating class of 2016, minus one.

PART III

The Garden

★ ★ ★

The Thanksgiving Surprise November 7, 2018

*I'm very familiar with unfortunate activities that have been
happening down in my part of the state.*

JOSH MALCOLM, STATE ELECTIONS BOARD VICE CHAIRMAN

Late on election night in 2018, while Mark and Beth Harris celebrated their victory with campaign supporters at the Monroe country club in the western side of the expansive Ninth District, the person who'd done the most to make it all happen sat at his kitchen table on the eastern side. McCrae Dowless was celebrating the only way he knew how: chain-smoking and calling people to see if they'd seen that shit. It wasn't much different from the way McCrae approaches any other day. But this night was the pinnacle of his career in politics.

McCrae had worked lots of sheriff's races and district attorney races, but this year he knew that he'd been the difference in a congressional race. The frustrations, the lawyers and subpoenas of 2016, were all long gone, he thought. Now he'd licked a sitting congressman in the primary, and then he'd done it again to the rich Democrat and his longtime Bladen Improvement PAC rivals in the general. On top of that, he did it for Harris, someone he genuinely liked.

At 2:04 in the morning, McCrae sent Harris a text. They exchanged several messages over the next few minutes. Then Harris went back to his crowd of donors and well-wishers, and McCrae went back to smoking and seeing who was still up.

In Raleigh, the state board of elections team was up late too, in a "war room" of their own, looking for cyberattacks and other potential hacks of the results. This was the first national election night after 2016, and Robert Mueller's investigation into Russian interference was underway. In North Carolina, the state board had requested federal assistance from the National Security Agency and the Department of Homeland Security. "We had a number of breach attempts from former Eastern Bloc countries,"

Josh Lawson, the state board's general counsel at the time, told us. "They weren't successful, but that's partly potentially because we had in real time, you know, twenty National Guardsmen, all IT National Guardsmen, actively patching the systems during the process."

While Lawson watched all of that high-tech security work play out in the war room, he periodically opened his phone to refresh the Ninth District results out of Bladen County, where the greatest threat to democracy was sitting at his kitchen table jabbering into a flip phone.

McCrae called Harris again at 3:49 A.M., and again Harris answered. They talked for about two minutes. McCrae had a suggestion: maybe Harris should come to Bladen County for a celebration? McCrae would organize something.

"I have to go to Washington," Harris said, laughing. New-member orientation for the 116th Congress was the following week.

Maybe it was the feeling of not being in the room. Maybe it was his excitement. Maybe it was just his chatty nature. Whatever the case, McCrae Dowless called Mark Harris four more times before he went to bed: 3:52 A.M., twice in a row at 4:33 A.M., and again at 5:51 A.M.

Each of those went unanswered. Then, with less than an hour before sunrise, he finally went to sleep.

Twelve hours later, Dan McCready finally acknowledged his defeat. The Democrat's campaign called a press conference for 5:30 that evening. Reporters and TV cameras crammed into a small press room in the back of his campaign office on the first floor of a generic midrise office building.

McCready stood shoulder to shoulder with a small group of supporters. His wife and children were to his left. He stood behind a lectern with the same "COUNTRY OVER PARTY" sign from the Marriott ballroom the night before. Taped on the wall behind him was a makeshift backdrop with a set of not-quite-Carolina-blue Dan McCready campaign signs arranged in a square.

The Democrat began his speech with his toddlers making noise in the background. He was conceding the election. "The theme of our campaign was country over party," McCready said. "To me, now, country over party means offering my help to Mark, which I did earlier by phone."

He told his supporters it was OK to be tired and disappointed. He was. But it was not OK to give up fighting. As he continued the concession, his voice cracked. He started to cry. He thanked his wife and told his four kids they were the reason he ran.

McCready looked like a man who'd set out on an ambitious mission to take a seat nobody thought he could take, before falling short by a margin that, at the time, was about 1,500 votes. (As more provisional ballots came in, the margin would shrink to 905.)

It was time to rest, he told his supporters, and take his family to Disney World.

That weekend, Mark Harris went back to Bladen County, which is its own sort of amusement park sometimes.

McCrae threw a little celebration together to welcome the congressman-elect back to Bladen. He called up Lu Mil Vineyards, a winery that makes a syrupy-sweet wine from scuppernong and muscadine grapes. Named for the late husband-and-wife farmers who owned the land—Lucille and Miller—the winery's vines may not yield merlot or chambourcin, but the vineyard stretches across fifty-eight acres, with a barrel room in a renovated barn, and an 8,000-square-foot tasting room. It's one of the pleasantest places in Bladen County.

Unlike with the meeting at the furniture store eighteen months earlier, this time all the local dignitaries came out to see Mark Harris: Congressman David Rouzer, whose Wilmington-based district bordered the Ninth; Jim McVicker, the sheriff; Judge Marion Warren, the state's courts director, who had introduced Harris to McCrae in the first place.

This who's who of southeastern North Carolina politicos sat on the terrace with their glasses of sweet wine while Harris took his place at the front. Sunlight flickered through the slats in the pergola as he grabbed the mike.

One of McCrae's top workers, a blond-haired woman with long lashes and sparkling blue eyes named Kayla Smith, recorded video of the Harris speech, which was, in its own way, historic. It was his last celebration in North Carolina before he was due in Washington. A few days later, he would be at the Capitol being ushered into meetings, briefings, and interviews for staff. For now, though, he was here, on a terrace on a crisp fall day with his people, and his message was that places like Bladen County mattered.

"There's something special about Bladen County. I had the opportunity to see it up close," he said. "That's what the people of Bladen County do: they're willing to stick together, they're willing to stand together, and they're willing to speak up together. And I like to think that this election was an opportunity for Bladen County to send a message not only to North Carolina, but to the nation."

Smith posted that video to her Facebook page, celebrating her new congressman.

While Harris was sipping scuppernong wine with the sheriff, McCready, too, was keeping in touch with the far corner of the Ninth Congressional District. Just two days after his tearful concession speech and pledge to rest and support Harris, McCready called Josh Malcolm.

Malcolm, if you recall, was the influential state board of elections member who grilled McCrae Dowless in the 2016 hearings. Malcolm's questions had led to McCrae invoking the Fifth Amendment on the stand, before he implicated the outgoing governor or, worse, himself. *This American Life* had recorded the interaction and broadcast it for the world to hear. McCrae was the accuser who became the accused, the slow-witted country boy who filed a complaint against his enemies, only to say too much and become the subject of a two-year-long investigation. For Malcolm, the influential Democrat from the county next door to Bladen, it was an especially sweet turn of events. He and McCrae had been political rivals for years, slap-boxing each other on a playground nobody cared to monitor. Now, under the new Democratic governor, Roy Cooper, Malcolm had ascended to become vice chairman of the state board of elections. He'd gone from the playground to the principal's chair.

Cell phone records show that on November 9, two days after the election, McCready's first call to Malcolm came just after 1 P.M. They spoke for eleven minutes. Then they had another twenty-one-minute conversation around 4:45 P.M. A third call from McCready to Malcolm at 8 P.M. lasted another twelve minutes.

That weekend, concern about election security and disputed races filtered into national headlines, but North Carolina had not yet attracted notice. Attention was focused farther south, on Georgia and—what else is new?—Florida. Brian Kemp had a narrow lead over Stacey Abrams in the Georgia governor's race that was still not called, and in Florida the Senate race between Republican Rick Scott and Democrat Bill Nelson left the candidates just 0.18 points apart, setting up a recount scenario in a state that's familiar with uncertain outcomes. But the national panic attack about election fraud had barely begun, and Dan McCready and Mark Harris's race was still just a local story. Josh Malcolm was considering whether it was time to change that.

Malcolm knew that throughout the 2018 general election, state and federal investigators had conducted interviews in Bladen County. He also almost certainly knew that a district attorney had told the state board of elections on October 19, two weeks before the election, that there was "significant fraudulent activity affecting the current election." Josh Lawson, the staff's highly reputable attorney, had written that much down on a notepad.

Truth was, Josh Malcolm didn't need sworn affidavits or an attorney with two law degrees to tell him what happens in Bladen and Robeson Counties.

Malcolm was just eighteen on February 1, 1988, the day his home county became the scene of a gripping national news story. That's the day when two armed men identifying themselves as Tuscarora-Cherokee Indians stormed the offices of the *Robesonian* newspaper, taking seventeen people hostage. The gunmen, Eddie Hatcher and Timothy Jacobs, were painted as lunatics at the time. But their mission, they said, was to draw attention to local corruption by public officials, especially the sheriff's department. And they wanted to bring attention to the death of a Black man in a local jail, whom Hatcher and Jacobs said suffered an asthma attack and begged for help for nearly an hour.

A news anchor from WRAL in Raleigh called the newspaper office, and an employee named Renee answered. In most hostage situations, a woman in Renee's position might've been distraught. But this was Robeson County, arguably the most corrupt place on earth, and Renee seemed to empathize with her hostage-takers' demands. She calmly told the television reporter, "They've been civil. . . . All they want to do is talk to Governor [Jim] Martin."

Then the reporter asked to speak to one of the hostage-takers. She handed over the phone and the man said, "Eddie Hatcher?" as if he were answering a call about house paint.

The reporter asked Hatcher what he wanted. In response, Hatcher launched into a rant that, in hindsight, explains just about everything that was breaking down in eastern North Carolina in the last half of the twentieth century.

We demand that John D. Hunt, who is a prisoner in the Robeson County jail on frivolous charges, be transferred to another county jail, at least seventy-five miles away, until the governor can set a special prosecutor and task force to investigate the charges against him. This man's in jail, been in jail for fourteen months, for doing something under the direction and guidance of the State Bureau of Investigation. But the reason they did it, is that when they found out when he was getting too close to one of the county commissioner's brother's drug ring, they wanted to keep him shut up in jail where he couldn't tell anybody. We demand that the governor of North Carolina immediately initiate an investigation into the corrupt Robeson County government, including the sheriff's department, district attorney Joe Freeman Britt, and the SBI agents in this area.

A little more than a decade later, the Robeson County sheriff's department found itself in the largest investigation into police corruption in North Carolina history. Operation Tarnished Badge ended with twenty-two lawmen, including the former sheriff, being charged with crimes ranging from pirating satellite television signals, kidnapping, perjury, drug trafficking, and armed robbery to money laundering.

This was the political environment in which Josh Malcolm came of age. He graduated in 1992 from UNC Pembroke, a school in the middle of the county during the middle of the most corrupt period in the county's history. A young man can go one of two ways from there—or maybe, in this land where right and wrong so often mingle, you can go both ways. Eddie Hatcher, of course, was absolutely right in demanding help to clean up his home county. But the way he went about it was technically wrong.

So now Malcolm was in a position of power, a position to, as he often said, try to clean up the mess in his home county. And finally he had the close election he needed to prove that corrupted absentee ballots made the difference.

Malcolm and McCready kept touch throughout November: text messages on November 17 and 19. Another thirteen-minute phone call on November 18. Malcolm sent his final two messages to McCready on November 25.

We don't know what any of these text messages said. For nearly two years, Nick has tried to obtain information about Malcolm's communication through a public records request and lawsuits. What we do know, though, is that two days after his last texts to McCready, Josh Malcolm from Robeson County threw the bomb that blew up the Ninth Congressional District, starting the process of overturning a congressional election because of suspected fraud for the first time in U.S. history.

The agenda for the November 27 state board of elections meeting was lengthy but boring. They would vote on appointments to local boards, consider fines for some delinquent campaign finance filings, and canvass the results of the election a few weeks earlier. Besides, few were paying attention to a run-of-the-mill meeting of the state elections board in Raleigh.

Kim Strach, the elections director, finished discussing her staff's efforts to canvass the vote totals and audit provisional ballots—an exercise, she said, that resulted in an extra 200 provisional ballots being counted. Most anyone would've guessed she was ready to recommend the board motion to approve the results of all the state's elections. Josh Malcolm, though, fidgeted in his chair.

Then, seventeen minutes in, he spoke: "So, um," he cleared his throat, "It's my request that the Ninth Congressional District, to be clear, the Ninth Congressional District, will not be part of this motion."

His timidity was unusual. Malcolm always spoke at board meetings in a confident, self-assured tone. Not here. The words came out softly from the hole in the center of a dark goatee, topped by a shiny bald head and decorated with rimless glasses. The same official who had cockily made slop of McCrae Dowless two years earlier now seemed to be quaking as he said, "The Ninth Congressional District shall not be part of this certification vote that this board is going to take, at least, in my opinion, that's going to be my motion: that the Ninth Congressional District not be included."

After a few more sentences, Malcolm's voice regained its normal conviction. His southeastern North Carolina twang built to a crescendo.

"I'm very familiar with unfortunate activities that have been happening down in my part of the state," he said. "And I am not going to turn a blind eye to what took place, to the best of my understanding, which has been ongoing for a number of years, that has repeatedly been referred to the United States Attorney and to district attorneys for them to take action and clean it up and, in my opinion, has not taken place."

The chairman, sounding somewhat surprised, took the meeting into closed session. They spent several hours hidden away. When the five Democrats and four Republicans returned, they voted unanimously to certify the election results throughout the state with a fairly big exception: the Ninth District.

They gave no explanation. No mention of McCrae Dowless or the Bladen County Improvement Association PAC. They simply voted to reconvene by phone that Friday to decide what to do next. That Friday, after calling the roll, they adjourned to a closed session to consult with their attorney and hear details of a criminal investigation.

When they reemerged, Josh Malcolm made a motion to hold an evidentiary hearing into the Ninth Congressional District election by December 21, "to ensure that the election was determined without taint of fraud or corruption and without irregularities that may have changed the result of the election."

The motion passed. Five Democrats and two Republicans voted for it. Two Republican board members opposed it. Nobody gave reasons.

Afterward, McCready issued a statement. "The right to vote is the foundation of our democracy. Any effort to rob a person of that right should be met with the full force of justice. Today's decision takes a strong step forward ensuring that the people of the Ninth District have the answers they deserve and any bad actors are held accountable."

The idea of taking his family to Disney World was gone, and Dan McCready suddenly sounded like a man ready for a fight.

Harris released a statement of his own.

"Today, after meeting behind closed doors for almost three hours, the State Board of Elections not only refused to certify our election results, but again refused to provide any details to the public as to what exactly is being investigated," the statement said. "Make no mistake, I support any efforts to investigate allegations of irregularities and/or voter fraud, as long as it is fair and focuses on all political parties. But to date, there is absolutely no public evidence that there are enough ballots in question to affect the outcome of this race. Accordingly, the Board should act immediately to certify the race while continuing to conduct their investigation. Anything else is a disservice to the people of the Ninth District."

Media outlets scrambled. Soon everybody was finding a number that confirmed their preconceived notion of the other side. Nate Silver tweeted a counterpoint to Harris's argument that there weren't enough votes in question to make a difference, saying that "with 1,364 absentee-by-mail ballots cast between the two counties [679 for Harris], and 1,675 absentee-by-mail ballots requested and not returned, it may be impossible to conclude whether voter fraud across both counties changed the outcome."

Within hours of the meeting, the chairman of the state board of elections, a Democrat, resigned, saying that he didn't want his "partisan views to undermine a widening investigation."

It looked, for a moment, like a huge national story was about to explode. That same day, though, former President George H. W. Bush died, and the nation's eyes turned to him.

As the weekend carried on, only local reporters and political observers were looking into the numbers around the election fraud investigation. So were, of course, the staff and lawyers of Dan McCready and the Democratic Party. The candidate's team ran throughout eastern North Carolina, looking for people to sign affidavits, which they'd then send to local media to raise the alarm.

★ ★ ★

The Bad Draw November 30, 2018

★ ★ ★

*The whole time we're treating this like this is still
the civilized old days, and it wasn't.*

BETH HARRIS

On the Tuesday after Thanksgiving, Mark Harris's phone buzzed with a text message from his son John. The same son who'd won awards for his integrity as a teenager, and warned his father nineteen months earlier about working with McCrae Dowless, now wrote, "What in the world is going on?"

He included a link to a news story with a headline that said the board of elections was holding up his father's certification.

Mark was in Washington, and at that moment he was with Beth and his newly hired chief of staff interviewing a job candidate. Mark looked down at the phone and back up at the job candidate, then wrapped up the interview. Beth hurried to the National Republican Congressional Committee offices, where she could use a private phone to call her lawyers. "They were just incredulous," Beth recalls.

Separately, Mark called a well-known Republican campaign consultant who'd helped Thom Tillis get elected to the Senate. The consultant told Mark not to worry. "This is Josh Malcolm wanting to grab this spotlight," the consultant said. "We're going to get it straightened out."

Everyone in his circle advised Mark to keep on with the business of settling into Congress. He enjoyed freshman orientation, something only a select few people in this country get to experience, and something even those who have the privilege only get to experience once. No matter how many terms you serve, there is only one first term. He didn't want to miss a moment.

The next day, November 28, the Harris campaign posted a tweet to try to calm supporters' concern: "We were surprised by yesterday's developments at the State Board of Elections, but our legal team is fully engaged. We trust the process. This morning, we sent a letter to the SBOE asking for clarity. We continue to prepare in DC to serve the constituents of the 9th District!"

For nearly every person who was in Washington taking part in orientation, there was another person back home wishing he or she was there instead. In North Carolina that person was Dan McCready. His team, too, was altering their plans and rounding up lawyers.

McCready's team settled on two actions: First, lawyers and investigators would fan out across Bladen County. Then they would lay the framework for a new campaign. They needed to prepare a narrative about a most unsexy kind of fraud—tampering with ballots is hardly as exciting as robbing a casino—in a way that would be easy for people to understand.

On Thursday, November 29, the night before the hearing, someone sent six signed affidavits to the Charlotte television station WSOC. The same day, the local NPR affiliate reported that the North Carolina Democratic Party had sent affidavits to people asking them to help.

In one affidavit, signed October 29, a Black woman named Datesha Montgomery said that a "white lady" she didn't know came to her home and said she was collecting ballots, which is illegal. Montgomery had already filled out her picks for board of education and sheriff, she told the woman at her door. And the woman responded by telling Montgomery that "the others were not important." The woman then told Montgomery to just sign the unfinished ballot, give it to her unsealed, and that she'd finish it herself. If true, it would be a most brazen crime.

And it would be damning to Harris and his supporters. Other affidavits came with similar concerns. People said they'd received absentee ballots in the mail even if they hadn't requested them. They said they'd received visits from the same "white lady."

All the affidavits implicated McCrae Dowless. WSOC's popular reporter Joe Bruno began tweeting about the affidavits, with screenshots, during the five o'clock hour that evening.

Three hours later, McCready was tweeting too. He issued his first statement just after 8:30 P.M. that Thursday night, starting it with words he'd repeat often when talking about the scandal: "I was as shocked as anyone."

Harris, meanwhile, was either aloof or in denial. He simply stuck with freshman orientation. He didn't answer interview requests. Entranced by the inner recesses of Washington's politics machine, he laughed as the assistants told him where he should turn and what he should say. He enjoyed the club, and the excitement, even though most of his classmates were newly elected Democrats.

"You're the elected congressman, but truthfully you're being told where to go, when to be there, what to do, and how to do it," he says. "Congressional staff runs the United States Congress. . . . I would come home and tell

Beth, 'Listen, the whole country is riding on these twenty-three-, twenty-four-, twenty-five-year-olds who just graduated from American University or Georgetown, and they're running this nation.'"

Mark and Beth were prepared to fly home and carry on with normal business. Parades. Christmas banquets and sermons at church. Speeches. Who had time to worry about whether your election was in jeopardy? It's not like the state board had ever thrown out an election result.

That Friday, the same day the board of elections met in North Carolina to decline to certify his election, the same day George H. W. Bush died, Mark Harris was in a room with all of his new colleagues—white and Black, Republican and Democrat—taking part in one of the last great Washington ceremonies: the office lottery.

Each freshman congressperson stuffed a hand into the same mahogany box.

The box contained eight-five chips with numbers on them. If you drew the number 1, you had the first pick of offices on Capitol Hill. Number 2 got second pick, and so forth. If you drew number 85, of course, you took the last remaining space. It's a lighthearted rite of passage, one that takes adult politicians who are about to steer this country and makes them look like kids in gym class again. There's no way to appear cool and collected when you stick your hand into a random box of chips.

The drawing comes with real consequences. In some offices, mice have longer leases than congresspeople. So the quest for a good one, while it has no bearing on your ability to govern, makes for a fun giddy-up.

The office lottery for the 116th Congress took place on Friday, November 30, 2018. In the same hour that Josh Malcolm was making his motion to investigate the legitimacy of Harris's seat, the pastor was waiting to see what number he drew. His freshman class included four women who would become known as the Squad—Alexandria Ocasio-Cortez, Ilhan Omar, Ayanna Pressley, and Rashida Tlaib. All were Democrats, all were women of color, all would one day be interchangeable in the eyes of Trump supporters.

But for the duration of the orientation, everybody came together to join in the fun. Tlaib celebrated when she picked the coin that had the number 8 on it. Another freshman did pushups before stuffing a finger into the mahogany box, for luck; and still others had spouses pick for them, for luck.

The national photographer Al Drago documented the day, and in a photo essay that appeared on Bloomberg News, two back-to-back shots told a hell of a story. In the first, Ocasio-Cortez, the political phenom in her late twenties who's beloved by progressives and despised by conservatives, reached her right hand into the mahogany box with her eyes closed.

In the very next photo of Drago's photo essay, there is Mark Harris.

He's wearing a pinstriped suit with a red and blue tie and a lanyard around his neck. In the still shot, Harris has both hands on the stomach buttons of the suit jacket. He's turned to the left, to face the crowd of people he so desperately wants to join. He grimaces. He scrunches up his face. The photo is a work of art, showing in a single frame playfulness and deep-down frustration about something that didn't go his way. It is the look of a person who's stuck with the worst player in gym class or with the worst cabin on a camping trip, or the college student who draws the oldest dorm. Yeah, he's bellyaching about it for the cameras and the sympathy, but the truth is, he's just happy to be on campus.

It is the reaction of a man who's just drawn the number 76 out of 85, meaning he was probably on his way to one of the offices with the mousetraps.

McCready was building his message. Each time it started with some version of the same sentence he used in his first statement.

"I was as shocked as anyone," he wrote.

Maybe he was. Maybe the seven texts and calls he shared with Josh Malcolm during the month of November were about something other than the investigation. In any case, that sort of message promised to serve as a fairly good foundation for a campaign looking to position itself on the right side of public empathy. In a district where most voters are inherently distrustful of government and its processes, he could be the clean one. He could keep reminding them that he was the one who served overseas in the Marine Corps. He would use his image as a righteous young man to cast himself as the counterpoint to Harris, who was all of a sudden put into the very believable role of dirty, lying preacher.

McCready would tell voters that he didn't serve his country just to come home and see people's votes stolen.

"Let's bring democracy back to North Carolina," McCready would say.

Over the next few months, McCready didn't waver from those lines. In selfie videos and national interviews, he returned to the same three points over and over and over: (1) He was as surprised as anyone. (2) He served in the military and loved this country. (3) He believed part of loving this country was to say that people's votes mattered. The message mushroomed, first to local media then to national.

On the other side, Harris remained quiet. He and his team focused on the legal side of the investigation and ensuring that he hadn't broken the law. He'd later regret their silence. The law, they'd learn, works slower than public opinion. "There's so much that is in my personality and, and, my ability to know what to do in a crisis, that I think about now," Mark told us one day at his kitchen table, about eighteen months after the election was halted. "And I'm thinking how I wish I would have done things very different. The calls I would have even made, people I would have talked to."

There were plenty of people wanting to talk to him. Anderson Cooper's team called. Local media vans came to his big brick south Charlotte home and parked out front. Some knocked on the door. That weekend, Beth turned the deadbolt and waited to hear from the attorneys.

One day passed. Two days. A few more. As they waited, the story turned harshly against them. In a country where the Republican president was a fire-breather for unsubstantiated voter fraud claims, Democrats clung to the story of the North Carolina Ninth. They shouted from every corner of the internet, and in front of every camera they could find: "See! The real fraud is being committed by Republicans! And it's not some pitiful little number of individuals; it's a coordinated effort that goes right to the top."

While Harris waited for his lawyers to clean the mess up behind closed doors, the public outrage was growing out of control. The Democratic Party rallied around McCready, but Harris's phone stopped ringing with calls from Republicans. By the time the attorneys knew what to do, Mark Harris's political future was over.

"The whole time we're treating this like this is still the civilized old days, and it wasn't," Beth said, thinking back on those frenzied days of early December 2018. "It was the new ball game of the manufactured scandal, and we had no idea that's really what was going on."

Mark nodded along beside her while she talked. "He's said that many times, says, 'It was a failure of leadership on my part; I should have investigated McCrae more.' I have a lot more mercy on that, just based on, you know, when six county officials vouch for the man and everyone says he's okay, I don't know what else you're supposed to do," Beth continued, getting worked up again.

"But also he has said many times, 'I should have dropped everything the day they did not certify. I should've immediately flown home. I should've immediately got in front of the press.' Your lawyers don't want you to do that."

Instead, the Harrises stayed in Washington and didn't meet with their lawyers until nearly a week after the vote to not certify the election.

What the Harrises didn't know at the time—what very few people outside of the board of elections staff knew—was that investigators had already made a connection between McCrae Dowless and Mark Harris.

A little more than a week before the decision to not certify, over Thanksgiving weekend, one of Dowless's workers brought the whole thing down the way so many things are brought down these days: with a Facebook post.

Kayla Smith, the blond-haired woman with the long lashes who'd enthusiastically recorded Mark Harris's victory speech at Lu Mil Vineyards, typed into the "What's on your mind?" box that she'd been paid by the consulting group that had been paid by Harris.

"The way we knew that there might be some link between Red Dome group and McCrae Dowless was that one of his workers posted on *Facebook*," Josh Lawson, the attorney, would later say, putting a heap of emphasis on the word *Facebook*, "that she just got a job with Red Dome group."

When Lawson and the board of elections staff and investigators saw the post, it had been more than a month since the Wake County district attorney had told them about the "significant fraudulent activity affecting the current election," as Lawson wrote it on that notepad. But that district attorney hadn't told them who was benefiting from the fraud, or who was perpetrating it.

Elections officials would later tell us that their lead investigator, Joan Fleming, had selected McCrae Dowless as her main target. And they would openly admit that they didn't pursue much in the way of Bladen Improvement PAC in their investigation that fall. It appears that the State Bureau of Investigation's inquiry was heavily favoring Dowless in its investigation, too.

Just a few weeks before Election Day, around the same weekend as the October 2018 Beast Fest, an SBI agent interviewed a handful of people about the work they did for McCrae in the 2016 election.

First was a woman named Tonia Gordon. She told the agent that McCrae had given her several blank absentee request forms. She said McCrae paid her five dollars for every form she returned. Then she'd go back to the house after the absentee ballots were mailed out, sign as a witness on the outer envelope, then collect the sealed envelope and return it to McCrae. He would then pay her another five dollars.

The agent heard a similar story the next day from a woman named Kelly Hendrix.

Months later, Matthew Matthis, the young man who had McCrae's number saved in his phone as "McCrae Boss Man," told the agent a similar story about the process McCrae used to collect ballots in 2016.

Three witnesses had said pretty much the exact same thing: that they'd been paid by McCrae to pick up ballots.

Still, as of November 30, the day Harris drew his number 76 office and McCready issued his first statement, none of that was public information. What information was getting out at the time was pulled by local and national reporters, who that weekend started setting up temporary residence in Bladen County.

One name that popped up over and over again was that of a thirty-nine-year-old woman who called McCrae her fatherlike figure, a woman with more than 100 criminal filings on her record, a woman who eluded investigators because she had at least three different last names in three different background searches, a woman who eventually settled on one name to sign on dozens of absentee ballot requests that fall, a woman who, despite all of those reasons to not trust her, was about to become the star witness: Lisa Britt.

Or, as she was known in the signed affidavits, the white lady.

★ ★ ★

The White Lady December 2018

This is not the day to ask that. This is not the week to ask that.
VALERIA MCKOY, ELECTIONS BOARD STAFF MEMBER,
WHEN ASKED HOW SHE WAS DOING

She became McCrae Dowless's stepdaughter the way a lot of people became his stepchildren: suddenly.

It was the late 1980s; she can't remember the exact year and neither can he. Lisa Britt—or Lisa Kitchens, depending on the identification she chooses to give you these days—was Lisa Gray back then. She would've been about nine or ten, and just along for the journey to her new life with her mother's on-again, off-again significant other, who just happened to be McCrae Dowless. Her mother is Sandra, the only woman McCrae says ever broke his heart, in that classic love story of two souls drifting apart after they commit a six-figure life insurance fraud together.

Lisa says McCrae was the only true father of her childhood. She was born on August 9, 1979. Her story is representative of a good number of kids from that time.

North Carolina's divorce rate peaked in the 1980s, with some stats showing that six in ten marriages ended up legally dissolved. Now, one could look at that stat and say that someone like McCrae Dowless and his nearly dozen marriages were merely a product of whatever larger systems contributed to it. Or one might look at it and say that McCrae Dowless is more responsible for the high divorce rate than just about any other groom in North Carolina.

He laughs about the marriages now, and so do his wives, but the reality is kids like Lisa Britt were caught up in them.

She started showing up in criminal records with larceny charges in 1997, just after turning eighteen. As an adult, she's been in and out of jail. She was charged with felony larceny and forgery around 2010 and sentenced to five years' probation. By the time Lisa Britt's name started showing up in news reports in early December 2018, she had more than 100 criminal filings in her record.

But through it all she remained close to McCrae. He wasn't the best father figure, but she was drawn to his loyalty, and he was drawn to hers. As she passed in and out of jail, in and out of addiction, and in and out of relationships, he always gave her a place to stay.

Even the strongest loyalty has its limits, though. Prosecutors and investigators understand that. To them, bonds like McCrae's and Lisa's are the ones to put through the stress test.

On the Monday after the election was frozen, the Charlotte television reporter Joe Bruno received a batch of 159 absentee ballots unexpectedly. Bruno and his producer printed the ballots and flipped through each one and took note of the witness lines. They were all ballots that supported the claims being made by Democrats. That night WSOC aired Lisa Britt's name for the first time, as part of a list of people who signed multiple ballots as witnesses. She had signed forty-two.

She wasn't the worst offender in the batch—there was a man who signed forty-six. But she became one of the most suspicious, because when Bruno visited the homes of those witnesses, she didn't even live at the address she had given. He did, however, meet up with another woman who signed twenty-eight ballots. Her name was Ginger Eason, and the clip of Bruno interviewing Eason on the front porch of her modular home went viral. "I was helping McCrae pick up ballots," Eason said in the clip. "I don't know nothing [about] what happened after I dropped them off. . . . I dropped 'em off. What they do, that's on them."

The clip, for all the good it did to help investigators trying to reveal McCrae's misdeeds, became the singular moment most outsiders used when they made fun of the place: Eason, in her lime-green T-shirt and hair tied in a rough-shaped bunch, talking through a smoker's voice and a southern accent in front of a storm door. It was the clip Colbert used on his show, and countless others replayed it too.

They descended on Bladen from all over the country, knocking on doors and looking for ballots. Nick and Michael were among them. In fact, that Tuesday night outside the Bladen County courthouse, we ran into each other. We were working for two very different outlets for very different purposes, Michael as a long-form writer and Nick as an investigative television reporter. We certainly had no idea it would be the first of hundreds of hours we'd stand on Bladen County soil together.

It was clear early on that, for all the important work others were doing, Nick was the only one who was able to get close to people who knew the inner workings of McCrae's absentee program. This reality became clear to Michael in a most awkward way. Michael was interviewing Pat Melvin in his real estate office, and Melvin was getting worked up and red-faced. Michael landed the interview because of his past work with *Our State* magazine, the lifestyle publication that highlights the beauty of North Carolina and that Melvin loves. But still Melvin considered Michael a member of the "liberal media." It was a reasonable accusation, considering Michael grew up the grandson of a Democratic Party leader in Maryland and, although he's unaffiliated, he's admittedly participated only in Democratic primaries his entire voting life. Melvin insisted that Michael agree with him that McCrae hadn't done anything illegal, and he was getting frustrated about receiving no more than polite nods in return. Just before Melvin burst, his phone rang. He looked down at it and smiled.

"That's McCrae right there," Melvin said.

"Oh, really?" Michael said in a recording of the conversation. "Go ahead and get it if you need to."

"Hey, McCrae," Melvin said.

McCrae, who had eluded reporters for more than a week and had assumed the unofficial title of "Republican operative," spoke.

"What's happenin', *buuud*?" McCrae said.

"Well, actually I'm in the middle of an interview with a guy from Politico. Name is Michael."

A couple of seconds passed before Dowless spoke again, this time softer and more difficult to hear on the tape. "There's a guy, Nick, wants to interview [you] too," McCrae said. "He's the man trying to help us." Unlike Michael, Nick grew up as a Republican and was involved with the college Republicans during his time at Elon. That easy-to-Google background offered him entry into places in this story that no other reporters could go, though it also left him shut out of places others could go. Nick had simply told McCrae he would be fair and offer the other side of the story, and McCrae believed him. In several of our recorded conversations with McCrae over the years, Nick attempted to define their relationship as reporter and subject, but still McCrae calls both of us "*buuud*."

That day in his office, Melvin responded: "Yeah, Nick. I'm aware of that. Ok-, Osch-... what is it, Oschner. Yeah. OK, that's fine. Just tell him to give me a call on my cell number."

Michael called Nick that night and told him what he'd heard in the room, and warned him to be careful. Nick laughed and said he knew he couldn't truly trust anyone there when it came to this story.

Somehow that conversation in early December in Bladen County, a conversation between two reporters who came up in vastly different political households but who shared a love of this unbelievable place with these unbelievable people, became the foundation for this book.

Meanwhile, conversations similar to it—between investigators and elections board members—were becoming the foundation for an unprecedented investigation.

While we were in Bladen that week, Mark Harris sat at home awaiting information from his lawyers, watching news trickle out.

The most interesting stuff wasn't yet public, though. There was still a binder of information and a file sitting on the U.S. Attorney's desk, untouched. And now the Wake County district attorney had her own binder filling up, as did the state board of elections investigators.

One little snippet, dating back to just a month before the election, tells of when board of elections investigators started to focus on Lisa Britt. And it serves as a pristine example of how corrupt Bladen County's elections had been, and how much of a role race played in those elections and the power that came with them.

On October 3, state board of elections investigators went to the Bladen elections board office to inquire about the high number of absentee ballots that were pouring in. There they met Valeria McKoy, a Black woman and the deputy director, and asked if she'd noticed anything strange.

Yes, McKoy told the investigators, she'd noticed that several of the containers were signed by the same name. Actually, a lot of the containers were signed by the same names. The investigators asked to see the ballot request forms in question, but McKoy hesitated. "You're getting me in trouble," she said quietly, then turned away to go get them, according to the investigators' report. That report also noted that she may have said, "You're scaring me."

Either way, she said it in a low tone before coming back with the forms. Several were signed by James Singletary. And several were signed by Lisa Britt.

When the investigators ran a check on Britt, they found several different versions of her last name, including Lisa Kitchens and Lisa Gray.

After Britt's 2011 conviction, while still serving her five years' probation, she voted by absentee ballot in the 2014 election. That's a crime in North Carolina. She was then convicted of another felony in 2016, this one felony possession with intent to sell. Nevertheless, she voted once again in the

2017 municipal election. And, most relevant to this story, she voted as a convicted felon in the May 2018 primary, casting a ballot for Mark Harris.

A clear-cut case of voter fraud.

The investigators now held absentee ballot request forms signed by Lisa Britt. It should have been enough to raise concern in the Bladen board of elections. But five days after the investigators' visit there, the county's elections director, Cynthia Shaw, called the investigators, furious that they'd been to the office and taken the forms. Based on what she said, the investigators had indeed gotten Ms. McKoy, the Black woman working the front desk, in trouble.

Shaw demanded to know how the investigators became aware of Lisa Britt. "There was an insistence in the way Shaw asked about the source of Britt's name," says the investigator's report we obtained.

The investigators told Shaw that they'd seen Britt's name on the absentee forms handed to them that day. Shaw calmed down, at least momentarily.

As it happened, those same investigators had already talked to Shaw a week earlier. And Shaw told them the office had received over 600 absentee requests, which she said was a high number. The investigators asked her how that might have happened and who might've been responsible.

Shaw told the investigators that the spike was undoubtedly due to the Bladen County Improvement Association. "Shaw made no mention of any other political groups working in Bladen County," the report said.

These days and in this part of the country, many white people bristle when they hear the term *systemic racism*. They think it's a buzz phrase used unfairly and unjustly against whites, as if part of some reverse-discrimination plot. Pat Melvin flat-out believes it's a conspiracy against white people.

But here was a striking example. Here was a person in power—the director of the local board of elections, a white woman—who had learned that investigators were looking into the behavior of a white woman she knew, a woman who happened to be a felon multiple times over. And on learning this, the director called the investigators, but not to help with their investigation. Rather, she demanded to know how they came across Britt's name, because she wanted to find out if the Black woman in her office gave it to them. And on top of that, just days earlier, when those same investigators asked that same director who was doing illegal voting things in Bladen County, she essentially heaped blame on *the Black people*, while making no mention of McCrae or his mostly white team.

The truth is that people working for McCrae and people who were being paid by the Bladen County Improvement Association PAC had each signed dozens of absentee ballots. But, depending on who you are, one side was likely breaking the law and the other side was helping the good guys win. And the head of the local board of elections was acting as the judge and jury on that, until the state caught her.

It gets worse. In fact, throughout the fall of 2018, most of Bladen County's racial and political tensions played out inside the walls of the board of elections offices. Shaw, the director, resigned abruptly on December 3, just days after the state board held up the election. She said it had nothing to do with the ongoing controversy. And maybe that's true.

Affidavits from one of the elections board members, Jens Lutz, show that McCrae Dowless was given full access to the board's offices during the 2018 campaign. On one occasion, Lutz said in an affidavit, he'd learned that McCrae's operation had turned in request forms for dead relatives of one of the board's *own members.*

It is worth remembering that in Bladen County, you can't trust anyone. And worth remembering, too, that Lutz had started a political consulting firm with McCrae years earlier, only to have a falling-out that eventually led to his attempt to run McCrae over with a motorcycle.

Now Lutz, a Democrat, was signing affidavits that said he'd heard second-hand that Dowless told Shaw that he'd "added a new trick" to his operation in 2018, and that when Shaw asked what the trick was, McCrae had said, "I am throwing ballots into the trash."

It made for an enticing story, but if McCrae said something like that—which he was likely to do—it was a joke. Months later, state board of elections director Kim Strach would say in a presentation at Davidson College: "What we did not find during this investigation was that there were ballots that were harvested that were not turned in, generally. There was only one or two cases where that potentially happened."

The believability of Lutz's testimony was in question long before that, though.

On December 7, one week after the election was held up, Michael visited the Bladen elections office to pull some old records from the 2010 sheriff's contest. He was greeted by Valeria McKoy. She was now on her fourth full day as interim director after Shaw's sudden resignation.

Michael asked Ms. McKoy how she was doing.

"This is not the day to ask that," she said. "This is not the week to ask that."

As it turns out, by complete coincidence, in that same hour, there'd been another resignation on the board of elections. It was just five days after the resignation of Shaw, the Republican. And now news was breaking that

Lutz, the Democrat who accused Shaw of wrongdoing, was also stepping down.

The main players in the election fraud scandal of 2018, McCrae Dowless and Mark Harris, received most of the attention. But for all of their faults and blindness to their own offenses, it's worth remembering that this dysfunctional board of elections office was actually in charge of securing the election they wanted to bend.

The following week, Lisa Britt talked publicly for the first time. She'd also just learned she was pregnant, about eight weeks. She would have the child in July, her doctors told her, just weeks before her fortieth birthday.

Lisa was living in Columbus County now, about forty-five minutes south of Bladenboro in a town called Fair Bluff. Sitting on the Lumber River, Fair Bluff took the two hurricanes worse than any other town in the state. Twice the storms sent water up and over the banks. The pharmacy was flooded twice, along with every other business in the main strip. The pharmacy owner's father, a minister, took a small boat to try to save what he could during Florence, but when he opened the door a bunch of the merchandise went rushing out. As he watched a pack of diapers float down Main Street, he said, "There goes Fair Bluff." The residents there are trying to keep the town from dying, but scientists and meteorologists have used Fair Bluff as an example of a town that will soon be another climate-change ghost town.

That's the town Lisa Britt moved to when she found out she was pregnant.

"Everything's so cheap here," she said.

For more than a week, Nick had been trying to convince McCrae to talk with him on camera. He wouldn't. Nick asked if any of his workers would. McCrae gave up Lisa's number, but she shot down the initial request. But then she called on December 12, a Wednesday, and told Nick she was ready. She told him to meet her at McCrae's house between 4:30 and 5 that evening. A strange request, but any person who's spent time in Bladen County knows not to expect anything less than strange.

Nick showed up to McCrae's house as instructed that evening at 4:30. While Nick was sitting in McCrae's kitchen, someone knocked on the door. McCrae answered. It was another TV reporter. Her producers had sent her to ask McCrae if she could just take his picture. "No, ma'am, I can't do that," he responded.

An hour later, Lisa still wasn't there. She took so long that Nick and his producer had to do a live report for CBS News's streaming channel in

McCrae's backyard with a generic batch of trees as a backdrop. A network producer texted afterward and asked if he had just gone live from the middle of the woods. "You have no idea," Nick responded. "If only I could tell you where I'm at right now."

Finally, nearly two hours after the meeting time she'd scheduled, Lisa arrived. She apologized. Said she had to take care of her kids getting home from school. She asked if she had time to put some makeup on and do her hair.

Sure, Nick said. And then, as the producer put Lisa's mike on, she asked one more question: "Can McCrae stay in the room to watch?"

Sure, Nick said again, whatever she was comfortable with.

In the run-up to the interview, both McCrae and Lisa, father and stepdaughter, smoked relentlessly. It felt like a big moment for them.

She spoke like a person who'd practiced her answers. She was wearing a light green, long-sleeved T-shirt and faded jeans. And in the wide shot of the two of them talking, it revealed her sitting in the corner of a room with wood-paneled walls, next to a table dressed in a winter tablecloth with snowmen and cartoon penguins. On top of the penguins was a pack of Newports.

"There are people who say that you've committed crimes."

"Yes, sir."

"What do you say to that?"

"I haven't committed any crimes."

"How would you describe what you did in the 2018 election?"

"We basically went to areas of people who do not have a vehicle and would not actually be able to make it to the polls to vote. So that way they would have the option to vote. We wanted to make it so everyone had the option to vote. . . . We did go to several of the homes of people who'd received absentee ballots in the mail. We did go witness them."

"Did you ever take someone's ballot from them?"

"No, sir," she said.

"Did you ever change someone's ballot?"

At that question, Lisa Britt made a sour face and shook her head *no!* as if the question was crazy. It was a sincere moment.

Their conversation lasted nearly thirteen minutes. It was the first extensive interview with anyone close to McCrae, certainly the first one that was in his house. If McCrae thought it would do him any favors, or if he thought it would do Mark Harris any favors, he was mistaken. In fact, had Lisa Britt not participated in that interview, Mark Harris might very well be in Washington today.

Because what McCrae didn't know, and what Nick didn't know, was that Lisa Britt had already talked to investigators and told them the exact opposite of what she'd told Nick.

Investigators had the interview with Nick transcribed word for word. They'd save it for the right moment. Like, say, during a public hearing to decide the fate of the Ninth District.

Two days later, Nick's phone rang again as he was walking into the studio in Charlotte late on a Friday morning. It was supposed to be a short day. He'd been working for two weeks straight and planned to skip out early on a family trip to Washington. He didn't recognize the number on the phone, so he ignored it.

Then came a text from that number: it was Beth Harris, Mark's wife. After two weeks of media frenzy, of accusations of lawlessness and speculation of his role in stealing an election, Beth said Mark had decided it was time to answer questions and explain himself on camera.

Nick immediately called back. Mark Harris picked up and, after a few minutes of introductions, asked Nick if he'd like to do an interview. Harris wanted to do it that afternoon, December 14. So much for Nick's family trip. About two hours after that call, Nick pulled up the long, curvy driveway at the Harrises' south Charlotte home and rang the doorbell.

Beth answered. Mark was a few steps behind. Nick's photographer was already there and had been arranging chairs and setting up lights. Nick helped Mark put on his microphone. Nick expected the interview to be tense, maybe even hostile. He expected Harris to be evasive on questions about his personal relationship to McCrae Dowless. Instead, he got the opposite.

Nick started the interview by asking Mark if he'd personally hired McCrae.

"I did," Harris responded, without any hesitation.

This was the first time Mark Harris had admitted to even knowing the man. Harris went on to explain—for the first of what would be many times— the story of Judge Marion Warren calling him after his narrow loss in the 2016 primary, and the introduction to McCrae in the furniture store.

Nick was stunned. Before this conversation, reporters had gone all over the place to tie Harris to McCrae. Now Harris was just talking about it as a matter of fact.

"Did you have any indication that McCrae Dowless was doing something that might be illegal?" Nick asked.

THE GARDEN

"No, absolutely not," Harris replied, in an answer that brushed aside the direct warnings saying that very thing from his son John.

Harris said he was frustrated. That wasn't surprising, but the focus of his frustration was. He wanted to say, in public, that he was disappointed by the lack of support from the Republican Party. Democrats rallied around McCready, he said, but where was his backup?

Nick ended the interview by asking Harris if he was preparing for a new election. Harris demurred and said he was staying busy with Christmas parties and preparing to go to Washington.

"So again, we feel like we won this race by 905 votes," Harris said.

A week or so later, McCrae let a photographer into his home. The *Washington Post* had been all over the story, and all over McCrae's house. He'd posed for a photo with the *News & Observer* the previous week. Those portraits, three or four with the backgrounds faded, gave McCrae the air of a distinguished and thoughtful man pondering the future or the past or both.

This time the *Washington Post* photographer came inside the kitchen. And although this portrait wasn't nearly as flattering as the *N&O*'s shot, it was masterful in its accuracy of the scene and McCrae's existence.

In it, he's sitting in his swivel chair and his lightweight jacket, like usual. He's looking up toward the camera. The tablecloth is that same snowscape scene for Christmas, gray with little penguin-faced snowmen. There's a Styrofoam cup next to a plastic cup with Pepsi. Right beside that, next to his left elbow, is an ashtray filled with cigarette butts. Underneath the ashtray is a stack of papers. The top sheet has a header that reads, in big block letters, "ABSENTEE VOTERS. KNOW YOUR RIGHTS."

It's the mailer the state board of elections staff sent to voters in October, warning them, pleading with them, not to hand their ballots to anyone.

★ ★ ★

The NAACP at First Baptist Church
December 18, 2018

★ ★ ★

I've got a song that the angels can't sing.

T. ANTHONY SPEARMAN

It had been four years almost to the day since the gathering to raise up the family of Lennon Lacy. Now people came from just down the street, from clear across the district, from as far away as Las Vegas. Wherever they hailed from, on a cold Tuesday night a week before Christmas, they all—the state NAACP, the Southern Coalition for Social Justice, the North Carolina Black Alliance, Blueprint NC, and Progress NC Action—came together at Bladenboro First Baptist, filling every pew and lining every wall to talk about stolen ballots.

Lennon Lacy's mother, Claudia, sat in a pew near the front, while the speakers brought up her son's name time and again. "The Lacy case is a cold case now," said T. Anthony Spearman, president of the state NAACP. "The investigation of the stealing of Black votes—you see, 'harvesting' is a fancy term they use for 'stealing,' but I'm here to tell you we gotta call a spade a spade. Stealing. An investigation of the *stealing* of Black votes would bode well to review the 2014 campaign that was the context for Lennon's mysterious death in late August, just as the campaign for sheriff was heating up."

Sitting in the front row, the former sheriff who lost that race, Prentis Benston, nodded. Spearman continued to build on that point, raising his voice and dropping it for effect. He went back and forth in time, from Reconstruction to today. The gathering happened to occur on the eve of the 148th anniversary of the day in 1870 when seventeen Black legislators issued their "Address to the Colored People of North Carolina," telling Black constituents they had a "right to go to the polls unmolested."

Now they were back again. Black people had gathered to address Black people about fighting through a modern-day form of voter suppression.

"Black voters have to be nice, extra nice, when we register to vote, go to the polls, and even cast our votes in some polling places," Spearman said. "We know. You've told us long enough that we are in the minority. And we have to win white votes to ever get a majority. I believe they call us minorities to remind us that we need white friends and neighbors to win an election. I'm here to tell you tonight that's not wholly true. Since news of Mark Harris's piecework payment scheme, it's reported that every *stolen* ballot from an African and Native American voter was worth good money."

By now the people were standing in the church and cheering.

"I want to leave you tonight that although they have stolen your votes, don't ever let them steal your song," Spearman said. People were whooping now. "I've got a song that the *angels* can't sing," he exclaimed, causing people to leap from their seats, as he started singing:

My hope is built on nothing less
than Jesus' blood and righteousness.
I dare not trust the sweetest frame,
but wholly lean on Jesus' name.
On Christ the solid rock I stand
all other ground is sinking sand.

Just before Michael returned to Charlotte after his first reporting trip that month, he stopped at Melvin's in Elizabethtown for lunch.

In the parking lot, he met an elderly Black man who was getting into his car after a stop at the hardware store. "Got some spray," the old man said. "Roaches tryin' to get in the house." William Tatum was eighty-two, retired from the logging industry, carrying around a bad leg but bright and trusting blue eyes. He lived in White Oak, a few miles from Elizabethtown.

Michael asked William what he thought of all the election fraud mess. William said someone came to his house, too. "Three head of 'em," he said. Then he shook his head, worried he was doing something wrong. "They asked me, did I want to early vote?" he said. "And I didn't know. Yeah."

He said all three were Black women. He said they came back weeks later. He doesn't remember their names. But he remembers telling them he wanted to vote for all Democrats.

"They filled it out for you?"

"Yeah, they filled it out," he said.

He said he later saw one of the women on the news. "I really don't know what happened. . . . I don't know if they tried to get the old people that didn't know nothing or what. You know how that can be," he said. "I know it ain't right. If it's wrong, it can't be right."

Inside Melvin's that day, a line stretched out the back door. Right in the middle of it was the newly reelected sheriff, Jim McVicker, waiting for a flat-top burger with his wife. The previous day, McVicker had stood Michael up for an interview. When Michael approached him this time, the sheriff gave a "not now" glare. McVicker and his wife went on talking and shaking hands with other customers in line.

McVicker was a popular man at Melvin's, but he isn't popular everywhere.

In the earliest days of the election fraud story, as news continued to break and ordinary people became more and more worried that their ballots hadn't been mailed, the most concerned were Black Democrat voters who had voted against McVicker.

Black voters enthusiastically supported Hakeem Brown, a chiseled twenty-eight-year-old who grew up here and went off to become a West Point leadership graduate. He's one of the few people in his generation to return to Bladen County after they left. He became a deputy and school resource officer (SRO), and ran on a platform of building trust between children and officers through SRO programs. He believed the program could solve a great many Bladen County ills, from opioids to larceny.

Brown gained a following. Few events in Bladen County draw more people of color than the Martin Luther King Jr. parade in Elizabethtown each January. Brown entered the 2018 parade with a pickup truck with his campaign sign on it. But instead of riding he just walked behind it wearing slacks and a lightweight wool coat with a fedora, smiling and shaking hands with everyone along the route. His support built that summer in typical small-town fashion, through fundraisers like seven-dollar plate dinners of chicken and rice.

In the November election against McVicker, Brown performed well, especially for a young man trying to unseat an incumbent. He lost 55–45, and by a total margin of just less than 1,400 votes out of 12,500 or so cast.

Back at the First Baptist Church of Bladenboro, Hakeem Brown, wearing a yellow sweater vest, was next up after Spearman. "It's a great day in Bladen County!" He exclaimed. "We gonna say that one more time 'cause it's hard to get people to come out to a Baptist church at this time [of night]: It's a great day in Bladen County!"

Brown's enthusiasm took over the room, in the same way that Spearman's did earlier.

"As a young Democrat candidate for Bladen County sheriff, I'm a little bitter tonight," said Brown. "But as Rev said, I still have a song."

During the course of the nearly two-hour meeting, several people gave speeches expressing their frustration and sharing their stories. Michael Cogdell of the Bladen Improvement PAC told the story of Emma Shipman, the eighty-seven-year-old Black woman who said someone took her ballot from her house. And Linda Baldwin told her story, too: the retired educator was at home when one of her old students, Matthew Matthis, came to the door using a fake name. She told the story again of how he took her ballot and never returned with it. "I'm standing tonight so my children, my grand-children, great-grandchildren, so forth and so on may have the opportunity to vote and their votes will count."

Less than a mile away on the same night, the best lawyer in town was having a small Christmas party. Cindy Singletary, the same little girl who remembered the firebombing at the Bladen County department store in the 1970s, grew up to run the local Democratic Party. Now she's a classic southern small-town lawyer, usually in makeup, her accent syrupy, and quick to welcome you into her home.

Her house is 5,540-square-feet of something out of an old *Southern Living*. Here she keeps a portrait on the wall of her grown son, Zane, who's in his midtwenties and recently graduated from pharmacy school and still lives upstairs. The home feels like a playhouse, with a secret staircase coming off the second floor, and a wood-fired brick oven in the center of the kitchen.

It's a great place to entertain. And Cindy loves to do that, especially around Christmas. Her buttered ham rolls are famous all across the county, and they were flying off the tray that night. So was the booze. Cindy stock-piles a bar for the party. In other years, Cindy would have thrown a big shindig.

But with everything going on, the hurricanes and the election fraud, that night Cindy had just a few people over. Employees and their spouses. A couple of good friends. And McCrae Dowless. He was there, too.

If he'd have pressed his ear against the air on the front porch, he might've heard his name being called out in the church just a few streets away.

Spearman, the Black pastor, made it known what he wanted to see happen to McCrae Dowless. And it's not what you might think. He didn't want Mc-Crae to pay the ultimate price.

"We trust that the Wake district attorney will be able to persuade Dowless to turn state's evidence for a possible reduced sentence if he'll show how, when, and who he and the paymasters worked out the scam with," Spear-man said, drawing a rousing applause.

In other words, he didn't want McCrae prosecuted, necessarily. Instead he wanted an indictment of the system that leaves some people partying with ham rolls on a Tuesday night and other people in church asking for their votes to be counted.

Hakeem Brown continued his speech, acknowledging his loss but hanging on to hope. "It's one thing to lose when it's fairly done, but it's another thing to lose when unjust is done," he said, and returned to the theme from earlier: "I'm bitter tonight but I still have a song."

He picked it up from there in his most preacherly voice. "Dr. Martin Luther King said a man cannot ride your back unless you bend over and let him. Tonight is not the night for us to bend over and let the man ride," he said. "I have a song that justice will be served. That our votes in Bladen County and surrounding counties will not be stolen. I have a song that says more young people will stand up for justice. And just know we shall not sit quiet. We shall not sit quiet, because justice will be served."

★ ★ ★

Time Check 6:30 P.M. on a February Night

★ ★ ★

What happened in Bladen County is a disease.
A disease that, if it's not cured, can infect a country.

JOHN LEWIS, CONGRESSMAN AND CIVIL RIGHTS ICON

Pat Melvin had been pissed all winter. Not the kind of pissed where you punch walls. Not the kind of pissed where you go for long runs. But the kind of pissed where you smile, smile at everyone, tell 'em you're doing just fine, fine, yep, fine, but inside you're burning, and behind that smile the back of your throat tickles and every food tastes like nickels.

Most of the news crews were gone, having swiped a white glove across the Bladen County shelf and deemed it dusty. But nobody seemed to want to stay and clean it up. He'd watched as the board of elections—led by Josh Malcolm, someone he considers an earthly enemy—delayed its evidentiary hearing from December 21 to January 11. The new date was after the swearing in of the 116th Congress, which makes someone like Pat Melvin use his "welp" words. As in, "Welp! I guess Mark Harris won't be there!"

Just before the new year, a three-judge panel said the board of elections hadn't submitted sufficient evidence for the date change. This was the same three-judge panel that previously ruled the board had been illegally created by Republican lawmakers. Now the judges had seen enough, so they dissolved the state board of elections right then, with one day left in 2018. Poof, Josh Malcolm was out of the job. Poof, all the people who went along with him were too. This should've been a victory for Pat Melvin, but . . . *Welp! Now we have to wait for a new board!*

A new board couldn't be seated until late January, at the earliest.

Pat was out of welps.

Up in Washington on January 3, 2019, 534 people took an oath of office as members of the 116th Congress. They included 280 Democrats, 252 Republicans, a record 127 women, and a record 120 nonwhite members. The clerk

197

of the U.S. House called out each name on the certificates of election, until she reached one outlier.

"The clerk has not received a certificate of election for the Ninth District of the state of North Carolina," she said.

Finally, later that month, the new board came on and set a hearing date for mid-February.

A week or so before the hearing, Pat Melvin's phone rang with a call from the executive director of the state Republican Party, Dallas Woodhouse.

Melvin, probably the best organizer and biggest donor to Republicans in Bladen County, wasn't fond of Woodhouse or the state Republicans at that point. He thought they'd abandoned Mark Harris. He was sick with envy of how Democrats rallied around McCready, both in message and in money. But on the Republican side, Woodhouse had gone so far as to say that he wanted to thank the media, of all the scoundrels, for their help uncovering the bad seeds in Bladen County. Woodhouse appeared to be a bipartisan peacemaker in that moment, and shit like that pisses Pat Melvin right off.

Still, Melvin answered the phone call from Woodhouse. He listened as the state's top Republican message-maker said he wanted to come to Bladen County to talk to the Republicans there. Woodhouse suggested the time: 6 P.M.

"OK, well," Pat said, "that's about the time everybody wants to get home and eat supper."

Pat said he'd see what he could do.

On a cold winter weekend in January—the same weekend as a polar vortex sent most of the country into a deep freeze—everything in Mark Harris's life came to a stop.

What started as a sickness quickly became much worse. By the end of that freezing weekend during that frozen election, doctors told Mark he had sepsis. It's a blood condition where the body responds too vigorously to an infection, and the release of chemicals becomes so intense that everything's out of whack, or worse. Sepsis kills about 40 percent of the people who get a severe case of it.

Mark Harris went into septic shock on the Sunday of MLK weekend. He was in the ICU in Charlotte. His son John called Beth each day, but initially he was afraid to visit his father, for fear that their conversations might come up in the hearings. In the end, however, he chose being a son over a witness.

When he saw Mark, frail and weak, John pulled his mother out into the hallway. "Mom," he said, "Dad cannot go to that hearing. Dad cannot go to that hearing. Whatever you do, Dad cannot go to that hearing."

She listened, somewhat. John knew McCready's lawyers were an accomplished bunch, led by Marc Elias, who'd served as lead general counsel for John Kerry's 2004 presidential campaign and Hillary Clinton's 2016 bid. John looked at his deteriorating father and envisioned Elias turning the screws, turning him into a fool or a liar. "Healthy people get extremely confused under cross-examination," John said. "Mark Elias's entire goal will be to destroy Dad and get him confused."

Beth was at her wit's end by that point, though. She waved her arms in the hallway and said, "What do you want me to do? It's happening. We're subpoenaed. We have to go."

That was the last they talked about it.

Most people need about six months to recover from sepsis. When Mark got home from the hospital in early February, he had only two weeks left before the hearing of a lifetime.

Six o'clock came and went.

Pat Melvin looked around at the people he'd gathered to meet with the state Republicans. All local Republicans who'd rather be at home eating supper, but who'd traded that to be in the presence of Dallas Woodhouse.

Dallas is a raspy-voiced North Carolina native with a hawkish nose and deep eyes that always look tired. But he's always on, and always moving. He talks like a used car salesman who's trying to make up for an entire month of sales on the last day. He's passionate and, at times, crazy as shit. (He does not dispute this statement.)

His brother, Brad, is equally passionate about politics. Only, Brad's on the Democrats' side. Their relationship is as entertaining as it is confusing. Once they were on the same C-SPAN politics roundtable, arguing and bickering, when the host stopped to take a call-in question.

"Let's go to Joyce from Raleigh, North Carolina," the host said.

"Hey!" Dallas said. "Somebody from down South."

A woman with a southern accent started, "Well, you're right I'm from down South . . ."

Before she said the next line, Dallas put his face in his hands, "Oh, God, it's Mom."

"And I'm your mother," the caller went on. "And I disagree that many families are like ours. I don't know many families that are fighting at Thanksgiving. I was very glad that this Thanksgiving was the year that you two were supposed to go to your in-laws. And I'm hoping that you'll have some of this out of your system when you come here for Christmas. I would really like a peaceful Christmas, and I love you both."

The host asked her what it was like raising those two boys.

"Well, it hadn't been easy," she said.

At 6:05 P.M., Pat Melvin could identify with Dallas Woodhouse's mother.

At 6:10 P.M., he was walking around the room, smiling at all the other people there, mostly farmers and developers.

By 6:15, that tickle returned to the back of his throat.

Welp!

At 6:30 P.M., finally, Dallas Woodhouse burst into the room.

Pat walked up to him, put out a hand for a shake, and gave him that Pissed Pat smile.

"Dallas, I'm Pat Melvin," he said. "I want to ask you something: Can I get you anything, like maybe a fucking watch? You've wasted thirty minutes of my fucking time."

Woodhouse had entered the Bladen nest as an outsider, and no red sweater was going to grant him a pass for disrespecting their evening. So he got right to it, his update on what the future looked like for the congressional race and for the people here.

"The one thing we know," he said, "is McCrae Dowless is going to jail."

Pat, who'd grown up playing pool with McCrae in the back of his father's arcade, felt the blood rushing to his bald head.

"No, he's not!"

★ ★ ★

The Hearing's Opening Lies February 18, 2019

★ ★ ★

Mr. Chair, we would call McCrae Dowless.

KIM STRACH, ELECTIONS DIRECTOR FOR NORTH CAROLINA

When it opened in 1969, the Holiday Inn in downtown Raleigh was heralded as the "area's first round inn." It is a twenty-story cylinder that shoots out of the pavement just a few blocks from the capital city's few skyscrapers. The elevator shimmies up and down the core of the building, and the rooms fan out of a central, circular hallway. It looks like a cross between an old World's Fair exhibit and an alien spaceship's landing pad in an old sci-fi movie, only it happens to be one of the main spots to stay for visitors to one of the fastest-growing cities in the South. It also happens to be where several key Bladen County witnesses checked in on February 17, 2019, the night before the evidentiary hearings.

Lisa Britt and a handful of others who worked with McCrae Dowless pulled into the hotel on a Sunday afternoon, about eighteen hours before the opening statements. The state paid for her room for two nights, Lisa says, and "told me to go check out some of the stuff in the area." It was a questionable gesture, she thought, but when you're a person who collects absentee ballot requests for $150 a stack, you don't turn down a paid-for room.

Every helping hand comes with a catch, however. That Sunday evening, Lisa was in her hotel room, barefoot on the matted blue carpet, when her phone rang. It was Joan Fleming, the state board's top investigator. According to Lisa, Fleming was calling because she wanted to swing by, bringing a board staffer to go over what to expect during the week.

When Fleming arrived, they went into a meeting room. Lisa noticed a thick binder on the table. It included "stuff that had been told and the answers that they wanted me to use in court, pretty much," she says. Lisa was now being coached by the people who'd investigated her, she says. As you can imagine, what the investigators wanted her to say was contrary to what McCrae Dowless hoped she'd say. She was a pregnant thirty-nine-year-old with two boys already at home, and she was being squeezed between two different kinds of power.

As Lisa remembers it, here in the room was Fleming, a college-educated professional from the big city, complete with three decades' experience as an investigator with the FBI. To Lisa, Fleming represented the very systems that had excluded her and her neighbors for decades. But reluctantly, she'd grown to know Fleming and her team over the past three months. A few weeks before she sat down with Nick to say she didn't take ballots, she'd told Fleming's team the opposite. A few days after Nick's interview aired, Lisa says Fleming knocked on her door. Her two boys were running around the living room. Fleming told her that she'd better cooperate. And if she didn't? "She said I'm gonna miss out on my boys growing up," Lisa told us.

That nearly broke her.

Meanwhile, back home in Bladen was another form of power, the main target of the investigation and the public's disdain, and a man who just happened to be the only father figure she ever knew.

Choosing between Fleming and McCrae would be a lot for any person to handle. But Lisa didn't have much choice. She stuck with Fleming.

The next morning, the investigator told her, Lisa Britt would be the first witness. The hearing would take place in the North Carolina State Bar office at the corner of Blount and Edenton. Built in April 2013, it's a sparkling arena compared to other government complexes—LEED Gold certified with 60,000 square feet across four floors, a rotunda on the corner, and Corinthian columns stretching down the sides.

Lisa arrived early, wearing a light tan sweater with elastic wrists. She passed the TV trucks circling the building and the crowd of reporters with their microphones and cameras and notepads, thrusting them at every person who walked by. Capitol Police officers screened every person who entered, and they waved her into the $18.4 million building—which, if sold, could pay for just about all the hurricane repairs her new town of Fair Bluff needs.

Along the way, she saw all the characters she'd come to recognize. There was Joe Bruno, the reporter she didn't care much for. There was Nick, the reporter she'd lied to. Mark Harris. McCrae Dowless and Joan Fleming. And the lawyers. Good lord, the lawyers.

Inside the boardroom, Bob Cordle, the board's new chairman, brought the hearings to order. After some opening statements and necessary introductory notes, state elections director Kim Strach laid out some of the numbers: in Bladen County, 1,323 people requested absentee ballots, and of those, 728 were returned and 595 were not. In Robeson County, 1,493 ballots weren't returned, and 776 were. Strach told the board that McCrae Dowless's operation included a process of helping fill out absentee requests forms, then returning for "phase 2," which was picking up the actual ballots.

Then she called the board's first witness: Lisa Britt.

"Madam court reporter," Cordle said, "will you swear the witness, please."

Lisa raised her right hand and swore to tell the truth. And then the first word she uttered under oath wasn't entirely true.

"And where do you live, Ms. Britt?" Chairman Cordle asked her.

"Bladenboro," the Fair Bluff resident said, and we were on our way.

"I want to start by showing you a part of an interview you did late last year, if you could watch," Strach began.

The first thing presented in the hearing was a clip of Nick's interview with Lisa, in which she said, "As far as I'm aware of, no, there's not been any crimes committed. We did not go pick up absentee ballots."

"Do you recall that interview, Ms. Britt?" Strach said.

"Yes, ma'am. . . . I was in Mr. Dowless's kitchen."

Strach: "Did you know you were going to be interviewed prior to arriving at Mr. Dowless's home that day?"

Britt: "No, ma'am."

Nick sat in the crowded hearing room with a notepad, stunned. He felt the stares. He wanted to stand up and say that Lisa was lying. Lisa had been the one who called him that day in December to say she was ready to talk on camera. She was even late by more than an hour. He couldn't do that, of course, so he just texted Josh Lawson, the board's attorney, who was sitting next to Strach, and said she wasn't telling the truth. Twitter was already lighting up with reactions to Lisa's opening grenade. "Whoa—Lisa Britt says she lied in a TV interview with another CLT station," Bruno from WSOC tweeted.

Here on the stand, Lisa claimed that McCrae had called her to come over and fill out some paperwork and that only then did he tell her she had to do the interview. That wasn't true either. She said Nick pulled up at the home after she did (also not true). And she said on that witness stand that McCrae told her Nick was "a friend of his."

Then came the question, "After looking at that and recalling that interview, Ms. Britt, were all the statements you made during that interview truthful?"

"No, ma'am," she answered honestly.

Lisa went on to explain that she had spoken with investigators before Nick's interview with her and that she'd told them she'd picked up absentee ballots from voters. (Again, just for clarity: in North Carolina, picking up absentee ballots is a crime. Picking up absentee ballot request forms is not.)

From there Strach warmly guided Lisa through her life story, starting with her time living with McCrae when she was a young girl. Lisa explained that she'd been through a very bad relationship in late 2018 and had left it to go to a shelter with her two-year-old and four-year-old. She said McCrae opened his house for her again and didn't charge her rent.

She then explained McCrae's operation from the inside. She said she and others got paid per absentee request form. And she said she got paid for every ballot she went back to pick up. One strange part about that: she said McCrae paid her less for the actual ballot—about three dollars per, compared to five dollars for a request form. That meant that he paid them *less* for the illegal part.

Her testimony lasted all morning until lunch. During the break, Britt says that rather than being taken to see the other witnesses, she was taken to a room where some of the board members were eating. Again, she says, she thought that was odd. But she carried on with it.

When it was finally over, at close to 3 P.M. that afternoon, Lisa Britt had answered questions for more than three hours total. She told us later that Fleming, the lead investigator, said she'd done a good job, and that it would "go a long way."

Before these hearings, if you saw a person from Bladen County in Raleigh dressed in a suit, there was a good chance it was to give witness testimony about pigs.

Ordinary people who lived next to industrial hog farms in eastern North Carolina had brought twenty-six lawsuits against Murphy-Brown LLC, the largest hog producer in the world, and a subsidiary of Smithfield Foods. They had legitimate nuisance claims, for sure, but after the payouts and attorney fees, the suits would put many small farmers out of business, while barely denting Smithfield's profits.

Juries reached verdicts in three of those cases by the time the election fraud scandal broke out, awarding $548 million in damages to eighteen plaintiffs. Because of the state's cap on punitive damages, the awards were reduced to about $97.6 million total.

Dean Hilton was one of the farmers fighting back. A fit man in his forties who runs at least three miles each morning, his farming operation started the slogan that would be plastered all over billboards and bumper stickers hanging in convenience store entrances: "Keep 'Em Makin' Bacon."

Dean is the co-owner of HD3 Farms of the Carolinas, which he runs alongside his father-in-law and operates like most modern farms in eastern North Carolina—in that it looks nothing like the family farms of old. The bulk of Dean's work involves keyboards and paper, managing production and profit. These days, it's about producing the best product at the lowest price and with the fewest number of employees. They have about sixty-eight employees and a management team of ten. Their operation is not huge but midsize. In 2005, he bought a ten-house facility in Bladen, and now they have about a million chickens and 220,000 finishing hogs.

A finishing hog is one that's in its last stage before production. Finishing hogs spend about three or four months with Dean's operation, until they're approaching 300 pounds, before being sent off to the slaughtering house. HD3 is one of dozens of contractors for Smithfield, the hog processor that employs most of Bladen County. This makes him one of the most connected people in the county. He also runs his grandfather's real estate business and was recently selected to serve on the White Lake town board of commissioners. Knowing people here means knowing power. And Dean, for all of his resources, has plenty of that, even if he feels helpless against the lawsuits.

Nuisance lawsuits aren't new. People have been filing official complaints about the stench of eastern North Carolina's hog farms since the early 1990s. In Bladen County, the conversations picked up in 1992, when people packed a county meeting to demand that each farm be more than 750 feet from the nearest residence. One commissioner who fought hardest to add to the distance was Delilah Blanks, who warned that people of color often seem to be the ones who have to live next to them. But the hog industry—particularly the North Carolina Pork Council—was and remains the most powerful lobbying organization in the state.

It took a quarter century, but eventually some of those poor people fighting the Pork Council finally got a helping hand. A group of lawyers from Texas began to put their boots in the Bladen County soil in the 2010s, around the time Smithfield sold to a Chinese food maker for $4.72 billion. At that point, the profits and the ownership of the company ceased to be real in any meaningful way. The owners are now safe and protected by layers of shell companies and international trade agreements too complex to make sense to most people. Losing a billion in lawsuits is its own sort of nuisance to them, but not the end of the business. To an ambitious lawyer, the new Smithfield looked like a natural spring for pulling money. They just needed a few willing participants, and they found them in Bladen County.

Over the past six years, big lawyers took their big swings at a big corporation by pitting neighbors against neighbors in Bladen County. In the end, the lawyers would win, the corporation would stay rich, and the relationships would be fractured forever.

Activists see the lawsuits as necessary steps to breaking down the powerful hog industry. But the middle managers of the industry, people like Dean Hilton, see the lawsuits as another disconnect between urban and rural America—one where perception is often stronger than reality.

Doesn't matter that the hog farmers are the first industry in the country to hire engineers who want to turn methane gas into natural gas. Didn't matter that they've worked with new regulations on waste lagoons, dramatically limiting the runoff with each hurricane. To people like Dean Hilton, the hog industry has already changed, but the disdain for it only grows stronger.

It is a dispute with no good answers. Yes, regulations on farmers are better for the environment. But yes, also, that leads to a situation where large corporations are better equipped to weather the regulations and thus more likely to gobble up small farmers. Hilton, for his part, knows that he could sell his operation today and be fine. But then he'd be just another who sold future generations of Bladen County to investors who've never even been here.

"If you took the hog industry out of Bladen County, all these counties, you're talking 42,000 jobs. I'd love for Amazon to come to Bladen County, but they're not," Dean told Michael once. "We rural North Carolinians have got to do a better job of educating metropolitan North Carolina on 'This is how we make a living, this is what we do, and this is how we feed you.'"

Here is one of the dozens of lines drawn between rural and urban North Carolina, one heavily marketed and promoted and the other abandoned. People in cities can make fine livings as influencers or promoters, their only skill being the person they proclaim to be. People in rural areas can come to the big city and sit on a stand and tell them exactly who they are, and some lawyer will tell them they're wrong about that. An influencer in Charlotte could become famous and adored by posting pictures with barbecue sandwiches, but the rural people who grow the hogs will always be just a bunch of nobodies.

You can, we hope, see the parallels.

After Lisa Britt stepped down from the stand, more Bladen County folks lined up to fill her seat, presenting themselves before the dozens of people in suits like live exhibits for rural America.

Kelly Hendrix was up next. As the attorneys started asking her questions, she swayed in her swivel chair and told them she was nervous. Then, when Strach asked her how she met McCrae Dowless, she broke down crying.

"I was working at Hardee's," she said, "and he come to the drive-thru, and from there I needed a ride to work one day, and a lady that knew him who I also knew told me that he might would give me a ride to work.

"And he gave me a ride to work that day, and just from there—he resembled my dad, [and] I just connected with him."

Hendrix then took jobs with McCrae working elections, and in turn he'd pay her in comfort. "He would never really say that he was paying me for the request forms. I would sometimes need gas, and he would give me money for gas."

Strach then showed her pictures of all the ballots Hendrix signed. One by one she went down the list and admitted to collecting them illegally, then turning them over to McCrae, the man who came through the drive-thru looking like her dad.

Sandra Dowless went next. She'd been married to McCrae in the late 1980s, and she was Lisa Britt's mother. The attorneys had just told her that her daughter had done well on the stand. Sandra, like she did nearly thirty years ago in the scheme to collect insurance money from a dead man, distanced herself from McCrae. She said she'd been in a room where he'd talked about the plan, but insisted that it was wrong. Delivering a well-rehearsed account of her righteousness, she told her audience, "I got up and I said, 'Why would he say to turn in an unsealed ballot?' I said, 'Who people vote for is none of your business, you know. That's not right. I don't want y'all picking up mine.'"

McCready's attorney then asked her if she knew about Red Dome, and she said she knew they'd paid her ex-husband. The attorney showed her the amount he'd been paid: $131,375.

"If those numbers are accurate, does it surprise you?" the attorney asked.

"Yeah," Sandra Dowless said.

"Why so?"

"Because he never did have any money."

After 5 P.M. a store clerk named Kimberly Sue Robinson took the stand and admitted that she turned in a blank ballot to one of McCrae's female employees. "I think it was Ginger, and I can't recall the other girl. I'm not for sure. They was in a van."

"You turned in a blank ballot?" Strach asked Robinson.

"Yes, ma'am," Robinson said.

"And why did you do that?"

"Because I was told that if I didn't fill it out, that it would be filled out for me."

The next witness offered a flickering glimpse past the stream of white people who worked for McCrae, around a corner that suggest more was going on beneath the surface of Bladen County election fraud. The board called Precious Hall, a Black woman. What ensued would be the only attempt by the board to show the full picture of the election fraud sickness in Bladen County. Under oath, Hall said that she opened her mailbox one day and found an absentee ballot. It was surprising, she thought, because she hadn't filled out a request form. She usually votes in person.

Then, a couple of days later, two women showed up at her door. She identified them as Lola Wooten and Sandra Goins, whom Precious knew as Squeaky. They worked for the Bladen Improvement Association PAC. Lola and Squeaky watched as Precious filled out her ballot. They didn't tell her who to vote for, she says, but when she was finished they witnessed it and left with it. That last part, leaving the house with the ballot, is against the law.

But when Harris's attorney asked the question "You voted for McCready, correct?" the Democrat's lawyers hopped from their chairs. And the board of elections chairman, Cordle, a longtime Democratic donor, said, "I don't think it's appropriate to ask the witness who they voted for."

The attorneys and Cordle argued while Precious sat patiently through the banter. The chairman determined she didn't have to say who she voted for with that illegally harvested ballot, because the hearing wasn't about Dan McCready, it was about Mark Harris. In other words, whether the organization working for the Democrat had committed the same crime in the same election didn't matter anymore, because the Democrats' activity wasn't in question.

Bladen Improvement had been granted temporary immunity, in a way. But McCrae Dowless wasn't. That much was clear with the next announcement from Strach.

"Mr. Chair, we would call McCrae Dowless."

McCrae sat quietly in the back of the room most of the day, watching the women he hired, women who looked up to him like their father, and the one wife he ever loved, and saw them roll on him one by one. If he had any friends, they weren't in this room. With one exception: his lawyer, Cindy

Singletary, the sharpest attorney in Bladen County and the woman who puts the black cat on her roof every Beast Fest.

When the board called McCrae's name, Cindy stood up and walked down the center aisle of the hearing room with McCrae next to her.

"I represent Mr. McCrae Dowless," she said, in a thick southern accent. Big, tall, hairsprayed blond hair and blue eyeshadow highlighted her expressions and intentions. "We are here under your subpoena, and we are complying in that we have appeared as the subpoena has directed us to do."

"Right," said Cordle, the board chair.

"Is he being directed by this board to testify?" she asked.

"No, ma'am, he is not. It will be the same thing I've said to the other subpoena witnesses."

What Cordle had said to each of them—to all the women who testified that McCrae was the ballot-harvesting king of Bladen County that day—was that he was excusing their subpoena and if they decided to stay and testify, they understood that they were there willingly and that they didn't have to answer questions.

"Are you saying he is not here willing to testify today?" Cordle asked.

Throughout the courtroom, heads turned as if it were a tennis match.

"I'm saying that he is willing to testify if he is so ordered by this board to testify under the provisions of 1391."

"That would be immunity to any testimony he might give," Cordle said.

After some commotion, Cordle took the board into closed session at 5:27 P.M. They emerged thirteen minutes later, and Cordle resumed by asking Cindy to give her name again.

"Cynthia Singletary," she said.

"Singletary?"

"Cynthia Singletary."

"Thank you."

"*S-i-n-g-l-e-t-a-r-y.*"

"Thank you," Cordle said.

"I'm pretty loud anyway," she responded.

"Well, I just don't remember names like I used to, so."

"You might remember it today," she said, causing chuckles.

"This board is unwilling to give a witness here, particularly Mr. Dowless, immunity from his testimony."

"Yes, sir," Cindy said.

"We would request him to come forward like all our other witnesses have come forward and testify voluntarily, and if he refused to do that, we have the right under our rules and our orders in this case to take negative inferences concerning his actions that we have had evidence about."

"Yes, sir."

"So it's your decision, Mr. Dowless," Cordle said.

Cindy again spoke for him, in the same sweet-but-don't-fuck-with-us twang.

"Mr. Dowless will only be complying with the subpoena he was given which was to appear without something further, so he will not be taking the stand."

"All right. Thank you, ma'am. I would say he's dismissed now."

Afterward, the herd of reporters swarmed Cindy. She answered their questions, reveling in being at the center of a fight. She was there to protect a friend who happened to be her client. She hadn't forgiven herself for not going to Raleigh with McCrae two years earlier, when he had been hoodwinked into testifying for the McCrory campaign. That wasn't going to happen a second time.

One reporter asked about the testimony from the women that morning and whether that meant McCrae had broken the law.

"Where'd you get your law degree?" Cindy fired back.

Then she and McCrae loaded into her white Mercedes and headed east toward home.

★ ★ ★

The Son's Sword February 20, 2019

★ ★ ★

We can all do a lot better than this.
JOHN HARRIS

Mark Harris glanced out the hearing room window and spotted the most surprising but comforting figure walking along the street. John, his oldest son, the one who never did any wrong, was now an assistant U.S. Attorney, and he was walking into the building. Because of his job, John and his family agreed not to communicate until after the hearing. They'd seen each other while Mark was in the hospital, but that was it. So when Mark saw John in an overcoat and bundled up against the cold February air, he smiled and tapped Beth.

"Looky there," he said. "He doesn't want us to know that . . . that he really does care."

But when the hearing started, Mark saw no sign of John in the room. *It is the State Bar*, he says he thought. *Maybe lawyers have their own little rooms that they go to.*

Few things are believable in this story about Bladen County, but the guilelessness of Mark Harris seems like it just might be genuine. He claims a lack of awareness too often for none of the claims to be true. So he sat through that first day of the hearings, watching his friend McCrae Dowless get slow-roasted for eight hours like a hog, and went home that night and called his younger son, Matthew.

"You know, your brother was there today," Mark told him. "I'm really glad that . . ."

He paused.

". . . that he came."

Matthew didn't say anything.

★ ★ ★

Day 2 broke with more Bladen County witnesses, and more gawking at the varieties of southernness on display.

The most interesting testimony was from Agnes Willis, a Black woman and poll worker. In 2018, her job was to hand out the "I Voted" stickers. Willis said that on the last day of early voting that year, a Saturday, she was helping wrap up when she heard another worker say, "Oh my God." She turned her head and looked, and he was running his finger down the results tape. It's illegal for people to view the tape before the election is complete.

She walked over to see what caused his outburst. He pointed to the results of the sheriff's race between Hakeem Brown and Jim McVicker and said, "I thought the Black guy had it."

After Willis, Andy Yates stepped to the witness stand. He's the leader of the Red Dome Group hired by Mark Harris to serve as a go-between for money between the candidate and McCrae Dowless.

Yates denied knowing that McCrae's operation included a ballot harvest. He denied knowing much of anything. He made fun of McCrae, in fact, for his incessant communication. Yates pronounced McCrae "a needy person who wanted validation to know that Dr. Harris was happy, [that] we were happy with the campaign."

Yates couldn't escape association with McCrae altogether. During his testimony, the state board posted screenshots of texts between McCrae and Yates, one of which read, "Happy Thanksgiving Andy Dandy."

Yates also claimed that he didn't know McCrae picked up ballots. But after sitting through a day and a half of the hearings, Yates admitted, "I don't know what to believe."

That night Mark and Beth Harris were driving home when their youngest son, Matthew, called to follow up on the call they'd had after the first day.

"Look," Matthew said. "John's not just there to watch. John's there to give testimony."

The words hung there for a second.

"I just, I couldn't stand for you and Mom to be, uh, shocked by that in the morning."

Thoughts streaked across Mark Harris's mind.

"Well," he told Matthew, "thank you for calling and telling me that."

In the Harris family, no topic was off-limits. They were frank and honest, and they had no fear of talking politics and religion at the dinner table. They fearlessly debated Scripture and elections, and Mark Harris loved that about his family.

But in the hearing room in Raleigh, on February 20, 2019, at 2:03 P.M., that fearlessness took a new turn. That's when Mark Harris, along with the rest of a tense audience, heard Kim Strach say, "The staff would like to call John Harris."

John walked to the stand and made an opening statement, telling the room that although his job was to be the assistant U.S. Attorney for the Eastern District of North Carolina, he was here as a citizen. He and Strach spent a few good minutes setting those boundaries, between citizen and professional attorney, just as John had done with his father before. He told the board that he had made his dad's attorneys aware of their communication about the Ninth District race over the years—all the way back to John's stern warning about McCrae Dowless in April 2017. He wanted to make sure it was known. What they did with it then was up to them.

In late December or early January, John said, he learned that his emails were in fact going to be part of the proceedings.

He went on to describe what he knew about his father's relationship with McCrae Dowless, how he found the 2016 results shady, and how he figured Red Dome would act as a buffer and oversee McCrae's operation to ensure nothing went wrong. Strach put up one exhibit after another, from the elections results to his emails. One was from the general election night in 2016, when then-governor Pat McCrory's campaign sent out an email to its list, saying they believed something was off with the absentee ballots in Bladen.

John forwarded that email to his father and said, "Preaching to the choir."

Walking into the building that morning, Josh Lawson had known that day's testimony was going to be big. He knew the public would be surprised when John's name was called. And he knew everyone in the room—even Mark Harris and his lawyers—would be jolted by the images of emails between father and son about McCrae Dowless flashed up on the screen.

Lawson had the emails because John Harris gave them up voluntarily, not because the Harris campaign had produced them. In fact, Lawson had asked the campaign's lawyers repeatedly whether there was any other evidence that needed to be produced. Even though they were subject to subpoena, they said no.

That changed around lunchtime on the third day of the hearing, when they knew what was coming. They knew John was taking the stand, and they knew Lawson already had the emails he'd asked the campaign for. They knew he'd caught them lying.

During the lunch break that day, two of Harris's lawyers abruptly shoved a stack of papers containing the emails into Lawson's hand. Lawson threw his hands up.

"I'm not taking those," he said.

Lawson would later use the interaction to cast doubt on the truthfulness of the Harris campaign during the course of the entire investigation.

Strach's questions to Harris were meant to prove one thing: that Mark Harris knew, despite telling people he didn't, that McCrae Dowless was doing something illegal. She brought up a damning email from John to Mark, in which the always-truthful young man wrote, "The key thing that I am fairly certain they do that is illegal is that they collect the completed absentee ballots and mail them all at once."

No longer could his father claim he hadn't been warned.

John's testimony was its own soap opera. He bantered back and forth with the lawyers about the Duke-UNC basketball game that night, then slipped back into talking about what communication was privileged and what wasn't. He detailed what his parents knew and what they didn't know. Every email between the two of them regarding the congressional race was now blasted out to the room and to political observers nationwide, who read into every word and inferred what they wanted, based on their blog's bias.

Then, toward the end, Strach directed a question to John that summed it up: "I just want to be clear with my understanding, not that your mom or your dad, but you're saying the campaign should have exercised better control over Mr. Dowless."

John said, "I certainly think in light of the concerns that I had expressed and that they were aware of, that I would have expected more control and oversight than what I have heard testified to here today or yesterday by Mr. Yates."

"Thank you," the attorney said.

It was late in the evening and getting dark outside. Unspoken throughout the room was that everybody wanted to be home for the Duke-UNC basketball game that night. The Tar Heels were ranked third in the nation, and Duke first. No hearing, congressional or otherwise, would overshadow that.

But John Harris said, "And—"

Cordle, the board chairman overseeing the meeting, looked at him, puzzled. Who would want to go through any more of this?

"Do you have something?" Cordle said.

"Well," John Harris said, "I was going to say if there's no further questions, I would like to just say something to wrap things up."

Cordle looked at the attorneys in front of him, "Any further questions?" They shrugged. "You may go ahead, Mr. Harris."

"Thank you, Mr. Chairman. I just want to say this in closing. I love my dad, and I love my mom. OK?"

Sitting on the left side of a row, Mark Harris had his left elbow on his chair's elbow and his hand on his mouth. "I certainly have no vendetta against them, no family scores to settle, OK? I think that they made mistakes in this process, and they certainly did things differently than I would have done them."

By now, Mark Harris's face was red and scrunched up, and he was crying.

"But the thing about all of this and engaging in this process and watching it all unfold, I've thought a lot more about my own little ones than my parents and the world that we're building for them.

"And I will be frank, Mr. Chairman, watching all this process unfold, we have got to come up with a way to transcend our partisan politics and the exploitation of processes like this for political gain. That goes for both parties, Democrats and Republicans and Libertarians.

"And frankly, when I'm coming out of this process, I'm just left thinking that we can all do a lot better than this. And that's all I have, Mr. Chairman. Thank you."

Cordle responded, "Thank you, sir. You are excused."

John's final words would be played across the country. Democrats loved them; Republicans loved them. About the only people who didn't love them were people from Bladen County—McCrae and his lawyer Cindy, and Lisa Britt—who thought John was a little too righteous, a little too snobbish. Nevertheless, they resonated across political lines, and across America.

But back in Raleigh, before they broke for the Duke-UNC game, Cordle turned to Strach, the board's director.

"Your next witness is scheduled to be Dr. Harris?"

And Strach said, "Yes."

★ ★ ★

The Pastor's Call for a New Election
February 21, 2019

★ ★ ★

His shoe broke!
BARACK OBAMA

Around the same hour John stepped down from the stand, Barack Obama landed in town. So did Spike Lee. And Hall of Fame baseball player Ken Griffey Jr. They'd all been lured to the Triangle by the greatest college basketball rivalry and a once-in-a-generation talent who captured the imagination of men and women young and old, a statuesque young man on the Duke roster by the name of Zion.

Zion Williamson was an eighteen-year-old college freshman, six foot seven and more than 260 pounds of muscle. His arms sprang from shoulders like live oak branches, and his vertical leap was already the stuff of legend. Just one week earlier he'd made a blocked shot hip with an immortal dash from the key to the wing against Virginia. He was twenty-five feet away from the shooter when the shooter got the ball. Zion made up the distance in less than two seconds and slapped the basketball back the other way, several rows deep. The highlight replayed time and again on sports shows and internet clips. Sports sites asked physics professors to dissect it.

On the night of February 20, Zion would take on the hated Tar Heels of UNC, from just eight miles down the road, in the tiny, hallowed box of an arena called Cameron Indoor Stadium.

A basketball game was the farthest thing from Mark and Beth Harris's minds as they passed the exit that would've taken them to the game right around the time the gates opened. They'd just listened to their son's gutting testimony, and now needed to hustle home to Charlotte so Mark could receive a round of antibiotics to fight his infection. They could only be administered intravenously.

The drive from Raleigh to Charlotte, North Carolina's largest cities, is about two and a half hours along Interstates 40 and 85. After you pass the Durham and Chapel Hill exits, you fly through Hillsborough, where artists and writers live quietly, and through the manufacturing row of Burlington and Greensboro and High Point and Thomasville. After you pass the wood-fired barbecue capital of Lexington, and around Dale Earnhardt Jr. Boulevard in Kannapolis, the Charlotte suburbs finally pull you in.

On this well-traveled road, Mark Harris called his son, and John answered.

Mark told him he was proud of him. Proud that he had the courage to testify. Proud to see his integrity and moral compass.

Mark, the emotional one of the family, says he wanted to clear the air. But Beth, the strategist and analytical one, couldn't help but wonder what she had missed. On the speakerphone she asked how she'd been so slow to see the warning signs their son had been trying to show them.

"I just want to make sure you didn't try to tell me something that I just blew off," Beth told John. "All you were looking at was an Excel sheet [back in 2017]. You never looked at the container envelopes. You never knew who witnessed any of those ballots. Literally, you only knew on [one day] six ballots came in, on [the next day] eight ballots came in."

"That's correct," John Harris responded.

It was a lucky guess, Beth thought. She still wasn't convinced that her son had enough evidence at the time he sent those emails for his warnings to be credible.

Besides, was it really the candidate's job to vet operatives so comprehensively? Shouldn't someone else be responsible for that? Maybe the firm he hired to funnel the money, Red Dome? Or maybe the investigators who had been camped outside McCrae Dowless's operation for eighteen months? Why didn't they alert the Harrises?

As the questions mounted, Beth's blood pressure rose: How on earth was her husband supposed to know to examine absentee ballots from elections past, in every county in the district?

But she stopped herself. She couldn't spiral, she thought. She had to focus on driving home, getting Mark his antibiotics, and going to bed. They had to be up early and back on the road again before 6 A.M. for Mark's testimony.

They pulled into their driveway right around the time the nation's sports fans fixed their eyes on Durham. Obama sat near the baseline in a black zip-up bomber jacket. Zion took the floor like a king. All of eighteen years old, and guaranteed to be the number one pick in the draft in just a few months.

But thirty-three seconds into the game, Zion was dribbling at the top of the key with his back to the basket. When he went to plant his left foot, his size 15 shoe split open. He fell to the court writhing with pain in his left knee. Nobody knew how serious it was. Obama pointed at the court and said, "His shoe broke!" Zion would be OK, but he wouldn't return to what was supposed to be the biggest night of his college career.

For Duke fans, it was a disaster, the loss of their star on a night when they planned to crown him. For UNC fans, it was an unexpected gift; with their toughest opponent sidelined, their path to victory was clear, and they won the night, 88–72. But for general fans of basketball, nonpartisan observers of this rivalry game who had no stake in one side or the other, it was just damn depressing.

The next day they arrived early, the preacher with the good hair and his strategist wife. He was in a pinstriped suit with a burgundy and blue tie, she in all black.

They sat in the audience for an hour while attorneys argued about his campaign committee's failure to produce John Harris's emails and text messages. Josh Lawson complained that the campaign was still producing documents that should have been handed over weeks, if not months, ago, and Marc Elias, the hotshot Washington lawyer representing the McCready campaign, got the Harris campaign lawyers to admit that they hadn't even searched for emails from Red Dome's staff.

But it was all trivial compared to what happened next.

Mark Harris finally took the stand at 10:07 A.M. and swore an oath to tell the truth. Strach, the elections director, started the questioning by asking Harris to tell the story of how he came to know McCrae.

Harris recounted the 2017 phone call with the judge and courts director from the southeastern part of the state, who told him he would've won the previous election had he hired a mysterious man from Bladen County. Mark recounted the meeting in the furniture store and explained how he wrote McCrae two personal checks to retain his services.

Then Strach walked Harris through the back-and-forth he'd had with his son the day after his meeting at the furniture store. Strach again read the contents of the emails and the warning John had given his father.

"How do you feel about that sitting here today?" Strach asked.

"Well, sitting here four days into this meeting, I, you know, my son was a good prophet in his statement that day," Harris said.

Several times after that, board members interrupted Strach with questions of their own, and all of them essentially distilled into one: *How did you not have any questions about what McCrae Dowless was doing?*

Harris's answer, over and over, was that he trusted McCrae and trusted the long list of locals in Bladen County who vouched for the man and verified his results. After two hours of questions, the board members were becoming frustrated.

Bob Cordle, the chairman, cracked first. "You didn't believe these emails were an attempt by John to warn you of problems with Mr. Dowless, problems in Bladen County, the way the absentee ballot program was working?" Cordle asked.

"I believed they were John's concerns. I did not take them—because, again, if you go back and look at the email, just about every sentence where he says this could happen, he would go back and say, 'But if it's done this way, then it's okay,'" Harris replied.

That wasn't good enough for board member Jeff Carmon, a Democrat who was growing increasingly frustrated by what he perceived as Harris's refusal to acknowledge any error in judgment.

"Dr. Harris, if I may, when I read those emails, it was painfully clear to me that your son was saying 'Daddy, don't mess with this guy.' It's painfully clear," the board member said. "He didn't just state, 'Stay away from this guy.' He said, 'This goes left instead of right; are you able to handle what's going to come out in the media?' This is beyond a red flag."

Carmon continued: "When you read those emails today, you still say that there were no concerns by you or no concerns by your campaign?"

Mark Harris answered: "Obviously I read these emails today in a very different, intellectual light than what I read then when my twenty-seven-year-old son who is a sharp attorney and very smart . . ."

"Extremely sharp," Carmon interrupted.

"Extremely sharp," Mark Harris agreed. "But I'm his dad and I know he's a little judgmental and has a little taste of arrogance and some other things, and I'm very proud of him; I love him with all of my heart, but this was a father and a son, and weighing out, and in all truthfulness today he was right."

Essentially, Harris acknowledged under oath that he trusted the local politicos in Bladen County over his son. It was an admission that would turn out to be a grave error.

Lawson, the board's attorney, asked a follow-up question. It was a seemingly obscure query about whether Harris knew his son's emails would come up in the hearings. Had he, Lawson asked, told anyone he didn't believe John's emails would be introduced as evidence?

"Again, I do not specifically recall a specific instance of making that statement," Harris said. "I'm open to being reminded of that, but I cannot."

With that peculiar exchange, the state board of elections said it didn't have any more questions.

Marc Elias, McCready's attorney, stood. The lights in the room reflected off his cue-ball head as he pulled the mike forward. "I don't believe in ambushed witnesses, so I want—you understand you're under oath?" Elias began.

"Yes, sir," Harris replied.

"And when you say you don't specifically remember, do you generally remember that you had that conversation?" Elias asked.

The question seemed so small, so insignificant. "I cannot imagine and cannot remember with all of the information over the last four days that I would've made a statement that the emails that John and I had communicated with would not be part of this," Harris responded. "Now, again, I will be very open to being reminded if I did, but I just don't specifically recall."

"That's why I'm giving you every opportunity," Elias said.

"Sure," Harris said.

The questioning about Harris's memory went on for another three or four minutes before Elias drifted into questions about the candidate's background. Where he went to school. His work history.

Then, seven minutes into Elias's questions, Harris's lead attorney shot up and asked to meet with the board behind closed doors. People looked at each other throughout the hearing room, wondering what unspoken words they were missing.

The attorney didn't say why.

Cordle decided it was time for lunch anyway. He called for a break.

TV photographers and reporters stood near the bank of cameras set up in the big marble rotunda just outside the door of the hearing room. Newspaper reporters tapped away on their laptops at tables nearly pressed up against the doors.

Few people could eat. A little more than an hour later, the room filled back up again, only to watch the board vote to immediately go into closed session.

More mystery.

More people talking to each other. More nervous eye rolls from reporters struggling to figure out what to tweet, what to say into the blank space.

Then at 2:45 P.M., the end of the 2018 election for the Ninth Congressional District began.

"We will come back into order as we wait for Dr. Harris," Cordle said. "Oh, here they come now."

Harris's attorney spoke next.

"Mr. Chairman, Dr. Harris would like to make two statements to the board."

Cordle, knowing what was to come, offered a reminder: "Let me just start by saying, Dr. Harris, you know you're still under oath."

"Yes, sir," Mark Harris said.

"And that you are here voluntarily still," Cordle said.

"Yes, sir," Mark said again.

"All right," Cordle said. "Thank you, sir. Go ahead."

"Mr. Chairman," Mark began, "I have a statement that I wish to make."

"All right, sir," Cordle said.

Mark looked down at a piece of paper and returned to that seemingly insignificant question about whether he'd talked to anyone about his son's emails. Of course, when the attorneys asked it, they already knew the answer. And now Mark would have to tell the truth.

Harris read the statement straight through, hardly looking up to acknowledge the eyes on him.

It's been brought to my attention that I talked to my son, my younger son, Matthew, that I referenced earlier two nights ago about the fact that I did not think John's emails would be part of the hearing. Obviously I was incorrect in my recollection, and I wholeheartedly apologize to this board.

On January 18th, I went into the hospital. After battling what we thought was bronchitis, I developed a severe infection that actually caused me to become septic. In the process of that illness I experienced two strokes from which I'm still recovering.

Though I thought I was ready to undergo the rigors of this hearing and I'm getting stronger, I clearly am not, and I struggled this morning with both recall and confusion. Neither I nor any of the leadership of my campaign were aware of or condoned the improper activities that have been testified to in this hearing.

Through the testimony I listened to over the past three days, I believe a new election should be called.

Heads that had been tilted down toward computers and phones all sprang up. People groaned and gasped. Harris didn't look once at the audience.

It's become clear to me that the public's confidence in the Ninth District general election has been undermined to an extent that a new election is warranted.

Mr. Chairman, that concludes my statement.

"Thank you, Dr. Harris," Cordle said.

Harris's attorney asked for his client to be excused.

"Yes, sir," Cordle said. "Thank you. We appreciate it. I hope you feel better."

"Thank you, sir," Harris said, and then he stepped down.

★ ★ ★

A Glass of Tea February 27, 2019

★ ★ ★

CS Faircloth and CS Barefoot had a visual on Dowless.
SPECIAL AGENT'S REPORT

A week after the hearings, McCrae Dowless was sitting in a tall chair at a high-top table outside a barbecue restaurant owned by his friend Terry Dove, drinking tea and flicking his Newport ashes into a Sprite can. It's a little takeout restaurant with a walk-up window and a drive-thru, stuck on the end of a hardware store. A lot of McCrae's life passes by at Terry's.

On the restaurant's red exterior hangs a sign with the "Fast-Food Worker's Prayer": "Lord let me remember that I am blessed to work in the mission field of fast food, where there are so many opportunities to show love to the lost and hurting, and forgiveness to the rude. . . . I pray for your grace to safely surround me, your direction to guide me, my patience to stay with me. And dear Lord I pray that today I have a nice day."

From his chair at Terry's, McCrae can watch the teenage boys grunt by in their big-wheeled trucks, holes in the mufflers to trick the engines into growling louder. "I hate that shit," he says.

The day Mark Harris called for a new election, McCrae started a Go-FundMe account to cover his attorney fees. He figured the fees would roll up to about $100,000, so he put that down as the goal. He'd already burned through his payments from the Harris campaign. He was still receiving a Social Security check each month for his disability—something that, like all things in this story, would come back to haunt him.

The flim-flam man begging for cash alongside parents of kids with cancer and other noble causes delighted the internet. When one of the reporters from the city tweeted about the GoFundMe page, it went viral, and McCrae had to take it down in shame.

On this day outside Terry's, though, it was warm and sunny. A good day for sugar, a smoke, and shit-talking.

Bored or curious or both, McCrae called Nick at 10:45 that morning. He sounded relaxed, especially for the man at the center of an election calamity that was still making international headlines. Now that the results had been thrown out, speculation mounted that criminal charges would be next. You wouldn't have known it from his voice.

"Just having a glass of tea," McCrae said, drawing out *tea* as a two-syllable word that rises and falls.

"If I were you, I'd probably need a bit stronger brown liquid in that tea," Nick joked.

Neither of them knew it at that moment, but a SBI surveillance team had already fanned out around Bladenboro to track McCrae's movement. When you think of undercover agents sliding in position to make a big arrest, you might think of El Chapo or Bernie Madoff, holed up in a faraway place or in a plush, fortified location. In this case, the most wanted man in Bladen County was just sitting at a high-top table with a pack of cigarettes and crushed ice in a Styrofoam cup.

The SBI's log for that day tracks the banal movements of a small-town political operative bumbling through his life. It reads like a scene out of a country comedy-drama.

> 10:20 A.M.—*The surveillance team dispersed*
> 10:35 A.M.—*SAC Ammons and SA Froman observed Dowless' vehicle was not at Dowless' residence*
> 10:37 A.M.—*CS Barefoot observed a black Kia Soul* [sic] *in the parking lot of the Hardee's. . . . SA Froman went into Hardee's and Dowless was not present.*

(Authors' note: Of course this story includes a sting operation in which the main target eluded the authorities at Hardee's, the holy sanctuary of two-buck sausage biscuits.)

> 10:54 A.M.—*CS Faircloth and CS Barefoot positioned themselves at the intersection of Highway 211 and Bladenboro Airport Road*
> 10:59 A.M.—*ASAC Long, SA Blue, and SA Warren positioned themselves at the opposite end of Bladenboro Airport Road*
> 11:10 A.M.—*SAC Ammons and SA Froman were parked in the Dollar General parking lot . . . and observed Dowless driving a black Kia Soul*

(Authors' note: The Dollar Store is next to Terry Dove's barbecue restaurant, a convenient location in the event he ever needs a stack of cups or napkins.)

11:15 A.M.—CS Faircloth and CS Barefoot had a visual on Dowless

Thirty-five minutes after he got off the phone with Nick, a week after the hearings, four months after the elections, twenty-two months after he met Mark Harris for the first time, McCrae Dowless was arrested. Right in front of that sign with the prayer ending in the words "And dear Lord I pray that today I have a nice day."

> *11:20 A.M.—Dowless was placed in the front passenger's seat of CS Faircloth's bureau vehicle. Dowless was agreeable for an NCSBI agent to drive his vehicle to his residence. SA Warren drove Dowless' vehicle to Dowless' residence.*

At his house, the agents let him inside so he could (1) take his blood pressure medicine and (2) smoke a last cigarette.

Then they loaded him into an SBI vehicle and drove him to the Wake County Jail in Raleigh. He was then booked on three felony counts of obstruction of justice, two felony counts of conspiracy to commit felony obstruction of justice, and two felony counts of possession of absentee ballot.

In short, they booked him on counts of election fraud.

While McCrae and the agents were still on their way to Raleigh, an email went out with the subject line "Dowless Indicted."

"These indictments should serve as a stern warning to anyone trying to defraud election in North Carolina," director Strach said in the statement.

The release also detailed McCrae's codefendants: Caitlyn E. Croom, Matthew Monroe Matthis, Tonia Gordon, and Rebecca Thompson. Strangely, all the charges were for his 2016 activity. There was no mention of his work in 2018.

Most curious to McCrae's attorney was that of all the people who worked for him, his most loyal and effective employee wasn't on the list of people arrested. Lisa Britt, his former daughter-in-law, had switched her statements on the stand the week before. When he learned that she wasn't arrested, McCrae jumped to the conclusion that she'd been given a deal for the story she told on the stand.

But now he had bigger worries. Most notably, he headed to jail and his bond was set at $30,000, money he most certainly did not have. Fortunately, the richest man in Bladen County did.

That afternoon, the richest man in Bladen County turned onto the ash-colored blacktop of N.C. Highway 87, speeding toward Raleigh with $30,000, all cash, in a bag.

The sky was cloudless and the temperature almost 70, warm for late February. White sandy soil, as fundamental to life in eastern North Carolina as heaven and the sun, twinkled through the patches of wiry Bermuda grass alongside the two-lane divided highway that led him out of the Mother County.

Nobody knows these roads better than Pat Melvin.

His daddy grew up here. His granddaddy grew up here, too. And his granddaddy's daddy. Starting when someone's daddy's daddy arrived in 1773, the family's power and patriarchy grew from one decade to the next. While George Henry White was growing up in the house by the swamp during the Civil War, and through the white supremacy campaign that ended White's historic political career, and through the Jim Crow era, and through the civil rights era that produced Black people like Harold Ford and Delilah Blanks, Pat Melvin's ancestors were buying up land and businesses, making babies and burgers to carry on the legacy.

A proud and rich man in a struggling and poor county will do questionable things to protect his family's standing. That $30,000 in the back of Melvin's car wasn't for a charity; it was to bail out the world's most recognizable small-town political operative. After all, if you didn't show up in his time of need, maybe that small-town political operative might just up and flip on you.

Melvin's lifetime of frustrations with local politics, warranted or not, were in the bag. He was talking to himself. *Everybody cheats, dammit. The Bladen Improvement folks were cheating for years, dammit. Look what they made us do, dammit.*

The frustration wormed into Melvin's soul. Now he was watching friends turn on each other. Now he was wondering if someone would turn on him. But even so, "I ain't done nothing wrong" is his default setting.

Now, on that late February afternoon as Melvin sped up the road, while investigators processed their first arrests in Dowless and four former employees, the question shifted: *Who's next to be squeezed?*

Melvin swung into the four-story parking deck at the Wake County Jail with a bag of hundreds. Deputies told him they couldn't take that amount of cash. They turned him away. This isn't Bladen County. His cash, it turns out, was useless outside the Mother County, out where people follow rules that he and his family didn't write.

Melvin had no interest in going through a bail bondsman. A bondsman adds a 14 percent charge. Even a desperate man has limits. Worse, Melvin knew, all that would do is start a paper trail that connected him to the man accused of rigging nearly a generation's worth of elections.

There are places friendships shouldn't go and places friendships won't go, and Pat Melvin's friendship with McCrae Dowless falls somewhere between the two.

Instead of returning with a check, signing the forms, and bailing Dowless out of jail, Melvin backed out of the garage and went home.

Dowless, his friend, or his friend to a point, would have to spend the night in jail.

That night Melvin gathered up prominent businessmen and Republicans, including Ray Britt, the county commissioner who owns Ray's Inc. Ray's furniture had been the vessel in which this whole thing launched twenty-two months earlier; now he would be the money mule. The next day, Melvin told him, he would go to Raleigh with a check from his banking account. Melvin would transfer the money that night to cover it.

Ray started up the road early the next morning.

When Cindy Singletary, McCrae's lawyer, learned of the arrangement to bail her client out, she jumped in her car and drove north too.

Cindy doesn't trust Ray under normal circumstances. No way did she trust him with a $30,000 check. She barreled out the back door of her hundred-year-old historic house and headed to Raleigh.

Cindy knew that if McCrae posted bond by 12:30 P.M., he wouldn't have to go to court that day. Cindy showed up just before noon, with plenty of time to spare. But when she looked around the jail lobby, Ray Britt was nowhere to be found. There could be only two reasons, she told herself: *He either stole the money, or his dumb ass got lost.*

She called him, and he confirmed that he was somewhere in the vicinity of Raleigh, a fact he knew because the highway had widened to four lanes on each side, and it was a little overwhelming. Ray Britt didn't have a GPS.

Nick was already at the jail, and other reporters were on their way, hoping to record the McCrae Dowless perp walk. Cindy spotted Nick and, in a microcosm of Bladen County's attitudes toward accepted decorum, she shoved her phone in in his direction and ordered him to help the bail-money man find the place.

Nick gave Ray Britt of Ray's Inc. turn-by-turn directions and assumed that would be the end of it. But it wasn't. Ten minutes later, Ray still wasn't at the jail and Cindy called Nick again to ask if he'd heard from Bladen

County's most esteemed county commissioner. Ray called back again for more directions soon after.

The calls went back and forth for nearly half an hour. Cindy grew more and more frustrated, her southern manners casting a glaze over her desire to tell Nick what she really thought about this man. But Ray was still lost. He called Nick one more time. Nick walked down the long driveway entrance to the jail, stood on the corner, and saw Ray. He was in the left turn lane at the intersection. Of course he needed to turn right. Nick waved him across the lanes and into the jail parking lot. Ray parked and speed-walked past the news vans and cars, then opened the door to hand over the check. He made it just in time.

Years ago, thanks to growing up in Pat Melvin's daddy's pool hall, McCrae Dowless became nifty around a pool table. He even won a big countywide tournament in 1979 with a shot experts dream of, an across-the-table slow-roller to tap the eight ball off the rail and let it waltz slowly toward the drop pocket.

"And I put it in," he says now.

After he won that trophy he took his game to Fayetteville, which, as an army town, had some of the best pool players in the state. He'd get there early and practice, study the way the ball rolled. Before each game he'd put his pool stick on the table to roll it around. Most anybody who's played the game before has seen someone do this: for amateurs, it's a way to make sure your stick isn't warped.

McCrae would tell his opponents that's what he was doing, checking the stick.

"But really I'm checking that table out," he tells us, always wanting us to believe he knows something we don't. He says he was looking for the bumps and irregularities. "Then you take the corners and see if they're hard or they're soft, to see how your cue ball is gonna react. Whether you can put top English or bottom English on it, to see how you're going to do it."

"Pool seems to suit you," Nick told him.

"Yep," McCrae said, "an old political pool shark."

About thirty minutes after Britt handed over the $30,000 check, McCrae made his way out of confinement through the basement of the jail, up a flight of stairs and toward the main doors. He had a plastic bag with his belongings in his right hand, and he stayed close to Cindy's side as they reached the lobby. There, reporters were lined up, cameras on.

Cindy turned through a row of chairs and eyed the route out. They had a plan. Just when they got close to the press gaggle and it appeared one of the reporters might say something, a voice chimed in.

"I'll be happy to give a statement," Ray Britt said. The cameras and reporters turned toward the voice to see who it was. They were confused, like people who showed up to interview an all-star athlete only to have the water boy pipe up to offer his assessment of the game.

In the few seconds Britt kept the reporters frozen and puzzled—*Who, exactly, are you, sir?*—McCrae Dowless, the old political pool shark, slipped out the door and was gone.

He collapsed into the passenger seat of Cindy's car once again. On their way out of the parking lot, McCrae saw something that made him speak up.

"Can we stop at that Chick-fil-A?" he asked Cindy.

He wanted to smoke another cigarette and buy an extra-large sweet tea.

★ ★ ★

The Chilling Chant July 17, 2019

★ ★ ★

Send her back.

A RALLY IN EASTERN NORTH CAROLINA

In the days after the hearing where he'd called for a new election, nobody seemed to know what to do. No congressional election had been called back because of fraud before, at least not in recent history, at least not in any documents the board of elections or lawyers could find. So there was some confusion. We knew there would be a new election. But what would it look like? Could new candidates run? Would Harris and McCready be required to face off in a redo?

In the middle of all of that speculation, Mark Harris looked at his phone one day and saw he had a message.

The United States and its democracy often operate under the shared belief that someone, somewhere, usually knows what the hell's happening. But on Mark's voicemail was proof that sometimes even the people closest to it haven't a clue.

"Mark, this is Dan McCready," the message began.

I know it's been a rough several weeks in and we've had uh, some strong disagreements. I just wanted to reach out and let you know that, um, I wish you the best in your recovery from your health issues. I was not aware of the, the severity of those. Please know that I wish you the best in your recovery. Um, and I'm also, uh, we're hearing that there's likely to be a lawsuit requiring a re-run of the general election, um, where you and I would both be required to be on the ballot. And um, was curious if you were planning on, on uh, joining that suit. Uh, thank you and I look forward to being in touch. Buh-bye.

Harris did not return McCready's call.

Beth Harris was beside herself. She compares herself in the weeks and months that followed to the people who lived in fear of the beast of Bladenboro. She's found kinship with them, and how they were lost and unsure what to do, while something dark and mysterious prowled around every tree.

For Republicans, what was lying in wait was more disgrace.

On April 2, 2019, Robin Hayes, the chair of the state Republican Party and a former five-term U.S. congressman, was indicted for his role in a scheme to bribe the state's insurance commissioner with a six-figure campaign donation. The specifics of Hayes's indictment have no direct link to the Ninth District mess, but it's a good indication that the Ninth is just one broken window in a larger wreck.

Beth's mind swirled when she saw the news. But nearly everybody in Bladen County, from Pat Melvin, to Cindy Singletary, to McCrae, came to the same conclusion immediately: the Republican Party officials must've known all along that Hayes was being investigated. They intentionally walked Mark Harris and McCrae Dowless out on the public plank.

"They wanted something else going on other than Robin Hayes catching all the damn flack," Melvin told us. "So what better, uh, subterfuge, would you have?"

As much as Melvin and the Bladen County Republicans now hated the state Republicans, they hated Dan McCready and the Bladen Improvement PAC more. The PAC's president, Horace Munn, had said that he was warned to stand down in 2018. *By whom?* the Republicans wondered. *And why weren't they told to do the same?*

But Michael Cogdell, an Improvement PAC member and longtime Bladen County commissioner, told us that everybody had been warned. "We were trained. The North Carolina State Board of Elections gave a workshop on absentee ballots," Cogdell told Michael in December 2018. "Everybody was invited, Republicans, Democrats."

Cogdell insisted that the PAC hadn't collected ballots—that year, at least—despite evidence that they had. Even after it came up in the hearings that a woman named Lola Wooten had gone around snatching them, Cogdell claimed no knowledge. "All I did was turn in things that came from churches that people were asking me to turn in," Cogdell said. "And I did two ballots, for my brother and my wife." (Spouses and siblings are permitted to turn in ballots under North Carolina law.)

Regardless, that May, three months after the hearing, a man who was McCready's opposite emerged from a twelve-person primary to earn the Republican nomination in the special do-over election. Dan Bishop is a slick-talking lawyer with a southern accent who stoked all of the rage burning in people like Melvin. He bashed the media and the Squad—honestly, anything the president bashed, Dan Bishop bashed. (In fact, a couple of years earlier, when Bishop was state senator, Nick put out a story that Bishop didn't like, and Bishop tweeted that Nick was part of the "media jihad" on Republicans.)

The day after Bishop won the primary, Dan McCready called a press conference at his headquarters in Charlotte. He set the time at 2 P.M. That morning, Bishop emailed reporters to tell them to arrive early.

At 1:30 P.M., Bishop kicked off the special election season outside the McCready headquarters, standing next to a life-size cutout of McCready.

"If you want to do your 2 P.M. press conference with this cardboard cutout, he'll have as much to say as Dan McCready will say," Bishop said.

Thirty minutes later, thirty feet away, McCready stood in front of microphones in the same cramped room with the same quilt of campaign signs where he'd given his tearful concession speech six months earlier.

"His agenda is quite possibly the worst thing that North Carolina's ever seen," McCready said of his new opponent.

Here's an important note about the beast of Bladenboro: many, many people in the county hate it.

They hate the story behind it, the festival in its honor, and especially the color of it. To the Black community of Bladen County, it's a myth that seems to be made up to represent something more sinister and racist. For nearly seventy years, their white neighbors perfected a story about a big, black monster lurking in the woods. A black monster who needed to be hunted.

"You'll notice about the beast of Bladenboro, you don't ever see Black people in that stuff. That's a myth that was perpetrated by our light-skinned brothers and sisters," the Reverend Gregory Taylor of First Baptist Church Bladenboro once said in a sermon. "The beast has always been black. We've always had a problem with that."

In the airing of grievances after the 2018 election, eastern North Carolina's racist history rushed to the forefront again. The irony was too obvious: after months of pushing to have Harris step down, the Democrats now faced a candidate who was even farther right, and a mini-Trump.

In mid-July, Bishop drove to join the president in Greenville, a few hours north of Bladen County and the home of East Carolina University. It was three days after Trump shot out a series of tweets telling the Squad—the four Democratic congresswomen of color who had gone through the same orientation class as Harris—to "go back" to the countries "from which they came."

Outside the arena, people sold merchandise that shared the sentiment.

"LET ME HELP YOU PACK!" one read. "FUCK OFF WE'RE FULL," said another.

About twenty minutes into Trump's address, he brought up "the four congresswomen," and 8,000 people in the arena booed. Then he named Ilhan Omar, the freshman lawmaker from Minnesota who's originally from Somalia but has been a U.S. citizen since she was seventeen. He talked about her for five minutes, characterizing her as someone who nuzzled with terrorists.

Then the chanting started. Not from Trump, but from the audience.

The Chant issued forth from the eastern North Carolina people who inherited this land from people like Furnifold Simmons. Not far from this arena, in March 1898, Simmons had authored his *Democratic Party Hand Book*, the 200-page document that launched the white supremacy campaign that led to the 1898 Wilmington Massacre. Now, 121 years later, people in the arena looked from side to side to see if their neighbors were saying the Chant—and if their neighbors were saying it, then it must be okay for them to say it. The Chant was contagious like that, like pages right out of the *Hand Book . . .*

"Send her back," they said.

"Send her back."

"Send her back."

The Chant chilled the heart of anyone who knew the history of these flat, swampy, marshy lands. But it didn't deter the president, or the congressional hopeful who accompanied him that day. The president carried on. Twenty minutes later, Trump said, "We're joined tonight by the Republican candidate who is really a special man, a great man, he's going to be a great, great congressman, Dan Bishop. Dan?"

Bishop bounced up in a blue suit and tossed out a right hand at the president whose agenda he promised to protect. Trump waved him to the mike, then stepped back.

"So as President Trump said, there are two Dans in this race. Dan McCready said that Donald Trump is the greatest threat to democracy ever and backed crooked Hillary."

Trump stood over Bishop's shoulder and smirked as the crowd went "*Boooooo.*"

"Dan McCready took money from Ilhan Omar."

BOOOOO.

"And Mr. President, Dan McCready wants to repeal your tax cuts."

Women behind him put their thumbs down.

"Now, he would be the wrong Dan. As for me, I'm going to go to Washington, and I'm going to stand with President Donald J. Trump, and that makes me the right Dan. And with the help of President Trump, we're going to win the Ninth District."

"Thank you, Dan," the president said. "Thank you, Dan."

The Garden of Good and Evil August 2019

McCrae Dowless: Political Operative

SLOGAN ON T-SHIRTS SOLD BY MCCRAE DOWLESS

On July 31, McCrae Dowless was indicted again.

This time the SBI didn't sweep him up. Instead, the indictment instructed him to turn himself in to the Bladen County magistrate.

This time the charges were for the 2018 election. (The February charges, remember, were for 2016 activity.) Six others were also called in this round: Lisa Britt, Ginger Eason, Woody Hester, James Singletary, Jessica Dowless, and Kelly Hendrix. But if the indictments beast was coming for Mark and Beth Harris, it wasn't coming that day. Instead, the cast of Bladen County's ballot opera made their way to the jail to be processed.

McCrae wore khakis, a blue shirt with a light check pattern, and a navy blazer. Hot for summer, but official. He told Cindy, his attorney, that two cars with Maryland tags had followed him there. He was quieter than usual. He'd chipped two bottom teeth a few days earlier in a fit of anger after learning this second indictment was coming.

McCrae had to wait outside the jail while one of the others was processed. Friends started to show up. Pat Melvin came with a pen. He asked McCrae for his autograph, then turned to the attorneys and the media and asked for theirs. Then he sat down and launched into a rant about North Carolina's Democratic governor, to nobody in particular.

Woody Hester arrived a few minutes after that in a teal polo shirt. He shook Pat Melvin's hand. "I thought about wearing my Trump hat," Woody said to Pat, "but I didn't want to drag him into this."

Then Woody walked in the door and turned around to wait outside. "I guess I have something in common with Trump now. We're both accused of obstruction and collusion."

Cindy was only there to represent McCrae. He'd promised her he'd figure out how to pay her. He had a new idea he'd told her about: he was going to sell T-shirts, and on the breast pocket they'd read, "McCrae Dowless: Political Operative."

During processing, several of the others wrote Cindy in as their attorney, even if they hadn't asked her. James Singletary walked out in a sport coat with sleeves nearly to his knuckles, faded blue jeans, and mullet-cut hair. He pointed at Cindy and smiled: "They said you could be my lawyer!"

Cindy rolled her eyes. The magistrate, she told Nick, is her godson. Signing her up for a bunch of nonpaying clients must've been his idea of a joke.

Then she asked Nick if he'd watched *Midnight in the Garden of Good and Evil* yet.

In the late summer along the Lumber River, the mosquitoes are lawless and the cicadas give them cover. And the kids are calling for their mama. At least they were in late August 2019, when Lisa Britt asked us to meet her there.

She wanted to tell Nick the truth about her testimony, she said. On the stand she'd told the world that she'd lied in her interview with Nick that December. She told the world that McCrae Dowless had set her up to talk to Nick, even though that wasn't the case. Nick received plenty of grief after that, with everyone from local media to national pundits criticizing his relationship with McCrae. Lisa Britt's testimony had made life difficult for several other people too, and now she wanted to tell Nick why. At least, that's what she said.

We met her at a gazebo in Fair Bluff on an August afternoon. The town had been flooded by two hurricanes in three years. It was hot, and she had a newborn in her arms and two other boys running around. A car drove by slowly while we talked, twice, the older woman inside eyeing us like we were mice in a field.

"That's just my mom," Lisa said. "She's just watching out."

Lisa started by telling us the state board of elections had paid for her room at the Holiday Inn. She said that the lead investigator had asked her to meet the night before, had told her what to say, and had told her that if she wanted to see her boys grow up, she'd better say it.

So she did.

"That's like with McCrae telling us all to stick together," she told us, drilling down to a key point in the hearings, one in which McCrae was actually the one who'd instructed Lisa on what to say. "They said, 'Mr. Dowless contacted all you guys and told you guys to all stick together, right?' So I mean, I agreed to it: 'Yeah, yeah, of course he told us to stick together.'"

Nick stopped her. "Did he do it? Did he do that?"

"*Nooooo*," Lisa blurted. "McCrae never told us to stick together. But that was one of them questions they tricked me up with on there."

Then she said that the lead investigator had called her after she was indicted and said, "This too shall pass."

Lisa rolled her eyes when she told us that.

And here's a big complication with the whole story, in our view: How is Lisa Britt a reputable witness, in any case? The answer, objectively, is that she's not. And McCrae Dowless knows that. So does Mark Harris. But someone must face penalties. The case was too well known, and too many careers had been ruined and lives changed, to let it sit.

"I saw we made a *Jeopardy!* question the other day," Lisa said. And that much was true. One evening in August 2019, you could turn on the quiz show *Jeopardy!* and see the prompt: "A new contest was ordered in 2019 due to election fraud in the Ninth Congressional District in this southern state."

But then Lisa laughed. What happened in Bladen could've easily happened in any of its neighboring counties too, she said. In fact, the gazebo where she was sitting is in Columbus County. She said investigators had asked her about her work there, in the controversial sheriff's race.

"All we did was register people to vote in Columbus County," she told us. "Columbus County's all messed up."

"Yeah, well," Nick said, "People could say that about Bladen."

"Yeah," Lisa said.

"Columbus has its own flavor," Nick said.

"Of messed up," Lisa responded.

"Yeah, it was messed up before McCrae," Nick said. "It'll be messed up after McCrae."

"And Bladen County will be too," Lisa said.

We drove back to Bladenboro after the conversation with Lisa to meet McCrae at Terry Dove's barbecue spot. Lisa had told him earlier that day she was having a sit-down with us. But when we pulled into Terry's and said we'd talked to her, McCrae said, "Oh, really? I didn't know that."

"You're lying to me," Nick said. "What was our deal?"

Nick and McCrae had made a deal in the early days of their relationship back in December 2018 that Nick could only be fair to him if McCrae was honest. It's the same deal Nick makes with anyone, only with everyone else it's unspoken. McCrae likes to think of the world in contracts, where there's a give and a take, so Nick made it explicit.

"I ain't lying," McCrae said, smoke coming out of his mouth and nose while he laughed.

He'd taken a new job helping Dove transition an old blueberry plant into a facility to smoke turkey legs. Dove planned to sell those turkey legs to a distributor in Japan that had a high demand for them.

The special election was only two weeks away. While we talked with him, his phone rang seven times. One call was from a man whose nickname is Boss Hog, just checking on him. One was from a friend who'd turned on the news to see that a Raleigh station was interviewing one of the people indicted, Ginger Eason. She was going on and on about how she'd witnessed McCrae throw away bags of ballots.

"Throwed away what now?" McCrae said. "Throwed away envelopes? Well, that's a lie. All I can tell you is she's a liar."

By now McCrae was woofing cigarettes. He flicked his fingers when he talked. He was using clichés about the truth setting him free, and being innocent until proven guilty. He turned away every time he saw a black car, believing he was being watched. He figured his whole house was bugged.

He was, in other words, having a breakdown.

On our way back to Charlotte that night, Nick's phone rang.

It was McCrae. He wanted to admit that he knew about our meeting with Lisa. He wanted to apologize for lying.

★ ★ ★

Peach Ice Cream September 9, 2019

★ ★ ★

A lot of illegal voting out there.
DONALD TRUMP

Another hurricane sawed north through the Atlantic toward eastern North Carolina. A week before the special election, Dorian laid waste to the northern Bahamas, leaving villages unrecognizable. As it approached the mid-Atlantic, it tilted north slightly, skirting past the southern coast of North Carolina around Wilmington.

Its western bands wielded tornadoes that flattened one neighborhood in Brunswick County, just twenty minutes from Bladen, but not much else. What Dorian missed in this part of eastern North Carolina, though, it made up for in a big way up the coast.

On the evening of September 5 on Ocracoke Island, friends gathered for drinks and dinner at the Back Porch restaurant. The island, all of sixteen miles long and with about 1,000 residents, had been evacuated, but the locals stayed. Locals always stayed. Around the table was the principal at the K–12 school that averages about eight or nine graduates each June, a motel owner, an electrician, and the restaurant owners. They joked about the storm, laughing when they compared it to the one that had come through the year before.

"This is no Florence," one of them said.

They ate crab cakes and sipped wine and cocktails deep into the night. By the time they woke up the next morning, they were panicking. It's the sort of panic that's now a yearly occurrence with the dateline SMALL TOWN SOMEWHERE IN EASTERN NORTH CAROLINA.

The restaurant owners lost their home and had to sleep at the restaurant. The school principal had water marks thirty-eight inches high in the gymnasium. The electrician lost power, like everyone else. The motel owner lost three-quarters of his rooms.

And yet . . . life went on in just about every other part of the state.

There's no way to quantify the damage hurricanes and climate change have done to the psyche of eastern North Carolinians in recent years. What used to be an every-half-dozen-years occurrence now rakes the region every fall. There are no calm falls, just the constant threat of wind and rain, until people's give-a-damn meters run empty.

The same thing can be said about the 2018 election, which became the 2019 election. By the end of it, many people had lost interest. Sure, there was the Right Dan v. Wrong Dan intrigue. And sure, Bishop's jingles calling his opponent "Greedy McCready" slithered into the language of toddlers in households across the district. And sure, national media were flying into the state for stories on McCready's twenty-seven-month campaign, but everybody knew the turnout would be down.

On the Monday eve of the election, McCready went to eastern North Carolina for one more visit in Fayetteville, the army town. He needed Fayetteville. He's a veteran. He'd played up his patriotism all this time. After the campaign stop, he sent his team home. The caravan went south out of the 'ville, then turned east toward Charlotte along the long and lonesome Highway 74.

For twenty-seven months, they'd driven this road—this road that doubles as Andrew Jackson Highway and the American Indian Highway, somehow. And for twenty-seven months, they'd passed a peach ice cream stand. This time, McCready spoke up: "Let's stop."

While the McCready team drove west, though, another person was headed east. Vice President Mike Pence was on a cross-district tour to rally votes for Bishop. If anyone was fatigued from this, the Republicans weren't going to show it. Pence's final stop would be in Fayetteville. There the vice president would meet not only Bishop but also another "special guest" who was flying in to be the last-minute closer.

President Trump was on his way.

Sometime around 8 P.M., Trump took the stage in a lively Crown Expo Center in Fayetteville, the town McCready needed, and the town he'd just left. There'd been rumors all week that a high-profile Democratic candidate might come to support McCready—maybe Joe Biden, Pete Buttigieg, or Kamala Harris. But none of them polled well in the Ninth District. So while Dan Bishop smiled and welcomed the walking earthquake of a president to wake up voters in Fayetteville on the last night of this longest election ever, Dan McCready's team was on the side of the road in the middle-of-nowhere North Carolina, eating peach ice cream.

THE GARDEN

The Crown Expo Center is a box of concrete best known for hosting gun shows, but on September 9, 2019, the familiar trappings of a Trump rally stretched across the room. The blue banners read "KEEP AMERICA GREAT!" The line had started to form on Saturday, two days before the event. Still, the space wasn't quite full.

He hit on his usual applause lines, although thankfully there was no chanting about sending anyone back this time. Instead he talked about the wall, and he called Elizabeth Warren Pocahontas. *What* he was saying, though, was less important than *where* he was saying it. He was on the doorstep of Fort Bragg, about thirty miles from Bladen County, and forty-five from Robeson County. He was in the urban center of the rural southeastern North Carolina corridor, where the race would be won or lost. He was way out here, telling them that they mattered.

Robeson, especially, was a focus. The Lumbee Tribe leans Democratic, for all the reasons marginalized groups usually tend to lean progressive. But Bishop had promised to be a champion of their quest for full federal recognition. He'd passed a statewide recognition bill while he was a member of the North Carolina Senate. That, and any support Trump could drum up, would give Bishop a decided edge.

As the crowd warmed to Trump, he kept hitting on local issues. He praised farmers and talked about reducing opioid abuse. Then he slipped in something he'd made a talking point everywhere, but here it carried a special meaning.

"A lot of illegal voting going on out there, by the way," he said, and the crowd went nuts.

★ ★ ★

The Last Lie September 10, 2019

Maybe the weasel will go home.
MCCRAE DOWLESS

At 6:27 A.M., three minutes before the polls opened, twenty-seven minutes before sunrise, McCrae Dowless became the first voter at the Old Spaulding-Monroe School polling place. As he waited for the doors to open, looking out across the field toward the dawn in the east, he was surrounded by ghosts.

Three-quarters of a century ago, Black teenage boys took swingblades to tall grass to clear a spot for an African American school here. The school was named for Charles Clinton Spaulding, CC Spaulding, the Black man who was president of North Carolina Mutual Bank in the early twentieth century.

Yes, McCrae Dowless's polling place is an old segregated school named for the man who founded the Durham Committee on Negro Affairs, which laid the seed for the Bladen County Improvement Association, the organization that gave him his start as a political operative and became the enemy he so desperately wanted to defeat.

He was surrounded by the generations of Black people who learned in this school, played football and basketball here, sang in the choir here, before the Court said separate wasn't equal. He was surrounded by the more recent history too, like the incident of 1994, when this was an integrated middle school where little white boys were taking home applications to join the KKK.

He didn't even need to look backward in time to see the ghosts of his life. From that cracked pavement, he could've just looked across the street. Over there was the First Baptist Church of Bladenboro, where William Barber called out for justice for Lennon Lacy in 2014, and where hundreds of people gathered on a winter night in 2018 to tell stories about how they'd been disenfranchised . . . by him.

Instead McCrae Dowless was thinking about grapes.

It was September, after all, and muscadines were ripe. His friends who own Lu Mil Vineyard hire him to help with the harvest each year. The vineyard has acres and acres of the super-sweet grapes, of which they only use a fraction for wine. The rest go to local food stores that turn them into jelly. So on the special Election Day he helped cause, McCrae wanted to vote, then rush over to the vines before sunrise.

Soon news crews learned that he'd been the first person to vote at his precinct, and the same internet that had mocked his GoFundMe now piled on this irony. Nick called McCrae that afternoon, and by that point all he wanted to talk about was the election.

His focus, as it had been for twenty-seven months, was on wishing the worst upon Dan McCready. "I don't think the man's got a shot in hell of winning," McCrae said. Then he admitted that he'd been on the phones again.

"Based on what I'm hearing coming out of Union [County], I predict Bishop will beat him by twenty-five hundred, three thousand votes," he said. "Might be a little more."

"Twenty-five hundred or three thousand votes?" Nick said, making a mental note for later.

"Twenty-five hundred or three thousand votes," McCrae confirmed. "Maybe the weasel will go home."

After all of our time inspecting the election fraud mess of 2018 and the environment that led to it, after hundreds of hours of interviews, after reading through thousands of pages of files and transcripts, we feel confident in saying about Bladen County that none of what you hear is all true, but all of what you hear is somewhat true.

Were ballots taken from voters illegally in Bladen County in 2018? Yes. We know that some low-level workers took ballots.

Was McCrae Dowless actively and knowingly directing them to do that? We don't know. He swears not. The best evidence to support it is in the words of people like Lisa Britt and others who have a history of drug abuse and other criminal offenses and who'd have reasons to give investigators what investigators hope to find.

Did Mark Harris spend campaign money that trickled down to people who illegally collected ballots? Yes. Should Mark Harris have known about that? The district attorney would say no two years later, declining to charge him with any crime. So should he have lost his seat in Washington? He certainly doesn't think so. In fact, his face turns red when he talks about it.

And what of Pat McCrory, the former governor who thrust McCrae into lodging a complaint in 2016, just to carry out McCrory's doomed quest to keep his office? Shouldn't he face some consequence? Not legally. But morally? God yes.

On the other hand, did Dan McCready do anything illegal in the 2018 election? Almost certainly not. In fact, a *New York Times* and *Serial* podcast about Bladen County showed that the Improvement Association was frustrated with McCready for *not* enlisting their services.

But did the Democratic Party that supported him support the growing rot in rural elections? They did send $6,000 to the Bladen Improvement PAC in 2018, the latest in a string of contributions in recent election years that totaled $21,500. Was all that money used to legally take voters to the polls? Perhaps. Did some of it end up in the hands of a woman named Lola Wooten, who floated door to door and was, according to several witnesses, collecting ballots? Probably, but there's no investigation in the works to prove or disprove it.

One thing was for certain on Special Election Day 2019: if arresting McCrae and his workers was supposed to clear everything up, it didn't. And if it was supposed to make people here more confident in the general state of democracy, well, that didn't happen either.

Just ask Pat Melvin. We spoke with him one last time, hours before the special election went final. He was in downtown Elizabethtown, near where his family started their hamburger empire, and he was looking at the Black Votes Matter bus. Founded in Georgia by Cliff Albright and LaTosha Brown, the Black Votes Matter Fund sends the bus to important places at important times in the election season, hoping to increase turnout. Albright said he was partnering with the Bladen Improvement Association to help connect with Black voters in the county. He said that church vans were going out to pick up voters and bring them. That's technically not illegal, unless the voter receives something of monetary value in exchange for getting in the vehicle to be carried to the polling place.

Throughout the day, people told us places where that might be happening. In Robeson County, Dan Bishop's people swore McCready's people were taking voters to the polls on the promise of coupons for five-dollar discounts at McDonald's. In Bladen County, McCrae Dowless was the Election Day Sasquatch, seen everywhere by Democrats, but without visual evidence.

As for Pat Melvin, his words from that September day in 2019 were consistent with the ones people said in the 2018 congressional race, and the 2016 Soil and Water race, and the 2010 sheriff's race. What Melvin said, in some form or fashion, had been said all the way back to when John Spaulding, ancestor of CC Spaulding, was elected as the first Black county commissioner in 1868.

"There's a Black Votes Matter bus here today," Pat Melvin said. "Maybe I'll go out and get us a White Votes Matter bus, and park it right beside 'em."

That night, Dan McCready booked the banquet rooms at the DoubleTree Suites in Charlotte's SouthPark neighborhood, right next to the outdoor concert venue where the Charlotte Symphony holds its summer Pops concert series. It was just a few blocks from where he'd been the previous November. People gathered around television screens. When the initial results posted, they clapped lightly: McCready was up by about 631 votes after early voting.

Bishop's watch party, meanwhile, was in a big room at a light-manufacturing facility in Monroe, with a large American flag hanging behind a lectern, not too far from where Mark Harris said the fateful words just ten months earlier, "Thank God for Bladen and Union Counties."

As night settled in, McCready's lead shrank, then vanished. People in each place clamored to see what precincts were left, looking for signs of a comeback or hammer drop. But people who knew how the district worked, they already knew.

In Robeson County, Bladen's neighbor and the home of the Lumbee Nation, the numbers told the story. Registered Democrats outnumber Republicans four to one in Robeson County—43,061 Democrats to 9,244 Republicans as of that night. McCready won the county, as you'd expect. But only by 281 votes. Barely a percentage point of the 21,000 or so people who voted.

McCready needed to cruise in Robeson to win the district. Behind closed doors at the DoubleTree and at the light-manufacturing facility, the candidates knew it was over.

At 10 P.M., Dan Bishop walked out to stand in front of that American flag. With pyrotechnics shooting sparks into the air all around him, he declared victory.

"I'm going to Washington with clear eyes and a steel spine," Bishop said.

After his speech, he told the crowd to hang tight. He called one number that didn't work, then another. He told the crowd to stick with him. Then he finally got through to someone who told him that the person he was trying to reach wasn't available.

"He'll call me back," Bishop said.

A few minutes later, around 11 P.M., Bishop returned to the stage and held his phone to the bank of mikes.

"I want to let you know that I'm putting on speakerphone the man I just told you is the greatest fighter ever to occupy the White House," he said. "Ladies and gentlemen, Donald Trump."

Trump spoke through the iPhone speaker.

"They had him written off and he didn't stand for it. CNN and MSNBC and all of the fake news, they were gonna have a big night tonight. And Dan handled pressure like the greatest athletes handle pressure. . . . What he did tonight is monumental, the comeback he made and the way he handled the pressure of that was great. It's an honor to be with you. And let me tell you what, we had some time last night. We had some time last night. That was a good indication of what was going to happen."

Bishop told Trump that the reason he won was the president's visit to North Carolina the night before, then he hung up and the audience cheered again.

Twenty miles away, Dan McCready took the stage to applause too. It had been twenty-seven months since Democrats had launched him into the Ninth Congressional District race. He'd become the darling of the national press but had fallen about 2 percentage points short.

"We may not have won this campaign, but that does not mean we were wrong," McCready said. His staffers were wiping away tears. Then he told the crowd he planned to sleep in the next day and take his four children out for ice cream.

That night, Michael was at the McCready rally and went to the hotel bar for a drink after the speech, hoping to catch what was left of the 11 P.M. news shows. The bartender said the last call was at 11.

"Even on the election night?" Michael laughed, then left.

Nick was one county over, packing up after the Bishop rally. He got into his car around midnight, and a few minutes later his phone lit up.

McCrae Dowless.

Nick answered.

"What was the final vote spread?" McCrae asked.

"About forty-one hundred votes," Nick said.

"That's what I told you it would be, wasn't it?" McCrae said.

Nick remembered their conversation from earlier. One of McCrae's many, many personality quirks is that he repeats himself, repeats himself.

So Nick remembered his words clearly: "Twenty-five hundred or three thousand votes," McCrae had said. "Maybe the weasel will go home."

"Yessir," McCrae was saying now. "I told you it was going to be about thirty-five hundred votes."

Nick shook his head and kept quiet.

"Yessir," McCrae said. "Thirty-five hundred votes."

Crossing the city limits, with the Charlotte skyline flaring in front of him and the sandy fields of Bladen County a hundred miles behind him, the reporter said to the flim-flam man, "Bullshit."

EPILOGUE

★ ★ ★

Letter from North Carolina Early 2021

★ ★ ★

Nick's phone buzzed around 7:45 one morning earlier this winter. The caller ID said McCrae Dowless. Nick didn't answer. It was too early for that. But when McCrae called again at 8:30, Nick looked at the date, December 4, 2020, and realized the urgency. It was the two-year anniversary of the day they met, McCrae standing in his driveway tapping on a piece of paper in his breast pocket, saying he had something Nick would want to see.

"You're one of the best friends I have," McCrae was saying now. He says that a lot. Nick always responds that he's a reporter first. But even as he's tried to keep a distance, Nick's grown to like talking to McCrae. The man's deeply flawed and broken. But for someone who could spend a good chunk of the rest of his life in jail, he's still an optimist, like someone who believes he's just one good scratch-off ticket away from glory.

You can't help but wonder what kind of life he's living when he considers a reporter he's only known a few years, one who lives more than a hundred miles away, to be one of his best friends. McCrae calls Nick once every few days now, a slower pace than the daily updates during the 2019 special election, but still enough to keep up with the Bladen County gossip.

On one of Nick's last trips to Bladen, before the pandemic, they sat in a garage next to Dove's barbecue while McCrae talked about an old friend named Snag. A light rain fell. McCrae said he'd seen ol' Snag use a switchblade once to cut a person who'd crossed him. He told Snag he knew then he wanted to stay on Snag's good side. Snag laughed and said he'd never hurt McCrae.

But, McCrae said, "I always kept an eye on him."

He seems willfully, gleefully unaware that people do the same with him.

McCrae's been indicted three times in the past two years: twice by a state grand jury on charges related to election fraud stemming from the 2016 and 2018 elections, and once by the feds for charges he scammed the unemployment system by working for Mark Harris. But as we write this, punishment is hardly imminent. As of that December 2020 phone call, McCrae hadn't made even a first appearance in federal court. And it'd been more than a year since he pleaded not guilty to the state charges. He rarely hears from his court-appointed lawyer. If anyone thought McCrae's crimes were so egregious, his guilt so clear, that he'd receive swift justice, they were wrong.

The public is convinced. He's become a meme for election tampering. Each time President Trump railed about fraud from Democrats during the 2020 election cycle, commenters replied with a McCrae photo and a reminder that he worked for Republicans.

In November 2020, McCrae was soundly defeated in his bid for a third term on the Soil and Water Conservation Board, winning only 18 percent of the vote. Still, McCrae looked at the number of people who voted for him, 2,656, and smiled. "I think I've done pretty good," he told Nick. "You can't say too many people who've gone through what I have in the past few years would be able to get so many people to still support him."

One of his closest allies, cousin Daniel Dowless, lost his race for county commission. Ray Britt won, though, somehow.

Still, McCrae sounds more defeated now than ever before. He's received the only sentence that could actually hurt him—no politician will hire him again. The precinct maps on his walls now have no purpose. His two decades of knowledge are now useless.

"They'll never take away what I know about how to win an election," he says.

The stench from 2018 nearly cost Michael Cogdell his job, too. Cogdell, a primary player in the Bladen Improvement Association, finished third in an at-large competition in which the top three claim seats. He was just eleven votes away from losing his seat and was bested by another Black candidate, Mark Gillespie, who launched a campaign outside of the Improvement Association.

The close finish is a clear example of why McCrae Dowless and the Improvement Association scratched the voting rolls raw for all those elections. Fact is, had McCrae been involved in the 2020 cycle, Michael Cogdell would probably have lost his job.

There've been no further investigations into the Bladen Improvement Association, even though a witness testified against them in the hearings.

Lawson, the elections board attorney who plays things fairly down-the-middle, has some regrets over that. He says the witness who claimed the PAC took her ballot actually wanted to withdraw her testimony the day after she gave it. "She went back home and people reached out to her mother, is my understanding," Lawson told us. "Her mother. This is like, as the hearings process, she testifies, I think on the first day of the hearing. By the second night of the hearing, we got word that she now wanted to recant all of her testimony and say she misremembered everything."

Zoe Chace's podcast *The Improvement Association* looked closely at the PAC and its leaders. Several of them expressed frustration on the show that Dan McCready didn't want to contract with them during the special election of 2019. McCready reached out to Michael and the two sat down for coffee outside his home in Charlotte. McCready had spent most of 2020 in Montana with his family, trying to set his mind right after the long election process. He'd been working on his own book, too, about how it all looked from his vantage point. The process wounded his idealism and left him as frustrated with Democrats as it did with Republicans.

Mark Harris took a pastorship at a Baptist church in Mooresville, North Carolina, a Charlotte suburb on Lake Norman known mostly for its big houses and NASCAR drivers. He still watches politics and wonders whether he can bounce back. He loved the brief taste of Congress. He still considers himself a victim. If only he hadn't trusted the locals who steered him to hire McCrae. If only the state board of elections had alerted him that they had open investigations into election fraud in Bladen County. If only he'd said something different on the witness stand that day in February 2019. If only he and Beth had called lawyers sooner. If only the Republican Party would've stood up for them. If only they'd fought more. If only he'd run in the special election.

If only he'd listened to his son.

"We regret giving up," Beth told us in June 2020. "But one of the factors in giving up was, this is, this is all revolving around our children. What is God trying to say to us? Is he trying to say, 'Get out. You don't, you don't have any business in this. This is hurting your family. This is bad.'"

Mark and Beth still can't decide what they think of McCrae. They're actually hoping for a trial, to see more evidence. They still believe investigators have hidden things from them.

"Like, was he really running a large-scale paid ballot operation?" Beth asked us.

"What does your gut tell you? Is he a con man or mostly innocent?" Michael replied.

Beth shrugged and Mark spoke.

"We don't trust our guts anymore," he said. "Honestly, I don't trust my gut anymore. In so many ways it has, it has ripped me apart. You know?"

Around the time of that interview, in June 2020, Black Lives Matter protests swept the nation in response to the murder of George Floyd. Each city in North Carolina had demonstrations.

In Raleigh, the descendants of Josephus Daniels ordered that a statue of the man be taken down. They'd long since apologized for his actions and turned the *News & Observer* into a progressive voice for the state, beginning with the civil rights movement of the 1960s. But this was the most public apology for the ruthless role their ancestor played in destroying a generation of Black prosperity in eastern North Carolina.

In Wilmington, the site of the brutal 1898 massacre Daniels helped incite, racial problems persist. In the days following the Floyd killing, a Wilmington police officer was caught on tape saying that he was ready for a civil war. "We are just gonna go out and start slaughtering them fucking n——rs. I can't wait. God I can't wait." The officer was promptly fired, and that night, the city ordered the removal of two Confederate statues in downtown.

Bladen County participated in the demonstrations too. During a march in Elizabethtown on June 1, 2020, right there on Martin Luther King Jr. Avenue, Sheriff Jim McVicker walked up to the line of protesters while they kneeled, and joined them. "I'm really encouraged about the police, the sheriff. I'm proud of him," a local woman named Asante Jones, who is Black, told the *Bladen Journal*. "I think that's awesome that they're out here to help us, to try to get things right. Especially around here in this county. Because we need help here."

That march resembled those that happened all across America. Protesters chanted all the familiar names—George Floyd, Breonna Taylor, Ahmaud Arbery. But here they also shouted a name that was personal, one that wasn't likely to be heard in any other city or town in the United States.

"Say his name," they chanted.

"Lennon Lacy."

That same year, PBS released a documentary on Lacy called *Always in Season*. It opens with the 911 call from the waitress who found Lacy hanging from a swing set, and from there its story is an indictment of faith and trust in rural America. Lennon's mother and brother are almost certain he was murdered. And they're definitely certain that police didn't care enough to try to investigate the homicide.

Almost to a person, Black people in Bladen County believe that too. They don't trust the local police departments, and certainly not McVicker. It'll take a lot more than one knee at a BLM march to change that; distrust here runs deeper. Roslyn Burden, a Black Bladenboro resident, put it concisely in the Lacy documentary: "We all have our skeletons, but honey, Bladenboro got skeletons that if you open the door they will scare you to death. Some things you see, you keep them to yourself, and you'll live longer."

On a 100-degree afternoon in September 2020, the president of the United States visited Wilmington and stood against the backdrop of the battleship *North Carolina*, a ship that Japanese radio reported sunk six times during World War II. It never actually sank, though. An *Our State* magazine writer once wrote it like this: "The Japanese hoped that saying something enough makes it come true."

So anyway, the president was next to that ship that was reported sunk but always has been above water, and he was saying absentee ballots weren't safe. This would be a significant thing if it were true. Especially in a state that had at that point had more than 1 million absentee ballot requests out of 7.1 million total registered voters.

"[People] will vote and then they are going to have to check their vote by going to the poll and voting that way because if it tabulates then they won't be able to do that," Trump told WECT. "So let them send it in and let them go vote. And if the system is as good as they say it is, then they obviously won't be able to vote [at the polls]. If it isn't tabulated, they will be able to vote."

In other words, the president encouraged people to test the system by trying to vote twice. It was an outrageous thing to promote, and it launched an outrageous presidential election.

But as we listened to it, we recalled the stories from the 2010 sheriff's race in Bladen County. On the first day of early voting in the primary that April, remember, Dr. Delilah Blanks cast a ballot at her polling place in the eastern corner of the county. Then a few days later she drove about thirty miles across the county to the main library and asked to vote there. The system worked; she was denied.

When the story got out that a powerful county commissioner tried to vote twice, Blanks told the *Bladen Journal* that she was "testing the system." But Blanks got down to a deeper reason to check ballots in this part of the country. She told the paper she went to investigate "voting problems for young Black voters." And she said, "It's my duty to do it."

It's often said that Donald Trump was a symptom, not a cause, of America's troubles. And if you know the story of eastern North Carolina, you'll better understand what that means. He didn't invent claims that people voted in nursing homes. He didn't invent the idea of ballot-collection programs. The falsehoods he spread throughout the 2020 election cycle, and after his loss, connected with his audience not because he was telling them something new but because he was telling them things they'd heard for years. He took their suspicions and turned them into rage.

In the prologue of her Serial Productions / *New York Times* podcast *The Improvement Association*, reporter Zoe Chace succinctly frames the story of the Ninth District and its role in the larger story of eroding confidence in U.S. elections: "Democrats like to talk about this scandal because it's Republicans who did it. Republicans like talking about this scandal without talking about who did it because it proves election fraud is real. It can happen. I like talking about this scandal because there's a story behind it that most people don't know, and it helps explain how we got here—'here' being how we, the United States, have become nearly undone by endless accusations of fraud and stolen elections."

For sure, in the weeks leading up to the podcast's debut in March 2021, the country's airwaves and front pages were consumed by debate over voter laws. Throughout the first few months of 2021, Republican-controlled state legislatures gave credence to Trump's wild assertions that the presidential election was "stolen" by rolling out election reform bills in statehouses far from Washington.

The most polarizing bill was signed into law by Georgia governor Brian Kemp. Depending on who you talked to, the law either protected and strengthened voting access or implemented changes aimed at eroding the minority vote. By any measure, the new law cut down on how much time voters had to request an absentee ballot and implemented new identification requirements for voting by mail. It also transferred some power over elections from county officials and the Georgia secretary of state to lawmakers.

New president Joe Biden called it "the Jim Crow of the twenty-first century." Republicans countered by saying the laws made elections more secure.

The election reform bills were in direct response to Trump's unproven claims of fraud in the 2020 presidential election, which followed the same script as former North Carolina governor Pat McCrory's claims in 2016: raise doubt and hope proof of fraud follows. And if it doesn't, never bother to go back and erase that doubt from your supporters' minds.

Marc Elias, the election lawyer from D.C. who represented Dan Mc-Cready in the aftermath of the 2018 campaign, spent nearly every day of early 2021 tweeting and talking on cable TV about the wave of new bills.

What nobody talked about, however, was what, if any, effect these new restrictions would have on people like McCrae Dowless and Horace Munn, people looking to gain political power and influence through small-town political operations.

Today, even after 2018 provided the country with a clear outline of how election fraud happens, most reform laws target individual voters, not voting operations. As for pundits, the debate remains mired in questions of good and evil, about which party is the sinner and which is the saint. But Bladen County showed us how those arguments prevent us from having a more meaningful dialogue about systems that lead to fraud, and the operations that remain intact.

On January 6, 2021, as we wrote some of the last pages of this book, a bus with forty people from North Carolina traveled up Interstate 95 to participate in a "Stop the Steal" rally in Washington.

The events of that day were the hard-boiled egg pulled from the pot of distrust bubbling in America. The country's polarization started before the Trump era, for sure, but was no doubt inflamed by it. The rage Trump built up now resulted in a full-fledged coup attempt that resembled Wilmington in 1898, with waves of white people carrying Confederate flags in an attempted takeover of the U.S. Capitol.

And it's entirely possible that some of the people involved were descendants of the 1898 coup.

One of the leaders of the group from North Carolina, listed as "Person Three" in a federal indictment, was armed, according to text messages sent between the rally's organizers. One national organizer whose text messages have been unsealed wrote, "Oathkeeper friends from North Carolina are taking commercial buses up early in the morning on the 6th and back the same night." Later she referred specifically to Person Three: "[He] is committed to being the quick reaction force [and is] bringing the tools if something goes to hell. [He] will have the goodies in case things go bad and we need to get heavy."

In the two years between the 2018 and 2020 elections, there were two politics-adjacent stories that mattered in Bladen and Columbus Counties in southeastern North Carolina: the election fraud fiasco that overturned the congressional race, and the growth of a budding group of Oath Keepers. The Oath Keepers movement was apparently the natural evolution of political operations after the 2018 scandal. It made ballot harvesting seem innocent.

The group trained in the woods of Columbus County, just across the Bladen line, not far from the land that's still in the Spaulding family, not far from where George Henry White was born. Here, in this part of the country where the population grows smaller each year, the Oath Keepers could blow up military-grade explosives without disrupting much. They had friends in law enforcement. The Columbus County sheriff was a member of their Facebook group.

The area became a national training ground for the Oath Keepers. A federal indictment revealed that several leaders of the attack on the Capitol had been to North Carolina in the months after the election to sharpen their skills. It gives us chills to think that these training grounds are the same swamps where rest the souls of countless unidentified Black people who fled Wilmington in 1898, the same swamps where, as George Henry White said, "many died from exposure, privation, and disease contracted while exposed to the merciless weather."

The indictment that revealed the connections between eastern North Carolina and the Washington insurrection was released on Wednesday, January 26, 2021. Two days later, on Friday, January 28, McCrae Dowless finally appeared in federal court on charges that he defrauded the Social Security Administration by hiding more than $100,000 of income earned during the 2018 election.

He pleaded not guilty.

ACKNOWLEDGMENTS

★ ★ ★

We'd been friends for a few years before the events of the 2018 election cycle transpired, but when we ran into each other outside of the Elizabethtown courthouse on the chilly evening of Tuesday, December 4, we'd never discussed collaborating on any project, let alone a book.

The idea came a few months later while we were sitting in camping chairs and having beers in the yet-to-be-furnished house Michael's brother, Kenny, was moving into. So we suppose we should start our acknowledgments there. Thanks for having us over for a beer, Kenny.

Authors, for some reason, often save their families for last in the acknowledgments. But nobody sacrificed more for this book than ours.

Sarah Blake Morgan is Nick's biggest supporter. In addition to enduring incessant chatter about Bladen County and election law, Sarah was a sounding board, often giving new ideas and feedback that helped make this book great.

And in the Graff house, Laura Graff gave birth to George Nevitt Graff on March 6, 2020, six months before this manuscript was due to our editors. She sacrificed sleep, friendships, and family gatherings to help make this book possible.

The process of writing this book inspired lots of sniffles and laughs and rolled eyes and headshakes from the people who love us most, and we wouldn't want it any other way.

Outside of them, we'd like to start by sending gratitude to the people of Bladen County. They were warm and welcoming and trusted us to be fair to their story and their home, despite decades of reasons not to trust people from the outside.

Josh Lawson and Pat Gannon have long set the standard for openness and transparency on behalf of the North Carolina State Board of Elections. Pat, who still works at the board, is a true professional who always does what he can to answer a question or produce a document, even if he doesn't always agree with the story.

Elaine Quijano of CBS News and the producers and bookers at CBSN helped Nick realize the story he was covering in Bladen County had national interest, which, in turn, helped spark the realization that maybe he should write a book.

Cindy Singletary is the quintessential southern small-town lawyer. She was instrumental in helping us navigate the people and places of Bladen County. If you're ever in Bladenboro, stop by her beautiful home and hope she has a fresh batch of ham rolls made up.

Thanks to Zoe Chace from *This American Life* for treating the people of Bladen County with dignity and care in her *Serial* series. Zoe was most kind to us, too, even as we pursued some of the same information and interviews.

We also each had mentors and friends who supported us to this point.

Nick's interest in journalism started his sophomore year of high school in Mr. Brian O'Neal's journalism class alongside classmate Chelsea Farelli, and it grew the following year in Mrs. Jennifer Czechowski's class alongside fellow students Paige Allmendinger and Caroline Thomas. Nobody knew it then, but that group planted the seeds for Nick to become an ornery journalist. Dr. Rich Landesberg played a key role in sparking Nick's passion for journalism at Elon University. No educator has had a bigger influence on Nick than Mrs. Nicole Jenkins, who remains a cherished friend and cheerleader nearly two decades after Nick first stepped into her class.

The good folks who have led WBTV—Scott Dempsey, Dennis Milligan, Kim Saxon, Molly Kelleher Dutton, and Mark Davenport, among many others—supported Nick's work and never shot down another story in Bladen County. Colleagues David Hodges and Corey Schmidt were always along for the ride, even when it got messy. Legendary newsmen Steve Crump and John Carter frequently lent Nick their considerable knowledge of North Carolina politics and history. Anchors Molly Grantham, Jamie Boll, and Maureen O'Boyle helped steer the ship.

Nick would also like to thank a number of friends and family who have lent an ear or sparked an idea as he worked on this book: Donald and Ruby Morgan, Drew Smith, James McClelland, Kourtney Hindman, Lyndsay Booth, Dan Glass, Michael Weisel, Dale Folwell, Matt Bales, Ray Martin, Mike Tadych, Lucille Sherman-Shockley, Ben and Lyndsay Williamson, Travis and Susanna Riley, Al Drago, Rob Tufano, Christy Steen, Ann Wyatt Little, Jay and Jan Gothard, Lauren Miller, Lacey Whidden, Mike Lano, Sam Pitts, Bud Harrelson, Brett Warner, Cameron Bowe, Seth Asbill, and Chris Nichols.

Michael would like to thank the two high school English teachers who told him he should pick a career other than writing—and the one college teacher, Mr. Michael Gaspeny, who did the exact opposite. Geeves, you're always MG1, and we're grateful.

Thanks also to Michael's colleagues at Axios Charlotte, particularly editorial team members Brianna Crane, Paige Hopkins, Katie Peralta Soloff, Emma Way, and Symphony Webber, for supporting him when he had to take time off for the book. And to Ted Williams, for constantly asking when it would be out.

To a string of colleagues, friends, and mentors who continue to inspire and motivate Michael, many of whom endured an earful about this book along the way: Greg Barnes, Sammy Batten, Jamie and Logan Cyrus, Brian and Lauren Castleberry, Kim Cross, Cristina Daglas, Bronwen Dickey, Kerry and Travis Dove, John T. Edge, Josh Ellis, Alix Felsing and Tommy Tomlinson, James Ford, Garrett Graff, Maxwell George, George Getschow, Brantley Hargrove, Eva Holland, Amanda and

Justin Heckert, Leigh Ann Henion, Scott Huler, Chris Jones, Greg Lacour, Thomas Lake, Brooke Jarvis, Greg Jackson, Lauren and Michael Kruse, Jeremy Markovich, Jen and Jim McGivney, Ben Montgomery, Michael Mooney, Tiff and Chris Mottram, JK Nickell, Brad Pearson, Katie Peralta Soloff, Jessica Reed, Tony Rehagen, Adam Rhew, Toussaint Romain, Melanie Sill, Andy and Sara Smith, Glenn Smith, Glenn Stout, Rick Thurmond, Matt Tullis, Don Van Natta, Kristen and Jon Wile, and Denise Wills.

Thanks to Bill Duryea, for assigning Michael to the Bladen County story in the first place. And to Luke Alexander, for always answering the call to explain the history.

Thanks to the other journalists and people who covered and helped push this story, including Joe Bruno, Michael Bitzer, and Amy Gardner.

Thanks to David Patterson and Aemelia Phillips from Stuart Krichevsky Literary Agency, who always saw something bigger in this small-town story. And to freelance transcriptionist Meagan Lynn, for noting every detail.

Thanks to all of the good people at UNC Press, especially editor Brandon Proia for his sharp touch and thoughtful notes.

We're also deeply in debt to the DoubleTree hotel in Fayetteville for always granting us two cookies apiece.

And to the barking mutts who came along for the writing trips, Murrow and Zara Ochsner and Gizmo Graff, for being very good dogs. Nick once took Murrow along on a trip to meet McCrae Dowless, who observed that Murrow was very well behaved.

And of course, thanks to Brigid Morgan and Sharon Houston for being the best mothers-in-law we could ask for—and for lending us a mountain cabin and a beach house to help complete this project.

And to Michael's mother, Patrice, who lives just forty-five miles east of Bladen County and whose home provided refuge on several reporting trips. And to Nick's mom, Ann, who unexpectedly housed him in Raleigh for the first impromptu week of his journeying back and forth to Bladen County in early December 2018.

And to our late fathers, Sergeant First Class Jim Ochsner and charter boat cap'n Fred Graff, who would be proud.

A NOTE ON SOURCES

This book started with conversations with people in Bladen County, and it ends with them. But it is by no means the last word on the Ninth District race—the people of Bladen County have much more to say, and this book certainly doesn't represent the thoughts and values and feelings of every last resident.

Much of our reporting was done face to face or on the phone, beginning in early December 2018, when we were assigned to cover the contested election results for two different media outlets.

Writing this book wouldn't have been possible without copious interviews with McCrae Dowless, and so it is worth elaborating on how, given his reputation and history as an unreliable fraudster, we approached such a complex figure as a key source. Because Nick talked with McCrae on the phone almost daily—sometimes several times a day—we made the decision early on that Nick would play a prominent role as a character in the book. But Nick did not process McCrae's claims and stories on his own: Michael served as a third-party witness to Nick's conversations with McCrae. After most of his phone calls with McCrae, Nick would immediately call Michael. Michael would then informally interview Nick about the conversation and take notes. We compared our notes on the McCrae conversations during the writing of this book.

Over the course of a year or so, we also conducted a series of recorded interviews with McCrae in his office and at his home. McCrae hated the recording device and was only half-fond of Michael. McCrae and Michael never talked in any setting that wasn't on the record.

In these McCrae interviews, as elsewhere, we aimed for transparency and relied on each other to check our blind spots and biases. That principle held not only in the McCrae interviews but in all of our interviews, including recorded conversations with Daniel Dowless, Pat Melvin, Irv Joyner, Delilah Blanks, Josh Lawson, Michael Cogdell, Mark and Beth Harris, Cindy Singletary, Harold Ford, Lisa Britt, Luke Alexander, and a handful of others.

"What'd you think?" we'd say to each other after each interview, and most often we had different opinions about it. Sometimes we'd debate the merits of a person's words. Even more frequently we'd debate their intent. And always we wondered, Why would someone say the thing they said . . . to us?

Those smaller conversations helped us reach the same conclusion about the big picture, that what happened in the Ninth District race in 2018 was a systemic failure rather than isolated wickedness.

We believe that conclusion is supported by our reporting, which draws on interviews, public records, criminal discovery files never before released, books, and social media posts.

We hope it's clear throughout the book that different people have different lenses for the same events. By now those people believe their side of the story is written-in-stone fact, even if it's only written in their mind.

We've also relied on newspapers, magazines, and other sources, especially for historical information. You'll see below that we have a source for each sentence and took no leaps for the sake of the story. But doing research in the year of COVID-19 was no simple task. We're grateful to the *Fayetteville Observer* for allowing us access to their trove of archives, both digital and physical. And to the Bladen County Library in Elizabethtown for permitting us to use the Wanda Campbell Room. And to our Newspapers.com subscription, without which this book would not have been possible. In the historical portions of the book—most of part 2—we made our best efforts to verify facts and details through the original sources and records. In a few spots we relied on secondary sources such as modern books from diligent journalists.

In other words, everything that happened in this book is true.

Where a quote appears, it either was told to us in an interview, was said in an official hearing transcribed by a court reporter, or appears in an official document. We're immensely grateful for freelance transcriptionist Meagan Lynn, who made note of every "uh" and "um" while navigating the most eclectic mix of southern accents.

For all the ways we are different and approached this work in different ways, we've always been guided by the same core principle, which is that this true story of Bladen County is more interesting than anything we could imagine or dream up.

With that, in the following pages is a selected bibliography of the sources we used, in case you want to look anything up yourself.

SELECTED BIBLIOGRAPHY

This list includes many of the sources of information we consulted in writing this book. While we took every effort to include all published works, it's far from an exhaustive list of everything we read or every person we talked to. Also, not everything we used in our reporting is accessible to members of the general public, including the criminal discovery files compiled by the N.C. State Bureau of Investigation, which we obtained in the course of our reporting. We also relied, generally, on the *Bladen Journal* and bladenonline.com's coverage of the 2010 and 2016 elections, but we do not list each story here.

We hope this selected bibliography is convenient and helpful for those who wish to study the story and the rich and complex history of Bladen County.

Interviews
Luke Alexander
Delilah Blanks
Lisa Britt
Bernard Brunson
Michael Cogdell
Daniel Dowless
Harold Ford
Mark and Beth Harris
Irv Joyner
Josh Lawson
Pat Melvin
Cindy Singletary

Books

Bradley, Mark. *Bluecoats and Tar Heels: Soldiers and Civilians in Reconstruction North Carolina*. Lexington: University Press of Kentucky, 2009.

Bridgers, John Luther, and Joseph Kelly Turner. *History of Edgecombe County, North Carolina*. Raleigh, N.C.: Edwards & Broughton Printing Co., 1920.

Brundage, W. Fitzhugh, ed. *Where These Memories Grow: History, Memory and Southern Identity*. Chapel Hill: University of North Carolina Press, 2000.

Craig, Lee A. *Josephus Daniels: His Life and Times.* Chapel Hill: University of North Carolina Press, 2013.

Justesen, Benjamin R. *George Henry White: An Even Chance in the Race of Life.* Baton Rouge: Louisiana State University Press, 2012.

Link, William A. *Righteous Warrior: Jesse Helms and the Rise of Modern Conservatism.* New York: St. Martin's Press, 2008.

Owen, Guy. *The Ballad of the Flim-Flam Man.* Wilmington, N.C.: Coastal Carolina Press, 1965.

Slap, Andrew L. *The Doom of Reconstruction: The Liberal Republicans in the Civil War Era.* New York: Fordham University Press, 2010.

Waddell, Alfred M. *An Address Delivered to the Colored People by Their Request at the Wilmington Theatre, July 26, 1865.* Wilmington, N.C.: Daily Wilmington Herald Office, 1865. https://archive.org/details/addressdeliveredoowadd /page/n5/mode/2up.

Zucchino, David. *Wilmington's Lie: The Murderous Coup of 1898 and the Rise of White Supremacy.* New York: Atlantic Monthly Press, 2020.

Government Documents

"Congressional District 9 Portal: Evidentiary Hearing Transcripts." North Carolina State Board of Elections. February 18–21, 2019. https://dl.ncsbe .gov/?prefix=State_Board_Meeting_Docs/Congressional_District_9_Portal.

"Letter of the Secretary of War." Court-martial records of E. W. Andrews and others. *Senate Executive Documents*, 39th Congress, 1st Session. Washington, D.C.: Government Printing Office, 1866.

North Carolina land grant files for Niell McGill, 1693–1960. Ancestry.com, https://www.ancestry.com/imageviewer/collections/60621 /images/44173_349225-01207.

North Carolina State Board of Elections and Ethics Enforcement. *Exhibit 2.2.2.1 in re: Investigation of Election Irregularities Affecting Congressional District 9.* Reports presented at evidentiary hearing on the Ninth Congressional District 2018 election results, February 18–21, 2019. https://s3.amazonaws.com /dl.ncsbe.gov/State_Board_Meeting_Docs/Congressional_District_9 _Portal/2.2.2.1%20Exhibit.pdf.

ReBuild NC. *Hurricane Matthew Resilient Redevelopment Plan—Bladen County.* May 2017. https://files.nc.gov/rebuildnc/documents/matthew/rebuildnc _bladen_plan_combined.pdf.

Strong, John M. *North Carolina Reports: Cases Argued and Determined in the Supreme Court of North Carolina.* Vol. 239, *Fall Term, 1953; Spring Term, 1954.* Raleigh, N.C.: Bynum Printing Company, 1954. *State v. Grayson.*

United States Department of Justice. U.S. Attorney's Office, Eastern District of North Carolina. "Nineteen Foreign Nationals Charged for Voting in 2016

Election." Press release. August 24, 2018. https://www.justice.gov/usao-ednc/
pr/nineteen-foreign-nationals-charged-voting-2016-election.

News Articles

1850–1859
"Twenty Dollars Reward." *Wilmington (N.C.) Journal*, December 20, 1850.

1860–1869
"Bladen County Democratic Township Meeting: Elizabethtown." *Wilmington
    (N.C.) Weekly Star*, August 20, 1880.
"The Escape." *Wilmington Daily Journal*, February 24, 1866.
"For the Standard: Bladen County Republican Convention." *Daily Standard*
    (Raleigh, N.C.), March 26, 1868.
"The Present." *Wilmington (N.C.) Journal*, November 11, 1868.
"The Result." *Wilmington (N.C.) Journal*, November 6, 1868.
"The Result." *Wilmington (N.C.) Post*, November 5, 1868.
"The Sykes Murder Case! Argument of Mr. Waddell on the Merits of the Case."
    Wilmington (N.C.) Daily Dispatch, October 26, 1865.
"The Views of a Radical: Correspondence between Alfred M. Waddell and the
    Hon. W. D. Kelley." *Wilmington (N.C.) Journal*, May 3, 1866.

1890–1899
Brief with a dateline "Raleigh, Sept. 11." *Sampson (N.C.) Democrat*,
    September 17, 1896.
"Fusion Is Effected." *Charlotte (N.C.) Observer*, August 31, 1894.
"Home Folks." *Wilmington (N.C.) Messenger*, November 13, 1898.
"Hon. George H. White, LL. D., the Only Colored Representative in the
    Fifty-Fifth Congress." *Gazette* (Raleigh, N.C.), June 12, 1894.
"Insulting His Own Race." *Wilmington (N.C.) Morning Star*, October 23,
    1898.
"Mrs. Felton Speaks: She Makes a Sensational Speech before Agriculture
    Society." *Wilmington (N.C.) Morning Star*, August 18, 1898.
"North Carolina's Negroes; Offices which They Hold in Several Counties of the
    State." *New York Times*, November 6, 1898. https://www.nytimes
    .com/1898/11/06/archives/north-carolinas-negroes-offices-which-they
    -hold-in-several-counties.html.
"The Republican Convention." *News & Observer* (Raleigh, N.C.),
    July 21, 1898.
"Sizzling Talk: Most Remarkable Speech by the Hon. A. M. Waddell." *Wilmington
    (N.C.) Messenger*, October 25, 1898.
"State Press." *Wilmington (N.C.) Semi-Weekly Messenger*, October 5, 1897.

"What Will You Be? Today White Men of North Carolina Must Declare Where They Stand." *Wilmington (N.C.) Messenger*, November 8, 1898.

"White Man's Ticket." *Wilmington (N.C.) Morning Star*, November 8, 1898.

1900–1909

Daniels, Josephus. "How It Works in the Black Belt: Amendment Leaves No Necessity or Excuse for Fraud or Force. Honest and Peaceful Elections Secured." *News & Observer* (Raleigh, N.C.), May 16, 1900.

"Latest Election News." *Wilmington (N.C.) Messenger*, August 4, 1900.

"Southern Negro's Plaint; Congressman G. H. White Forced to Leave North Carolina. Will Not Re-Enter Congress. Wife a Physical Wreck Owing to Attacks – Advises Negroes to Migrate West." *New York Times*, August 26, 1900. https://www.nytimes.com/1900/08/26/archives/southern-negros-plaint -congressman-gh-white-forced-to-leave-north.html.

"Under the Dome." *News & Observer* (Raleigh, N.C.), March 5, 1901.

1950–1959

"Boy, 17, Slain by Two Cops in Lagrange Break-In Try." *News & Observer* (Raleigh, N.C.), January 11, 1951.

"Milton White's Daughter Drowns at Elizabethtown." *News & Observer* (Raleigh, N.C.), September 21, 1955.

"Negro Confesses He Killed and Raped Woman in Bladen." *News & Observer* (Raleigh, N.C.), September 15, 1952.

"Patrolmen Will Protect Man during Bladen Murder Trial." *News & Observer* (Raleigh, N.C.), November 16, 1952.

"The People's Forum: Protest." Letter to the editor. *News & Observer* (Raleigh, N.C.), January 15, 1951.

"Supreme Court Grants New Trial to Bladen Rapist-Killer." *News & Observer* (Raleigh, N.C.), February 25, 1954.

1970–1979

"Elizabethtown Fires Investigated." *News & Observer* (Raleigh, N.C.), April 28, 1971.

"Unknown Gunman Kills 1, Wounds 6 outside Tavern." *News & Observer* (Raleigh, N.C.), April 27, 1971.

1980–1989

"Blacks Win Bladen Seats." *Fayetteville (N.C.) Observer*, June 1, 1988.

"Bladen Adopts Controversial Election Plan." *Fayetteville (N.C.) Times*, August 21, 1987.

"Bladen Blacks File Lawsuit over Elections." *Fayetteville (N.C.) Times*, July 30, 1987.

"Bladen Changes Sought." *Fayetteville (N.C.) Times*, February 4, 1986.

"Bladen Panel to Study Vote Districting." *Fayetteville (N.C.) Times*, July 8, 1986.

"Bladen Picks Voting Districts; Blacks Vow Challenge." *Fayetteville (N.C.) Times*, April 14, 1987.

1990–1999

"Klan Rallies in Bladenboro; Many Sing Out in Protest." *Fayetteville (N.C.) Observer-Times*, December 19, 1994.

"Placement at Issue in Book Controversy." *Fayetteville (N.C.) Observer*, March 17, 1993.

"Teacher Denies Distributing KKK Literature." *Fayetteville (N.C.) Observer*, December 7, 1994.

2000–2009

Tyson, Timothy B. "The Ghosts of 1898: Wilmington's Race Riot and the Rise of White Supremacy." *News & Observer* (Raleigh, N.C.), November 17, 2006. http://media2.newsobserver.com/content/media/2010/5/3/ghostsof1898.pdf.

2010–2019

Barnes, Greg. "Bladen Sheriff Part of Investigation into Election Fraud." *Fayetteville (N.C.) Observer*, December 12, 2019. https://www.fayobserver.com/news/20181219/bladen-sheriff-part-of-investigation-into-alleged-election-fraud.

Brockell, Gillian. "There Have Been Thousands of Lynching Victims in the U.S. Trump Isn't One of Them." *Washington Post*, October 22, 2019. https://www.washingtonpost.com/history/2019/10/22/more-than-people-have-been-lynched-us-trump-isnt-one-them/.

Bruni, Frank. "A Patriot's Guide to Election Fraud." *New York Times*, March 26, 2019. https://www.nytimes.com/2019/03/26/opinion/mccready-north-carolina-fraud.html.

Bruno, Joe. "Channel 9 Uncovers Similarities between Absentee Ballots in U.S. House District 9 Race." WSOC, December 4, 2018. https://www.wsoctv.com/news/local/channel-9-uncovers-similarities-between-absentee-ballots-in-us-house-district-9-race/882660808/.

"DA Office Ousted from Bladen Gaming Case." *Bladen Journal* (Elizabethtown, N.C.), January 14, 2016.

Drago, Al. "Check Out New Members of Congress Picking Their Offices through a Lottery." *Bloomberg News*, November 30, 2018. https://www.bloomberg.com/news/photo-essays/2018-11-30/check-out-new-members-of-congress-pick-their-office-through-a-lottery.

"Dan McCready Concedes District 9 Race to Mark Harris." WBTV, November 6, 2018. https://www.wbtv.com/2018/11/07/harris-mccready-take-nc-district-race-down-wire/.

"Dan McCready Concedes 9th District Race." WFAE, November 7, 2018. https://www.wfae.org/politics/2018-11-07/dan-mccready-concedes-9th-district-race.

Fain, Travis. "Bladen Town Hall Sparks Passion over 9th District Results, Little Evidence of Fraud." WRAL, December 19, 2018. https://www.wral.com/bladen-town-hall-sparks-passion-over-9th-district-results-little-new-evidence-of-fraud/18073737/.

"FBI to Probe Bladenboro Teen's Death as Questions Swirl and NAACP Organizes March." *News & Observer* (Raleigh, N.C.), December 12, 2014.

Futch, Michael. "Cape Fear Profile: Bladen County's Delilah Blanks Has Spent Her Life Fighting for Fairness." *Fayetteville (N.C.) Observer*, January 24, 2015. https://www.fayobserver.com/article/20150124/News/301249794.

Gardner, Amy, and Beth Reinard. "N.C. Elections Board's Warnings to Local and Federal Prosecutors about Alleged Election Fraud Drew Little Action." *Washington Post*, December 21, 2018. https://www.washingtonpost.com/politics/nc-election-officials-sounded-alarm-about-alleged-election-fraud-to-federal-prosecutors-in-january-2017/2018/12/21/240e09a0-0539-11e9-b5df-5d3874f1ac36_story.html.

Gerard, Philip. "River Runaways." *Our State*, August 2011. https://www.ourstate.com/runaway-slaves/.

Graff, Michael. "Hurricane Hazel." *Our State*, August 2012. https://www.ourstate.com/hazel/.

———. "The Story of the Greensboro Four and the Sit-In Movement." *Our State*, February 2011. https://www.ourstate.com/greensboro-four-sit-in-movement/.

———. "The Town Fighting the Climate Crisis to Stay Afloat, One Hurricane at a Time." *Guardian*, June 2019. https://www.theguardian.com/environment/2019/jul/21/fair-bluff-north-carolina-hurricane-aftermath-climate-crisis.

Harrison, Steve. "NC Democratic Party Submits Affidavits of Bladen County Voters Who Claim Wrongdoing." WFAE, November 29, 2018. https://www.wfae.org/politics/2018-11-29/nc-democratic-party-submits-affidavits-of-bladen-county-voters-who-claim-wrongdoing.

Hodges, David. "Bladen Co. Improvement Association President Says He Was Tipped Off about Absentee Ballot Investigation." WBTV, February 26, 2019. https://www.wbtv.com/2019/02/26/bladen-county-improvement-association-president-says-he-was-tipped-off-about-absentee-ballot-investigation/.

———. "Newly Uncovered Document Suggests Bladen Improvement PAC President Collected Absentee ballots." WBTV, December 20, 2018. https://www.wbtv.com/2018/12/20/newly-uncovered-document-suggests-bladen-improvement-pac-president-collected-absentee-ballots/.

"Hurricane Florence: 6 Months Later, by the Numbers." *Bladen Journal* (Elizabethtown, N.C.), March 14, 2019. https://www.bladenjournal.com /news/23291/hurricane-florence-6-months-later-by-the-numbers.

Knopf, Taylor. "Four North Carolina Cities Make Top 25 List for Opioid Abuse." *North Carolina Health News*, July 27, 2017. https://www.northcarolinahealthnews.org/2017/07/27 /four-north-carolina-cities-make-top-25-list-opioid-abuse/.

Kruse, Michael. "Trump's North Carolina Supporters Were Ready to Unload." *Politico*, July 18, 2019. https://www.politico.com/magazine/story/2019 /07/18/donald-trump-north-carolina-rally-227403/.

Maeser, Nadine. "State, Feds Investigate Elections Allegations in Bladen County." WWAY, May 11, 2010. https://www.wwaytv3.com/2010/05/11 /state-feds-invesitgate-elections-allegations-bladen-co/.

Mandel, Kyla. "Early Voter Turnout Is Down." ThinkProgress, October 24, 2018. https://archive.thinkprogress.org/north -carolina-hurricane-florence-early-voting-election-3ce3367681e4/.

"Melvin, Town Continue the Staring Contest." *Bladen Journal* (Elizabethtown, N.C.), August 25, 2015. https://www.bladenjournal.com/opinion/1187 /melvin-towncontinue-thestaring-contest.

Morrill, Jim. "Mark Harris Defends His Comments about Women." *Charlotte (N.C.) Observer*, October 24, 2018. https://www.charlotteobserver.com /article220557210.html.

Murphy, Brian. "Bladen County Election Fraud: McCrae Dowless vs. Jens Lutz." *News & Observer* (Raleigh, N.C.), January 29, 2019.

Newkirk, Vann R., II. "The Battle for North Carolina." *The Atlantic*, October 27, 2016. https://www.theatlantic.com/politics/archive/2016/10 /the-battle-for-north-carolina/501257/.

"911 Call Released in Lennon Lacy Death." WECT, October 14, 2014. https://www .wect.com/story/26809568/911-call-released-in-lennon-lacy-death/.

Ochsner, Nick. "Elections Board: Bladen DA Had 'Undisclosed Apparent Conflict of Interest' When He Sought Investigation Info in '17." WBTV, December 12, 2018. https://www.wbtv.com/2018/12/21/elections-board -bladen-da-had-undisclosed-conflict-interest-when-he-sought-investigation -info/.

———. "Prosecutors Won't File Charges against Harris in NC-9 Probe." WBTV, July 15, 2020. https://www.wbtv.com/2020/07 /15/prosecutor-wont-file-charges-against-harris-nc-probe/.

Ochsner, Nick, and David Hodges. "Democratic Party Chair, Group's Attorney Both Deny Knowledge of PAC Workers Collecting Absentee Ballots." WBTV, December 11, 2018. https://www.wbtv.com/2018/12/11/democratic -party-chair-groups-attorney-both-deny-knowledge-pac-workers -collecting-absentee-ballots/.

Pilkington, Ed. "Teenager's Mysterious Death Evokes Painful Imagery in North Carolina." *Guardian*, October 9, 2014.

Saxton, Scott. "Bladen Sheriff Says Only Way to Remove Him—'Judge or Death.'" WECT, July 6, 2010. https://www.wect.com/story/12762528 /bladen-sheriff-says-only-way-to-remove-him-judge-or-death/.

Smith, Charlotte. "Nail Biting General Election." *BladenOnline.com*, November 7, 2018. https://bladenonline.com/nail-biting-general-election/.

Specht, Paul A. "Affidavit: Election Office Gave Dowless Special Access." *Fayetteville (N.C.) Observer*, December 25, 2018. https://www.fayobserver .com/news/20181225/affidavit-election-office-gave-dowless-special-access.

Tomlinson, Tommy. "Reverend Resistance." *Esquire*, April 26, 2017.

Wagner, Adam. "Study Finds Hurricane Florence Harmed Survivors' Mental Health." *News & Observer* (Raleigh, N.C.), June 21, 2019. https://www .newsobserver.com/news/local/article231788928.html.

Wieland-Stanford, Georgia. "Hurricane Florence Could Impact Midterm Elections." *Daily Tar Heel* (Chapel Hill, N.C.), September 20, 2019. https:// www.dailytarheel.com/article/2018/09/hurricane-florence-voting-0920.

Websites and Online Sources

Benjamin and Edith Spaulding Descendants Association. "Spaulding Family History." 2017. https://www.spauldingfamily.org/history.

Capitol Broadcasting Company. "WRAL News Coverage of Robesonian Newspaper Hostage Siege." Media Assets, History of Capitol Broadcasting Company (website). https://history.capitolbroadcasting.com/media-assets /wral-news-coverage-of-robesonian-newspaper-hostage-siege/.

Howard, Philip. "The Civil War, Ocracoke, and Josephus Daniels." *Village Craftsman*, February 21, 2012. https://www.villagecraftsmen.com /civil-war-ocracoke-josephus-daniels/.

Newspapers.com.

Other Sources

"Address to the Colored People of North Carolina." Broadside in support of Governor William Woods Holden, December 19, 1870. *Documenting the American South*, University Library, University of North Carolina at Chapel Hill. https://docsouth.unc.edu/nc/address/address.html.

Bishir, Catherine. "Landmarks of Power: Building a Southern Past in Raleigh and Wilmington, North Carolina, 1885–1915." In *Where These Memories Grow: History, Memory and Southern Identity*, edited by W. Fitzhugh Brundage, 139–68. Chapel Hill: University of North Carolina Press, 2000.

Bladen Online. "An Interview with Harold Ford." YouTube video, 10:44, March 2, 2018. https://www.youtube.com/watch?v=kLQ_C4iwD28.

Bruno, Joe (@JoeBrunoWSOC). "Breaking – I have obtained 6 sworn affidavits related to the #NC09 investigation. A team of a dozen @wsoctv employees and I working on this. Huge allegations . . ." Twitter, November 29, 2018. https://twitter.com/JoeBrunoWSOC9/status/1068259440023998464.

Cameron, Rebecca. Rebecca Cameron to Alfred Waddell, October 26, 1898. Folder 2b: Papers 1898–1899, collection 00743, Alfred M. Waddell Papers 1768–1935. Southern Historical Collection, Louis Round Wilson Special Collections Library, University of North Carolina at Chapel Hill. https://finding-aids.lib .unc.edu/00743/#folder_2b.

Charlotte Observer. "Democrat Dan McCready Concedes after Tight Race for N.C. Congressional District 9." YouTube video, 3:02, November 7, 2018. https://www.youtube.com/watch?v=kQMCSfxm2dY.

C-SPAN. "Oh God, It's Mom." YouTube video, 2:37, December 16, 2014. https://www.youtube.com/watch?v=Q15xhG6pVUw.

"Dockery and His Supporters." Cartoon. News & Observer (Raleigh, N.C.), August 12, 1898.

"Durham Committee on Negro Affairs." Photograph. Image i020, North Carolina Collection, Durham County Library. Part of "And Justice for All: Durham County Courthouse Art Wall," photographic display in the lobby of the Durham County Courthouse, Durham, N.C., February 2013. http://andjusticeforall.dconc.gov/gallery_images/durham -committee-on-negro-affairs/.

"Good Morning! Have You Voted the White Man's Ticket." Cartoon. News & Observer (Raleigh, N.C.), November 8, 1898.

Harris, Mark (@markharrisnc9). "We were surprised by yesterday's developments at the State Board of Elections, but our legal team is fully engaged. We trust the process. This morning . . ." Twitter, November 28, 2018. https://twitter.com/markharrisnc9/status/1067828642653356032.

Hayden, Harry. "The Story of the Wilmington Rebellion." Booklet. 1936. Folder 41, Box 1, Wilmington Riot of November 10, 1898 Source Documents (SC), William Madison Randall Library Special Collections, University of North Carolina at Wilmington.

Jennet, Norman Ethre. "He Doesn't Like to Let Go." Cartoon. News & Observer (Raleigh, N.C.), May 26, 1900.

Kirn, Walter. Presentation at Mayborn Literary Nonfiction Conference, Grapevine, Texas, July 2019.

McCready, Dan. Interview by Rachel Maddow. The Rachel Maddow Show, MSNBC, December 8, 2018. https://www.facebook.com /watch/?v=207414540144688.

McCready, Dan (@McCreadyforNC). "I was as shocked as anyone to see the State Elections Board, in an unprecedented bipartisan 9-0 decision, delay certification of our election results. Our . . ." Twitter, November 29, 2018. https://twitter.com/McCreadyForNC/status/1068318605278879744.

Olive, Jacqueline, dir. *Always in Season*. Season 21, episode 11, of *Independent Lens*. Aired July 5, 2020, on PBS.

Pearson, Conrad Odell. Audio recording of interview, April 18, 1979. Interview H-0218, Southern Oral History Program Collection, Southern Historical Collection, Wilson Library, University of North Carolina at Chapel Hill.

Postcard of Holiday Inn, downtown Raleigh, 1969. "Raleigh's 'Second Round Building'—the Holiday Inn (Downtown)." Goodnight Raleigh (website), August 26, 2011. http://goodnightraleigh.com/2011/08 /raleighs-second-round-building-the-holiday-inn-downtown/.

Robert, H. Wooley. "Race and Politics: The Evolution of the White Supremacy Campaign of 1898 in North Carolina." PhD diss., University of North Carolina at Chapel Hill, 1977.

Spaulding, Asa T. Audio recording of interview, April 14, 1979. Interview C-0013-2, Southern Oral History Program Collection, Southern Historical Collection, Wilson Library, University of North Carolina at Chapel Hill. Transcript available at https://docsouth.unc.edu/sohp/html_use/C-0013-2.html.

Trump, Donald. Speech at rally in Greenville, North Carolina, July 17, 2019. Transcript available through Scribie, blog, July 22, 2019, https://scribie.com/blog/2019/07/president -trump-rally-in-greenville-north-carolina-transcripts2020/.

Trump, Donald (@realdonaldtrump). "So interesting to see 'Progressive' Democrat Congresswomen, who originally came from countries whose governments are a complete and total catastrophe . . . " Twitter, July 14, 2019. https://www.thetrumparchive.com.

INDEX

★ ★ ★

Bruce, John, 73
Bruno, Joe, 176, 183, 202
Bryan, Eric, 38–42
Burden, Roslyn, 252
Bush, George H. W., 174, 177
Butler, Marion, 134

Cain, Ed, 158
Cameron, Rebecca, 125
campaign donations, 51, 231
Cape Fear River: description of, 97; as
    escape channel, 98, 131; flooding
    of, 1, 53, 55, 83; industry on, 105–6,
    130, 158
Carmon, Jeff, 219
carnivals and fairs: ban in Bladen
    County, 17, 143; Beast Fest, 19–20,
    72; in Columbus County, 17. *See
    also* parades
cartoons, racist, 119, 127, 133
censorship, 153
Chace, Zoe, 21, 250, 253
Charleston church shooting (2015), 13
Charlotte, North Carolina, 12; civil
    rights movement in, 31, 33, 148;
    political rallies in, 55, 88, 89, 248;
    racial unrest in, 69
Charlotte Business Journal
    (publication), 88
Charlotte Journal (publication), 116
Charlotte News (publication), 66, 114
Charlotte Observer (publication), 88
Chavis, Ben, 146–49
chicken production, 7, 83, 145, 205
civil rights movement: Great
    Migration and, 137; in North
    Carolina, 30–31; school desegre-
    gation, 31, 145–49. *See also* Black
    Americans; Black Lives Matter
Civil War, 95, 96–97, 98–99, 106, 113
Clarkton High School, 145, 146
Clemmons, Lloyd, 66

Clinton, Hillary, 54, 55–56, 199
Cogdell, Michael, 195, 231, 249
Coinage Act (1873), 113
Colbert, Stephen, 2, 183
collard sandwiches, 20, 72–73, 92
Colored American (publication), 114
Columbus County, North Carolina,
    17, 237, 255. *See also names of
    specific cities*
Columbus County Correctional
    Institution, 17–18
Confederate flag, 153–54, 254
congressional elections. *See*
    U.S. Congress
congressional redistricting, 3, 35–36,
    48, 68, 151–52
Conservative Party, 112
constitution, 107–8
Cooper, Roy, 59–60, 170
Cordill, C. C., 134
Cordle, Bob, 202, 203, 208, 209–10, 219
Cotton Mill Hill beast incident (1954),
    66–67, 72, 232. *See also* Beast Fest
Counts, Dorothy, 31, 33
county commissioners, 109, 115, 125.
    See also Bladen County, North
    Carolina; *and names of specific
    persons*
Croom, Caitlyn, 56, 80, 89, 225
Cumber, Harvey, 147
Cunningham, Joe, 88

Daniels, Josephus, Jr., 116–18, 132, 134,
    138, 251
Daniels, Josephus, Sr., 117
Daniels, Mary, 118
Dare, Virginia, 3
David, Jon, 50, 52, 74, 161
David Walker's Appeal in Four Articles
    (Walker), 96
Deepwater Horizon spill (2010), 43
Democracy v. Bladen County, 5

U.S. Department of Homeland
    Security, 167–68
U.S. Department of Justice, 146, 151, 152

Vause, Johnny, 66
violence against Black Americans:
    1898 Wilmington massacre, 34,
    129–31, 233, 251, 255; Black Lives
    Matters protests on, 251–52; during
    Civil War, 95; legislative bills on,
    114, 132–33; by police, 69, 141–42, 147,
    163, 251–52; during slavery, 119; in
    Tulsa, 29. *See also* Black Americans;
    lynchings; white supremacy; *and
    names of specific persons*
violence against women, 88–89, 119,
    122–23, 132, 139
voter fraud: (1898), 128; (1900), 134;
    (1901), 135; (2010), 40–43, 157, 252;
    (2014), 51, 157; (2016), 56–65, 69–70,
    181; (2018), 72, 78–81, 194–95; Trump
    on, 2, 73–74, 249, 252, 253. *See also*
    Bladen County Board of Elections;
    Dowless, McCrae; North Carolina
    State Board of Elections
voter intimidation, 36, 61, 108, 111,
    127–28
voting rights: of Black citizens, 96, 101;
    intelligence tests and, 102; literacy
    tests and, 32, 133; of white citizens,
    133–34
Voting Rights Act (1965), 59, 151

Waddell, Alfred Moore: 1898 speeches
    by, 124, 125; congressional career of,
    111, 115–17; description of, 101, 138;
    legal defense of McGill and McMillan
    by, 102–4; massacre incited by, 129–31;
    self-promoted mayoral position of,
    131; on white supremacy, 101–2
Walker, David, 96
war. *See* Civil War; Korean War

Ward, Billy, 41, 42–43
Warren, Marion, 15–16, 169, 190
Washington Post (publication), 46, 55,
    71, 115, 134, 191
Watts, Alston, 136
Weaver, James B., 114
Wells Fargo building, Raleigh, 76
Wesley, Charles, 98
West, Cornel, 160
Westwood, Susan, 89
Wheeler, J. A., 141
Whig Party, 101
White, George Henry: antilynching bill
    by, 114, 132–33; death of, 138; early
    life and family of, 5, 105–7, 108–11;
    incident at circus show of, 124; last
    congressional speech by, 135–36;
    legal career of, 113; *New York Times*
    interview of, 134–35; political career
    of, 5, 29, 30–31, 113, 114, 119–20,
    129; racist cartoons about, 133; on
    Wilmington massacre, 131, 255. *See
    also* U.S. Congress
White, Milton, 140, 143
White, Thay Lewis, 139–40, 142
white backlash, 163; in 19th c. North
    Carolina, 109–11, 122–29; after 2010
    sheriff election, 47–49; 2018 election
    fraud as, 5; 161. *See also* racist
    politics; violence against Black
    Americans
white fear, 119, 121–23, 132, 134–35, 148
White Lake, Bladen County, 59, 205
Whiten Normal School, 110
White's Creek Missionary Baptist
    Church, 142
white supremacy: 1898 campaign of,
    114, 119, 120–21, 124–25, 127, 137; of
    Cameron, 125; of Daniels, 116–17,
    118, 132; KKK, 101, 108, 111, 112, 115–16,
    153–55; punishment for, 103, 104;
    U.S. Capitol siege, 3, 254–55;

white supremacy (*continued*)
of Waddell, 102, 116–17, 124. *See also* racist politics; violence against Black Americans; white backlash
white violence. *See* violence against Black Americans
white women: fear of Black men by, 119, 121–23, 134–35; fear of Black Panthers by, 148; in U.S. Senate, 138
WikiLeaks, 42–43
Williamson, Zion, 216, 217–18
Willis, Agnes, 212
Williston School, 147
Wilmington, North Carolina: 1898 massacre in, 104, 129–31, 233, 251, 255; 1898 white supremacy campaign in, 114, 118–21, 124–25, 127, 137; 1971 riots in, 147–48; Black population statistics of, 137; nightclub shooting in, 148; opioid abuse in, 78
Wilmington Daily Dispatch (publication), 103
Wilmington Daily Star (publication), 107
Wilmington Journal (publication), 101–2, 109
Wilmington Messenger (publication), 124, 127
Wilmington Morning Star (publication), 120, 121, 128, 138
Wilmington Post (publication), 109
Wilmington's Lie (Zucchino), 123
Wilmington Ten case, 142, 149
women. *See* violence against women; white women
Woodhouse, Brad, 199–200
Woodhouse, Dallas, 198, 199–200
Wooten, Lola, 208, 231, 244
work ethic, 145
WRAL, 171

Yates, Andy, 212

Zucchino, David, 123

Printed in the USA
CPSIA information can be obtained
at www.ICGtesting.com
LVHW041350060224
771068LV00003B/364